Speech
Communication

second edition

Speech
Communication

Raymond S. Ross
Professor of Speech
Wayne State University

FUNDAMENTALS
AND
PRACTICE

Prentice-Hall, Inc.
Englewood Cliffs, New Jersey

Library of Congress Catalog Card Number: 71–116614

Printed in the United States of America

13–827360–X

Current Printing (last digit):

10   9   8   7

PRENTICE-HALL INTERNATIONAL, INC., London
PRENTICE-HALL OF AUSTRALIA, PTY. LTD., Sydney
PRENTICE-HALL OF CANADA, LTD., Toronto
PRENTICE-HALL OF INDIA PRIVATE LIMITED, New Delhi
PRENTICE-HALL OF JAPAN, INC., Tokyo

**To the great teachers
in my life**

*Franklin H. Knower
William R. Duffey
Hugo E. Hellman
Alan H. Monroe
Paul E. Lull*

Preface

This book is an attempt to revitalize the time-tested arts and skills of good public speaking by adding to them a knowledge of modern communication theory.

In this, its second edition, certain additions and only modest deletions are found. Much feedback from many users indicated the utility and popularity of chapter one, "Speech Communication Processes." This chapter has been doubled in length. A strong call for a chapter on group discussion has been heeded also. I was delighted to write in this, one of my favorite areas. I have had the counsel and criticism of some of the best small-group people in our field and feel that it reflects the best and most current thinking. To keep the book a reasonable size most of the sample speeches have been deleted. Several fine collections of model speeches, many in paperback, suggest the practicality of such an action. These are the major changes. Less major changes, including critical updating, are found throughout the book. Some new things are found under language, logic and persuasion.

Speech training has always infused itself with fresh energy from other fields, a practice which has permitted the continual growth of public address and has also rescued it from countless fads and over-emphases. The new "theory" courses are usually good communication courses, but they are not usually speaking courses; consequently, the vigor which they have made available has not been taken advantage of by public speaking. Communication theory should be taught in the speaking course so the student can readily apply it to an actual speech.

This is primarily a public speaking book containing the best of the old emphasis on skills of language, thought, voice, action, and rhetoric. But it also updates and modifies the old with the best of the new theory and research. The distinguishing characteristics of this book are:

1. A behavioral view of speech and communication as a dynamic process, a system of coding, decoding and recoding ideas and emotions.
2. A re-emphasis on the role of language in speech including considerable discussion of abstraction and generalization as well as words, sentences, and context.
3. A historical as well as a psychological approach to persuasion, drawing on A. H. Maslow's classification of dynamic needs and Kluckhohn and Murray's writings on personality. The research findings of rationalistic or "both-sides" persuasion which have long been overlooked by authors of speech texts, have also been utilized.
4. Learning theory is related in an uncomplicated way to the presenting of information; the role of visual aids is emphasized; and Edgar Dale's "cone of experience" is the cornerstone of the discussion.
5. The problem of speech anxiety is discussed frankly, and a sound psychological explanation is given.
6. Group discussion is defined as systematic cooperative, reflective thinking and communication. A comparison of various agenda systems are clearly charted. Modern concepts of participation, leadership and interaction are explained.
7. The rigor of a traditional public-speaking routine is *not* de-emphasized in the face of these modern contributions. Purpose, delivery, preparation, outlining, arrangement, voice, action, and logic are all discussed fully.

In addition to the special people mentioned in the dedication, I am indebted to my colleagues and students at Wayne State University for their encouragement and support. Professor Elizabeth Youngjohn, our brilliant rhetorician, deserves special acknowledgment for her many hours of counsel based on her long experience as director of the basic speech course at Wayne State University. Professor William A. Boyce deserves thanks for his careful reading and criticism of the voice and articulation material. The Prentice-Hall team that sold so many copies of the first edition deserve credit as the persuaders who kept this professor writing and living well. And without the charming Ricky there would have been no point in either the writing or the living.

R.S.R.

Contents

ix

Speech Communication Processes 1

The Importance of Speech Communication in Society

Suppose you call in two of your friends and communicate a rumor; then suppose that they each relay the rumor to two of their friends. Allowing 15 minutes for each communication and assuming the chain was not broken, this rumor could theoretically reach every person in the world in only 8 hours and 30 minutes. Talk about a grapevine! If you have ever played the game of passing along a message orally to see how much distortion takes place by the time it reaches the last person at your party, you can guess what probably happened in our hypothetical worldwide grapevine. One wonders how we achieve any understanding at all.

The amount of communication that goes on is also fantastic. Surveys indicate that we spend some 75 percent of our waking time in communication activity, that is, listening, speaking, reading, and writing. When one considers the telephone and the mass media, the volume of emitted signals becomes astronomical. It is estimated that the American public alone makes 30 billion telephone calls a year.

Communication is of vital importance to business and industry. Research tells us that business managers may spend 75 to 90 percent of their

1

time doing nothing but communicating, and about three-quarters of that time is spent in oral face-to-face situations.[1]

One top executive pointed up the importance of communication when he said,

> Poor communications cost companies billions a year in ill-conceived actions based on misunderstandings and baseless rumors. If our corporations are to grow in size and complexity, then our managers will have to become articulate.[2]

The importance is further reflected in

> the establishment of communications departments in many companies and in requests for special training courses and increased number of professional consultants. Management is estimated to spend over $112,000,000 a year on publications.[3]

One division of a major automobile producer is estimated to spend over $75 million a year on advertising alone.

The information explosion, the amount of material to be stored and communicated in this period of man's history is truly enormous. It is probably true, as one scholar has estimated, that man has discovered more knowledge within the last 50 years than through all the centuries before, that human knowledge has more than doubled within the last century! Our present specialization of knowledge adds to our problems. Communication must somehow bridge these isolated islands of specialization.

Colleges and universities have responded to the needs of society by offering numerous courses in speech and general communication. Doctoral degrees in speech are being granted in ever increasing numbers and in more specialized aspects of the field. Strong graduate programs are being developed in all parts of the United States. A considerable literature is

---

[1] C. S. Goetzinger and M. A. Valentine, "Communication Channels, Media, Directional Flow and Attitudes in an Academic Community," *Journal of Communication,* March, 1961, pp. 23–26; also "Communication Patterns, Interactions and Attitudes of Top-Level Personnel in the Air Defense Command," *Journal of Communication,* March, 1963, pp. 54–57.

[2] *Steel: The Metalworking Weekly* (Cleveland, Ohio: Penton Publishing Company, June 28, 1965), p. 29.

[3] M. Joseph Dooher and Vivienne Marquis, eds., *Effective Communication on The Job* (New York: American Management Association, 1956), p. 16.

growing that is both behaviorally and rhetorically oriented. Many speech teachers and speech majors have become adept in numerous fields because of the growing awareness of the interdisciplinary nature of communication and speech training.

The importance of speech training to you, the student, is indicated by the requirement of the subject by many schools. Moreover, the testimonials of successful men have affirmed the value of speech training, and recent research has indicated its usefulness to you in better understanding your other university courses. Dr. Charles Hurst studied 157 college sopho- mores, 70 with speech training, 87 without such training. He sought to describe the educational implications arising from any relationships be- tween formal instruction in a basic speech course and increased readiness to undertake work at the next academic level. He discovered that a sig- nificant and positive relationship between these two factors definitely does exist. More specifically, the speech group showed a statistically significant gain in ability to demonstrate learning and reasoning on a standardized test of academic aptitude; the gain experienced by the nonspeech group was not found to be statistically significant. Further, the speech group was found to be significantly superior on a measure of study skills and practices. A finding of interest to all grade-point-conscious students was that improve- ment of the speech group in ability to achieve in classroom work, as measured by comparison of mean honor-point averages, was found to be superior to the improvement of the nonspeech group. In fact, the speech group showed a net gain as compared with a net loss for the nonspeech group. Hurst concluded:

> The data of this study clearly suggest that the basic speech course is an agent of synthesis, providing students with a schematic basis for orderly thinking and improved control of the multivariate phenomena constituting the total personality.[4]

One scholar defines speech as "a tool of social adjustment, which reflects the efficient personality . . ."[5] Wiseman and Barker suggest that, "Physical, social, and mental existence depend upon communication. Each affects the other until it would be foolish to try to distinguish where one

---

[4] Charles Hurst, "Speech and Functional Intelligence: An Experimental Study of Educational Implications of a Basic Speech Course" (Unpublished doctoral disserta- tion, Wayne State University, 1961).

[5] Elwood Murray, *The Speech Personality* (Philadelphia: J. P. Lippincott Com- pany, 1944), p. 10.

begins and the other leaves off. Communication shapes personality and personality determines the pattern of communication."[6]

Perhaps for our purposes we can say that speech training may have as much impact on personality as personality may have on speech.

The Process of
Communication

Before we can consider the serious communication skills involved in this type of training, we must understand how communication takes place.

When asked to define communication, many people reply that it is the transmission or transfer of meaning from one mind to another. To most speech teachers today, this definition is not only technically in error, but may actually impede the learning of more specific skills that must be acquired.

In dealing with definitions of speech and communication we range from "speech is the great medium through which human cooperation is brought about,"[7] to the more specific definition of the American College Dictionary, ". . . the imparting or interchange of thoughts, opinions, or information by speech, writing, or signs." Let us examine some others that are useful.

Communication is the eliciting of response and successful human speech communication is the eliciting of the desired response through verbal symbolization.[8]

Human communication is a subtle set of processes through which people interact, control one another, and gain understanding . . .[9]

---

[6] Gordon Wiseman and Larry Barker, *Speech—Interpersonal Communication* (San Francisco: Chandler Publishing Company, 1967), Ch. 1, p. 5; also Lee Thayer, *Communication and Communication Systems* (Homewood, Ill.: Richard D. Irwin, Inc., 1968), Ch. 2, p. 17.

[7] Grace A. de Laguna, *Speech: Its Function and Development* (New Haven, Conn.: Yale University Press, 1927), p. 19.

[8] From *Business and Professional Speech Communication* by Harold P. Zelko and Frank E. X. Dance. Copyright © 1965 by Holt, Rinehart and Winston, Inc. Reprinted by permission of Holt, Rinehart and Winston, Inc., p. 5.

[9] Alfred G. Smith, ed., *Communication and Culture: Readings in the Codes of Human Interaction* (New York: Holt, Rinehart and Winston, Inc., 1966).

Communication is social interaction through symbols and message systems.[10]

Communication has as its central interest those behavioral situations in which a source transmits a message to a receiver(s) with conscious intent to affect the latter's behaviors.[11]

Speech is ongoing multisymbolic behavior in social situations carried on to achieve communication. We define communication as a social achievement in symbolic behavior.[12]

. . . by "communication" shall be meant any occurrence involving a minimum of four sequential ingredients: (1) a generator of a (2) sign-symbol systems which is (3) projected to (4) at least one perceiver who assigns it meaning. . . . we are primarily concerned with the human organism's involvement in terms of his sign-symbol behavior.[13]

Communication is a social function . . . a *sharing* of elements of behavior, or modes of life, by the existence of sets of rules . . . communication is not the response itself but is essentially the *relationship* set up by the transmission of stimuli [signs] and the evocation of responses.[14]

All the above definitions are worth thought and even class discussion. It seems apparent that up-to-date definitions agree that ideas must be somehow with both parties before there can be any real communication, and most importantly that communication should be thought of as a process and not simply a transfer of meaning from one mind to another. Let us examine this process and attempt to develop a working operational, behavioral definition that will help us in this course, if not our lives.

---

[10] George Gerbner, "On Defining Communication: Still Another View," *Journal of Communication,* June, 1966, p. 99.

[11] Gerald R. Miller, "On Defining Communication: Another Stab," *Journal of Communication,* June, 1966, p. 92.

[12] A. Craig Baird and Franklin H. Knower, *Essentials of General Speech* (New York: McGraw-Hill Book Company, 1968).

[13] Robert S. Goyer, *The Proposed Interdisciplinary Doctoral Program in Communication at Ohio University,* Center for Communication Studies, Special Report #14 (Athens, Ohio: Ohio University, September, 1967), pp. 7–8. The position taken by Goyer on sign and symbol is that operationally they are both observable as substitute, or surrogate representatives of some other event.

[14] Related statements from Colin Cherry, *On Human Communication* (Cambridge, Mass., and London, England: The M.I.T. Press, 1966), pp. 6–7. Arrangement and selection and brackets are this author's. Cherry uses the word *sign* for any physical event used in communication—human, animal, or machine—avoiding the term *symbol.*

Although it is technically impossible to separate the parts of so integrated a process, for our purposes it may be helpful to divide it arbitrarily into sequential events. Let us assume we have a message (which might be referred to as an idea or concept or meaning) that we wish to convey to another person. Our brain or thinking apparatus now sorts through our storehouse of knowledge, experience, feelings, and previous training to refine and select the precise meaning we are seeking. Before it is transmitted, it goes through a phase that we may think of as a language-attaching or coding event; that is, the refined idea is now encoded or put into signs and symbols that we commonly think of as language. Gesture, facial expression, and tone of voice may also be considered as signs, symbols, or codes. Our meaning could, for example, be put into a sign language, a foreign language, or even international Morse code. This code is then transmitted, and it has meaning to you, the sender. The way in which it is coded, the way and finesse with which it is transmitted, and the medium or channel chosen for its transmission have much to do with the meaning it will have for the receiver. Assuming that the media for this illustration is simply the air between you and the listener, we now have the encoded message, the transmission, and the signal being received by the other person. The receiver now proceeds to decode the signal or at least attempts to recode it. If the signal is in a code with which he is not familiar, such as a foreign language, not much communication will take place. The listener proceeds, figuratively, to elicit, to sort and select, meanings from *his* storehouse of knowledge, experience, and training, until there has been created in his own mind a near replica of the images and ideas contained in the mind of the sender.

To the extent that this replication is similar to the sender's, we have achieved communication. The idea, concept, or meaning in the mind of the listener is therefore heavily dependent upon, if not restricted, to the knowledge and experience he can bring to bear on the code. The value of knowing your listener and the value of audience analysis now become evident.

We shall thus operationally define communication as *a process involving the sorting, selecting, and sending of symbols in such a way as to help a listener elicit from his own mind a meaning similar to that contained in the mind of the communicator.* We now see why seemingly obvious meanings (in *our* minds) are often distorted or misunderstood by others. Perhaps this is what is meant when we hear the saying, "One cannot teach a man what he does not already know"; and perhaps this better explains the old teaching rule of "Go from the known to the unknown."

Communication Models

The word *model* typically refers to the representation of a thing or a process. When producing a model of a physical object we have relatively little trouble. We can make model trains, boats, and airplanes and learn much about their physical behavior. However, when we attempt to make models of more abstract things, where physical measurement is so difficult, we have the very real problem of oversimplifying to the point of poor or dangerous representation or of simply being unable to agree on our observations.

We may use words, numbers, symbols, and pictures to illustrate our model of things, theories, or processes. In geometry we accept the theory that the "square of the hypotenuse of a right triangle is equal to the sum of the squares of the legs." This statement is a form of verbal model. If we

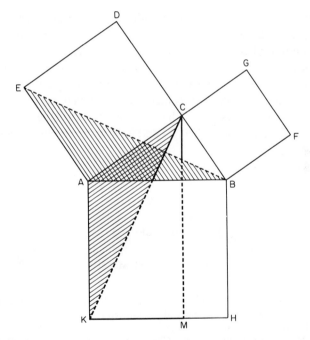

Figure 1. The Square of the Hypotenuse of a Right Triangle Is Equal to the Sum of the Squares of the Legs, or AKHB = ACDE + BFGC.

draw a picture of this theory as well, we have a verbal-pictorial model.[15] The advantages of using a model are quickly evident. The model gives you another, different, closer look. It provides a frame of reference, suggests informational gaps, points up the problem of abstraction and helps get a problem expressed in symbolic language where there is the advantage of the manipulative facility of that language.

Of course some drawbacks, such as oversimplification and other dangers inherent in gross abstraction, exist in the use of models. Campbell and Hepler warn us of yet another danger in their use.

> After a scientist plays for a long time with a given model he may become attached to it, just as a child may become, in the course of time, very attached to a doll (which is also a model). A child may become so devoted to the doll that she insists that her doll is a real baby, and some scientists become so devoted to their model (especially if it is a brainchild) that they will insist that this model *is* the real world.[16]

Communication experts have used primarily verbal-pictorial models in trying to give us a closer and more scientific look at the process. The working definition of communication suggested earlier for this text is really a verbal model, which will shortly be illustrated pictorially. First, let us look at several models that appear to be in essential agreement. Each one gives you just a little different perspective. The first is a simple verbal model posed as five questions. The last one shown (Figure 10) is the specific model for the writer's theories and is explained in more detail.

WHO
SAYS WHAT
IN WHAT CHANNEL
TO WHOM
WITH WHAT EFFECT

Figure 2. Lasswell Model[17]

---

[15] See especially, Ronald L. Smith, *General Models of Communication,* Purdue Communication Research Center, Special Report No. 5, (Lafayette, Ind.: Dept. of Speech, Purdue University, August, 1962).

[16] James H. Campbell and Hal W. Hepler, eds., *Dimensions in Communication* (Belmont, Cal.: Wadsworth Publishing Co., Inc., 1965), p. 18.

[17] H. D. Lasswell, "The Structure and Function of Communications in Society," in *The Communication of Ideas,* ed. Lyman Bryson (New York: Harper & Row, Publishers, 1948), p. 37.

Intentive	Encoding		Decoding	Interpretive
behavior of →	behavior →	Message →	behavior of →	behavior of
speaker	of speaker		hearer	hearer

Figure 3.   Carroll Model[18]

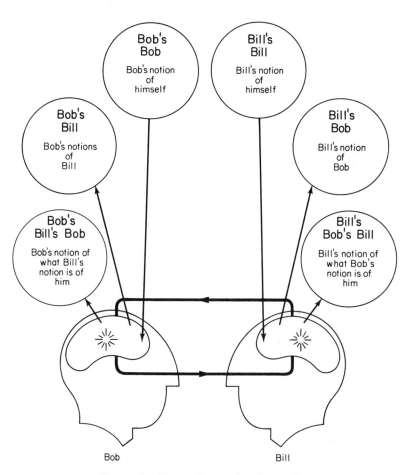

Figure 4.   Human Interaction Process[19]

---

[18] John B. Carroll, *The Study of Language* (Cambridge, Mass.: Harvard University Press, 1955), p. 88.

[19] From *Dimensions in Communication: Readings,* edited by James H. Campbell and Hal W. Hepler. © 1965 by Wadsworth Publishing Company, Inc., Belmont, California. Reproduced by permission of the publisher.

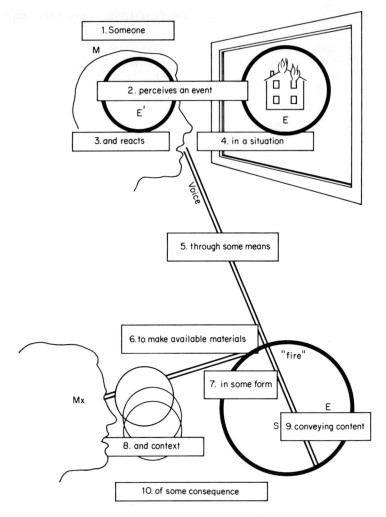

1. Someone

M

2. perceives an event

E'

3. and reacts

4. in a situation

E

Voice

5. through some means

6. to make available materials

Mx

"fire"

7. in some form

E

8. and context

S | 9. conveying content

10. of some consequence

Figure 5. Gerbner Model[20]

Key: E = event, S = signal, M = man. The events of someone seeing a fire and sounding an alarm are shown by the numbers:

Someone (1) is the communicating agent.

Perceives an event (2) indicates that a possibility of decoding and encoding exists, regardless of which of the senses did the perceiving.

And reacts (3) indicates that the message was received, decoded, and was being analyzed.

In a situation (4) indicates that a comparison was made to a frame of reference, stored in the communicating agent's experience and memory.

[20] George Gerbner, "Toward a General Model of Communication," *Audio-Visual Communication Review,* 34 (Summer, 1956), pp. 172–73.

Through some means (5) indicates that appropriate action is being taken, via some channel, commensurate with the seriousness of the situation, as defined by the agent's frame of reference.

To make available materials (6) indicates that some form of communication, voice, pressure, or some other form of signal is being employed.

In some form (7) indicates that a pattern, discernible to others was used to convey the material in (6).

And context (8) indicates that one or more than one of the senses is being alerted in the receiver, if his sense of values are comparable to that of the communicating agent.

Conveying content (9) indicates that the message has been sent and it is ready for reception and decoding if conditions at the receiving end are favorable.

Of some consequence (10) indicates that if conditions at the receiving end are favorable, and the receiver's sense of values are comparable to the communicating agent's, some type of action will be taken.

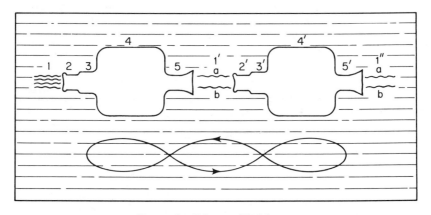

Figure 6. Johnson Model

Key: Stage 1. Event, or source of stimulation, external to the sensory end organs of the speaker.

Stage 2. Sensory stimulation.

Stage 3. Pre-verbal neurophysiological state.

Stage 4. Transformation of pre-verbal into symbolic forms.

Stage 5. Verbal formulations in "final draft" for overt expression.

Stage 1′. Transformation of verbal formulations into air waves (*a*) and light waves (*b*), which serve as sources of stimulation for the listener.

Stage 2′, etc.

Stage 2′ through 1″ (see diagram) correspond in the listener to stages 2 through 1′. The arrowed loops represent the functional interrelationships of the stages in the process as a whole.[21]

Figure 7.   Goyer Model[22]

Key: "G" represents a generator, "S" represents a sign/symbol stimulus, "P" represents a perceiver, "R" represents a differential response, ⟶ represents a projection in time. Communication thus occurs with reference to G and P whenever the response of P to the sign/symbol stimulus projected by G is consistent with the response intended by G; that is, when the referent responses of G and P to the sign/symbol stimulus are systematically correlated. The greater the correlation between the response intended by G and the response provided by P, the more effective is the communication.

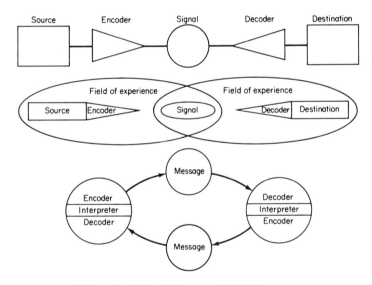

Figure 8.   Three Schramm Models[23]

---

[21] Wendell Johnson, "The Fateful Process of Mr. A Talking to Mr. B," *Harvard Business Review,* 31 (January–February, 1953), 50. (Rearrangement of quotation and parentheses are this author's.)

[22] Robert S. Goyer, *Communication Process: An Operational Approach,* Center for Communication Studies, Special Report No. 16 (Athens, Ohio: Ohio University, November, 1967), p. 5–6.

[23] Wilbur Schramm, "How Communication Works," *The Process and Effects of Mass Communication* ed. Wilbur Schramm (Urbana, Illinois: University of Illinois Press, 1955), pp. 4–8.

Key: 1. Encoding—Making the information or feeling into a form which can be transmitted.
  2. Sending—Transmitting the encoded message.
  3. Decoding—The relating of the message to the "picture in the mind" of the receiver.

The encoder and decoder can only perform their functions in terms of their respective fields of experience. In this sense, then, the decoder and encoder are each limited by their experience. There must be an overlap or some common experience, common to both decoder and encoder, for the communication to be meaningful and thus convey the intended message.

Finally, the decoding of a message by the receiver results in encoding. Whether this encoding results in an overt communication or not depends upon the barriers in the way. However, the process is constant and con-

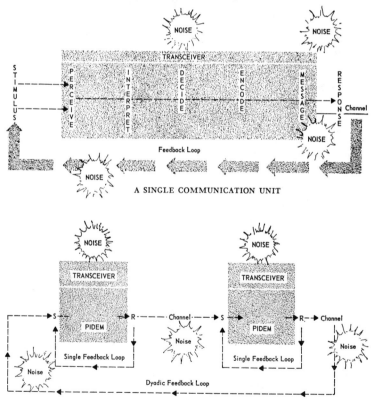

A SINGLE COMMUNICATION UNIT

TWO COMMUNICATION UNITS IN DYADIC SYSTEM

Figure 9. Zelko-Dance Model[24]

[24] From *Business and Professional Speech Communication* by Harold P. Zelko and Frank E. X. Dance. Copyright © 1965 by Holt, Rinehart and Winston, Inc. Reprinted by permission of Holt, Rinehart and Winston, Inc., pp. 6–7.

tinues. One individual communication is merely part of a greater network of communication.

The roles of encoder and decoder are interchangeable and each person involved in the process is both encoder and decoder as well as interpreter.

Since no model of anything, much less a complicated process, can ever be 100 percent accurate or complete, you are not expected to be in perfect agreement with the previous models or the one that follows. However, with the previous material as a background or frame of reference, perhaps more insights are now available to you as you elicit meanings from your storehouse of knowledge to decode the Ross model (Figure 10).

Let us return to our initial explanation of the communication process. You will recall the verbal model in the form of a definition:

> Communication is a process involving the sorting, selecting, and sending of symbols in such a way as to help a listener elicit from his own mind a meaning similar to that contained in the mind of the communicator.

In interpreting the Ross model, remember that its focus is primarily directed at that process that involves the *human* organism and particularly his sign-symbol behavior.[25] He is capable of being both sender and receiver at the same time; he is, as Zelko and Dance would say, a transceiver!

Let us now assume that our person on the left side of the model wishes to communicate a message (a concept or idea) to the other person. The idea is represented by the star on the model (inside his brain). Let us suppose the concept is an abstract one like *love*. The fan projecting from each brain represents, let us assume, a projection of man's 13½ billion brain cells. In this brain are stored his knowledge and his past experience, his feelings, attitudes, emotions, and many more things that make him the person he is. Our sender now proceeds, figuratively, to sort and select from among his storehouse of knowledge and past experience, choosing items that help him refine and define what he's trying to say. He has to have a basis or set of criteria for this operation, a program if you will. We can think of the brain in some ways as a computer. The forebrain, for example, becomes a kind of servo-mechanism or input regulator where we feed in the program. His program had better include at least three instructions or he's already in trouble! They are: (1) What do I have stored under love? (2) What do I know about the other person? and (3) What do I have filed

---

[25] Some writers are primarily interested in mathematical theories and models applied to electrical engineering, others to animal communication, and so on. See especially: C. E. Shannon and W. Weaver, *The Mathematical Theory of Communication* (Urbana, Ill.: University of Illinois Press, 1949), p. 98; and Jon J. Eisenon, J. Jeffery Auer and John V. Irwin, *The Psychology of Communication* (New York: Appleton-Century-Crofts, 1963), Ch. 10, William Etkin, "Communication Among Animals."

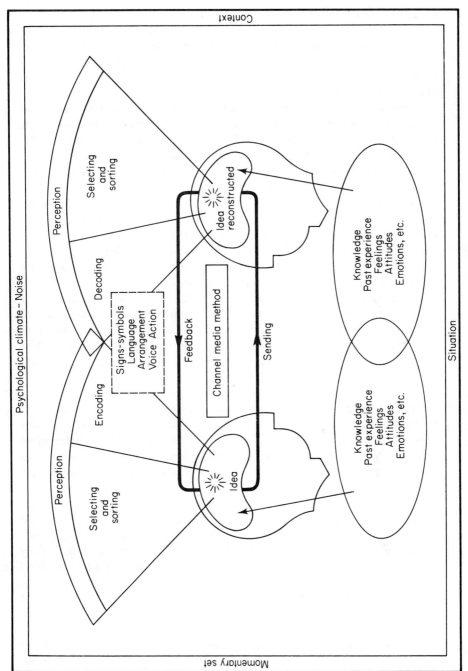

Figure 10. Ross Human Communication Model

15

for this particular situation and context? One can visualize the program assessing the storehouse, accepting, rejecting, cross-referencing, synthesizing—in short, selecting and sorting the appropriate knowledge, past experience, and so on.

While there is some confusion among scholars as to exactly how, and particularly *when* the encoding, or sign/symbol attaching event takes place, it is useful, if only for instructional purposes, to think of it sequentially. Our sender must now proceed, figuratively, to choose his codes and should apply minimally the same program or questions discussed previously. More will be said of this critical process in Chapter 3. The sender now emits the stimuli, which, let us presume, are primarily oral. He might, of course, have chosen to write a memo or use a blackboard.[26] Let us further assume that there is no unusual distraction or noise in the situation, and further that the sensory apparatus of both parties is adequate. Since our message concerned *love,* the situation and context factors may be fairly critical, not to mention the specific facts about the other person.

Finally (and this whole operation could involve but seconds), the stimuli strike the receiver's sensory end organs. This is the first part of human perception—*sensation;* the second part is the *interpretation* of what those sensations mean, again, in this highly specific situation. More will be said of the process of perception in the section immediately following.

The model now suggests that our receiver proceeds to *decode* the signs, symbols, language, and so on, ultimately drawing upon, and eliciting from, his storehouse of knowledge and experience, those meanings that will allow him to create a message concerning *love.* To the extent that this recreation is similar to the sender's intended message, we have communication. This reconstructed idea is then heavily dependent upon what a person already knows.

The term *feedback* in the model calls for a moment of important consideration. In engineering, feedback refers to some of the transmitted energy being returned to the source. The automatic pilot used in airplanes is an example of self-correcting machinery that uses feedback. The analogy to human communication breaks down a bit when one considers the kind of electronic feedback all of us have observed with public-address systems or tape recorders (a reentry of some of the sound from the speaker to the microphone, causing a howl or loud noise). For speech purposes, we may think of feedback as useful in a self-correcting sense, or perhaps we should say audience-adapting sense. As our transmitted signal is bounced off our receiver, it feeds back information that allows us to correct and refine our

---

[26] There are many interesting researches on media or channel selection. See especially: T. L. Dahle, "Transmitting Information to Employees: A Study of Five Methods," *Personnel,* 31 (1954), 243–46.

signal. A quizzical look, a frown, a yawn, the sound of our own voice—any of these may cause us to reevaluate and recode our own emitted signal. On the other hand, speech fright to the point of emotional disintegration (such as forgetting) can be compared to intense feedback of the howl or public-address system type, which momentarily—but completely—shorts out the sending device. The complicated phenomenon of speech fright will be covered in a later chapter. For now, let us think of feedback as something that we should make work for us.

Cartoonist McKee catches the problem of near zero feedback in the clever sketches that follow on page 18.[27]

Perception and Human Understanding

The other half of sending is receiving. An understanding of the way people receive, decode, and assign meaning is critical. Listening is much more than hearing acuity. All of our sensory apparatus may be involved in helping us interpret even a primarily oral signal. The perception process is for our purposes identical to the communication process except that the emphasis is on receiving instead of sending. The receiver or perceiver is thought to posit hypotheses, which he accepts or rejects. Postman[28] calls this a cycle of hypothesis involving information, trial, and check, confirmation or nonconfirmation. The meaning then is supplied primarily by learning and by past experience.

Sensation and Interpretation

Have you ever been on a train that is stopped between other trains in a railroad terminal? Have you then felt, seen, and heard all the signs indicating movement, only to find that it is the other trains that are moving? Perhaps you discovered this when the other train was actually gone, or perhaps you fixed your gaze on something you *knew* was not moving, such as the ceiling of the station, a roof support, or the ground itself.

The point is that perception involves essentially two acts: (1) the *sensation* caused by the stimulation of a sensory organ, and (2) the *interpretation* of the sensation. In our study of speech we are primarily concerned

---

[27] Drawings by David John McKee, by permission of *The Times Educational Supplement* (London), March 27, 1964. Published in the United States by *Saturday Review* (New York), Sept. 19, 1964, p. 68.

[28] L. Postman, "Toward a General Theory of Cognition," in *Social Psychology at the Crossroads* eds. J. H. Rohrer and M. Sherif (New York: Harper & Row, Publishers, 1951), p. 251.

Making a Point . . .

—Drawings by David John McKee.
—Times Educational Supplement, London, March 27, 1964.

SR/September 19, 1964

Figure 11

with the interpretation; as has been discussed earlier, it is primarily through our knowledge and experience that we interpret or attach meaning to a symbol.

The complexity of human communication is further indicated by the various levels of perception now thought to exist. We talk of subliminal or subthreshold perception, that is, a receiving below the level of conscious awareness. This is not to be confused with so-called extrasensory perception. Many experiments have been conducted in this field, most of them involving visual projections at speeds above our physiological level of perception, but below our awareness level, or in some cases, at our awareness level, but below our recognition level. They are complicated by the fact that people vary in their perceptual abilities not only one from another, but also in their own individual range of acuity. The best known of all subthreshold experiments[29] involved the projection of nonsense syllables. Meaningless combinations of letters were associated with electric shock. When these stimuli were later presented subthresholdly (at speeds too rapid to permit their conscious identification), the subjects' emotional reactions were more intense than their reactions to other nonsense syllables not previously associated with shock. The subjects had been able to identify the stimuli unconsciously before they could do so consciously.

During a six week experiment in a New Jersey theater in 1957, sales of popcorn and a soft drink allegedly were increased by the use of subthreshold messages superimposed over the regular film. No adequate account of procedures is available for verification.[30] A more recent study by Gibb involving subthreshold prestige suggestion superimposed over video tape did indicate some attitude change.[31]

A person's set, expectancy, or preparation to perceive[32] has much to do with his level of perception as well as his individual acceptance of a stimulus. The consciousness defends itself through an apparent refusal to accept certain messages. On the other hand, we may wish or desire so very much to hear something that, regardless of the actual code or words emitted, we attend, interpret, and attach meaning in terms of what we wish to hear. One of the great barriers to good communication is the tendency to

Also see J. S. Bruner, "Personality Dynamics and the Process of Perceiving," in *Perception: An Approach to Personality* eds. R. R. Blake and G. V. Ramsey (New York: The Ronald Press Company, 1951).

[29] R. S. Lazarus and R. A. McCleary, "Autonomic Discrimination Without Awareness: A Study in Subception," *Psychological Review,* 58 (1951), 113–22.

[30] H. Brean, "Hidden Sell Techniques Are Almost Here," *Life,* 44 (1958), 102–4.

[31] J. Douglas Gibb, "An Experimental Study of the Effects of a Subthreshold Prestige Symbol in Informative and Persuasive Communication" (unpublished doctoral dissertation, Wayne State University, 1966).

[32] Charles M. Solley and Gardner Murphy, *Development of the Perceptual World* (New York: Basic Books, Inc., Publishers, 1960), p. 239.

hear what we wish to hear, see what we wish to see, and believe what we wish to believe. This kind of behavior is called *autistic thinking*. Piaget defines autism as "thought in which truth is confused with desire."[33] In its extreme form, this kind of perception and thinking grows out of an abnormal emotional need for ego-satisfaction, and we actually have a mental disorder known as *paranoia*. The foregoing indicates that perception is a function of *internal* as well as external sources of stimulation. Signals that originate within us also enter into the problem, and can function to either stabilize or distort perception.[34]

Another closely related perceptual and communication problem arises because of a normal tendency to completeness. In communications that appear to be only partially complete, we often read in the unsaid part or complete the pattern. If we do not arrive at a sense of completeness or closure, we often feel upset, ill at ease, confused, and unhappy. This tendency can be an important factor in motivation. Perhaps you have had a teacher who communicates just enough knowledge in a stimulating way, motivating you to do further reading and research so that you can complete or close the pattern. The problem arises when we close incomplete communication patterns in ways not intended by the speaker. This tendency is illustrated by an incomplete triangle. We find it more reasonable, more comfortable to see Figure 12 as a complete triangle.

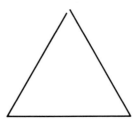

Figure 12. Pattern Closing Tendencies

Sometimes our habits and previous experience cause us to leave things out. Read the next three messages quickly.

Figure 13

---

[33] J. Piaget, *The Child's Conception of Physical Causality* (London: Routledge & Kegan Paul Ltd., 1930), p. 302.

[34] Solley and Murphy, *Development of the Perceptual World*, pp. 259–60.

Many people see nothing unusual about these messages even after two or three readings. The good, rapid readers seem to have the most trouble. Why should this be so? A group of second and third graders had no trouble finding the double words in each message. We perceive to a certain extent what our habits, our emotions, and our knowledge and past experiences let us perceive. A good reader has learned to skim and to ignore nonessential words. The beginning reader sees literally one word at a time.

Test your perceptual ability on the next two stimuli. Do you see anything familiar or identifiable? Do you see a message?

Figure 14

Figure 15

You should see words in white on a partial black field. Your experience is typically just the opposite—the area *between* the letters is in black instead of the letters themselves.[35] Even after you see the messages they may escape you momentarily as your longstanding habits and previous experience patterns fight to assert their influence.

Try reading this simple word! It's easier if you examine just the bottom half of the stimulus.[36]

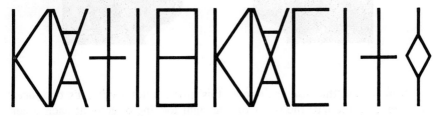

Figure 16

---

[35] This is referred to as a figure-ground transformation. The words are Left, and Fly.

[36] Nationality, the top part reads nationality too, only upside-down and backwards.

Experience should help you the next time, shouldn't it? Let's see. Can you decode or elicit meanings for the next stimulus? You've had practice!

Figure 17

Your mental set or disposition to interpret has a lot to do with what you "see." Look for a *vase* in the next figure! You should find it very quickly because that is, after all, what you were looking for.

Figure 18

Now look at the *vase* again, only this time it's not a *vase,* it's two *faces!* One face on the left, the other on the right looking directly at each other. Do you get the message?

Some patterns that seem to make no sense at all in terms of *what* we "know" can cause real irritation. Engineering students find the next one frustrating (Figure 19). It just can't be!

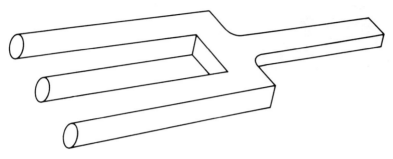

Figure 19

A group of professional photographers had an almost impossible time trying to "see" the following photograph. What do you see?

Figure 20

Don't proceed until you see a cow looking right at you! If you haven't seen it by now, you may actually regress, particularly if you've asked for help and your friends see it immediately. Communication is like that. We don't do our best where we begin to feel awkward, stupid, or left out . . . How are you doing with LEFT, FLY, and THE? Can you lose them? When things or experiences are new or novel to us, we may literally understand or "see" one moment and "not see" the next. This would be a good time to review the communication models again, wouldn't it?

Perception tends to be selective for many reasons, and we are well advised to remember it. The next three photographs are all reproduced from the same negative; each is shown as it might appear to:

A young man "on the town"

A person needing to cash a check

Someone who is late for an appointment

Figure 21.   Selective Perception[37]

[37] With permission of Kaiser Aluminum and Chemical Corp., "Communications" 1965, p. 7.

Figure 22[38]

Our friend, Charlie Brown, illustrates humorously how others' perceptions and subsequent communications affect our output if not what *we* see.

The communication of stereotyped or stylized portrayals of facial expressions and gestures has been studied experimentally. Landis performed an experiment designed to discover whether reported emotions are accompanied by definite and easily recognized facial expressions. A series of photographs were taken of his subjects while they were actually undergoing

[38] © 1960 United Feature Syndicate, Inc.

various emotion-producing situations, not simply portraying emotions as an actor would. Landis had a regular torture-chamber experiment, and after many comparisons he writes:

> With no verbal report of a given emotion did a muscle, group of muscles, or expression occur with sufficient frequency to be considered characteristic of that emotion. There is no expression typically associated with any verbal report.[39]

A study similar to the one described above was conducted by Feleky, but with one vital difference: the photographs of emotions were artificially portrayed or acted. The experimenter found in this case a remarkable agreement on the description of the poses, indicating that we may interpret an individual's emotional state with reasonable accuracy from a posed photograph.[40]

A study with more specific conclusions was conducted by Knower and Dusenbury. The design of the study was almost identical to Feleky's. Knower and Dusenbury concluded:

1. Interpretation of the facial expression of emotional tendencies and attitudes may be made with a high degree of reliability.
2. There are significant individual and group differences in ability correctly to interpret facial expressions of the emotions.
3. Women are more accurate in the interpretation of facial expressions of the emotions than men.
4. Patterns of facial expression extended in time, as on a short, moving picture, are judged more accurately than are still photographs of the same emotional tendencies.
5. Accuracy in the interpretation of facial expressions of the emotions is influenced by the conditions under which such expressions are judged.[41]

A more recent study by Williams and Tolch[42] indicated that there are two basic dimensions in the perception of simulated facial expressions, namely, *general-evaluation* and *dynamism*. By *general-evaluation* was

---

[39] "Experimental Studies of the Emotions: The Work of Cannon and Others," in Henry E. Garrett, *Great Experiments in Psychology* (New York: Appleton-Century-Crofts, 1941), p. 331.

[40] Garrett, *Great Experiments in Psychology*, p. 330.

[41] D. Dusenbury and F. H. Knower, "Experimental Studies of the Symbolism of Action and Voice—I: A Study of the Specificity of Meaning in Facial Expression," *Quarterly Journal of Speech*, XXIV, No. 3 (1938), 435.

[42] F. Williams and J. Tolch, "Communication by Facial Expression," *The Journal of Communication*, XV, No. 1 (March, 1965), p. 17; also see J. Tolch, "The Problem of Language and Accuracy in Identification of Facial Expression," *Central States Speech Journal*, 14 (February, 1963).

meant a perceiver's assessment of those qualities of an expression that reveal such things as goodness, gratefulness, kindness, and the like. *Dynamism* involves an assessment of qualities such as active-passive, fast-slow, interesting-boring, and so on. Stimulated facial expressions based only on these two dimensions did appear to be differentiated by viewers. However, a simulated "no message—neutral" expression introduced into the study tended to have both *evaluative* and *dynamic* qualities.

In one study, Moe and Savage cut up pictures of stereotyped emotions (for example, terror, love, hate) and asked students to look at the hand and face gestures separately. Recognition or identification was higher in both cases indicating that there are reasonably stylized expressions of the hands as well as the face.[43]

The study of the spontaneous small acts thought to reveal internal states is called kinesics by some experts.[44]

As far as communication (recognition) is concerned in these experiments, we can say that simulated or stereotyped emotions can be perceived or identified with some reliability. With recognition of real emotions one might just as well leave the judgment to chance.

Good actors and capable speakers appear to communicate emotions with regularity. The actor has the play, the set, the other actors, and the stylized conceptions of the audience to help him. If the cause of whatever emotion the actor is portraying is also perceived (for example, a gun and fear), the communication pattern is easier to follow.

But though certain peripheral patterns or expressions have become stylized, we still have a potential barrier to communication, for these patterns may vary so much from person to person, sender and receiver, that excepting perhaps skilled acting, it remains difficult to communicate the precise emotion intended.

The conclusion of all this research is that the "meaning" is in the eyes, ears, and other senses of the beholder to some extent, but it is more in his previous experience, learning, knowledge, feelings, attitudes, and emotions.

Listening

Nearly one hundred years ago in George Eliot's *Felix Holt, the Radical,* the Reverend Rufus Lyon counseled the hot-tempered hero: "Therefore I pray for a listening

---

[43] J. Moe and N. Savage, "Recognizability of Emotions as Expressed by Facial Expressions and Hand Gestures," (Unpublished pilot study, Speech 0726, Wayne State University, 1967).

[44] R. Birdwhistell, *Introduction to Kinesics: An Annotation System for Analysis of Body Motion and Gesture* (Washington, D.C.: Foreign Service Institute, Dept. of State, 1952).

spirit, which is a great mark of grace. . . . The scornful nostril and the high head gather not the odors that lie on the track of truth."[45]

From a discussion of the process of perception and its intimate relationship to the process of communication, it seems obvious that although speech training must put great emphasis on skills of delivery (encoding and transmitting), it must also be concerned with listening. We may think of listening in terms of the general discussion of perception and specifically as auditory perception. Once again we may profitably divide auditory perception (listening) into hearing (sensation) and listening (interpretation).

Our disposition, set (or expectancy), and attention once again become critical even before the hearing or sensation is actually registered or received by the brain. The interpretation of this *hearing,* as was explained earlier, is affected by our interest, motivations, and desires. When we think of speech as a communication and a perception process, we are also discussing listening. Listening is the most used of the communicative skills, and *good* listening is an integral part of the communication process; it is therefore an essential factor in *good* speaking. Surveys of communication habits indicate that man may spend as much as 60 to 75 percent of his time listening.[46]

Stuart Chase scolds Americans forthrightly:

> Listening is the other half of talking. If people stop listening, it is useless to talk—a point not always appreciated by talkers.
>
> Americans are not good listeners. In general they talk more than they listen. Competition in our culture puts a premium on self-expression, even if the individual has nothing to express. What he lacks in knowledge he tries to make up for by talking fast or pounding the table. And many of us, while ostensibly listening, are inwardly preparing a statement to stun the company when we get the floor.[47]

Robert Goyer indicates the following as factors and attributes of good, perceptive listening:

FACTORS

(a) An adequate hearing acuity.

(b) A recognition on the part of the listener of the problems and obstacles

[45] George Eliot, *Felix Holt, the Radical: The Personal Edition of George Eliot's Works* (New York: Doubleday & Company, Inc., 1901), p. 70.

[46] Ralph G. Nichols and Leonard A. Stevens, *Are You Listening?* (New York: McGraw-Hill Book Company, 1957), pp. 6–8.

[47] Stuart Chase, "Are You Listening?" *Reader's Digest,* December, 1962, p. 80.

to overcome in order to listen effectively, including such things as improper attitude, boredom, fatigue, and the like.

(c) A knowledge of the specific kind of listening situation and the listener's adaptation to it, including such kinds as casual listening and intent listening.

(d) The relationship between listening and vocabulary.

(e) The judging of what is heard—being able to think and analyze while listening.

ATTRIBUTES

(a) A readiness to listen.

(b) An ability to discriminate among sounds and ideas.

(c) The capacity to give meanings to selected sounds.

(d) The ability to relate meanings given to certain sounds to other experiences.

(e) The ability to evaluate properly the medium and manner of the sound presentations.

(f) The willingness to disregard prejudice.[48]

You listen with more than your ears, and you listen for more than sound—you listen with all appropriate senses to perceive the total situation or receive the total communication. This concept is far removed from a concept of listening which can be described as *auding* and which possesses and utilizes only an adequate hearing acuity. Cortright and Hinds have blended listening and perception in this way: "The listening process involves accurate perception and orientation, direction of attention toward digestion of the speaker's views, and integration of the meaning into objective concepts."[49]

In an article entitled "The Listening Spirit and the Conference Leader," Ernest D. Nathan attempted to diagram the process of perceptive listening and to develop functional definitions. His emphasis was on conference leadership, but the theory is equally applicable for almost all speech and communication situations. (See Figure 23.)[50]

---

[48] Robert S. Goyer, "Oral Communication: Studies in Listening," *Audio-Visual Communication Review,* II, No. 4 (Fall, 1954), 263–76; also see Sam Duker, *Listening: Bibliography* (New York: Scarecrow Press, Inc., 1964).

[49] Rupert L. Cortright and George L. Hinds, *Creative Discussion* (New York: The Macmillan Company, 1959), p. 117.

[50] Ernest D. Nathan, "The Listening Spirit and the Conference Leader," *Training Directors Journal,* XVIII, No. 1 (January, 1964), 24.

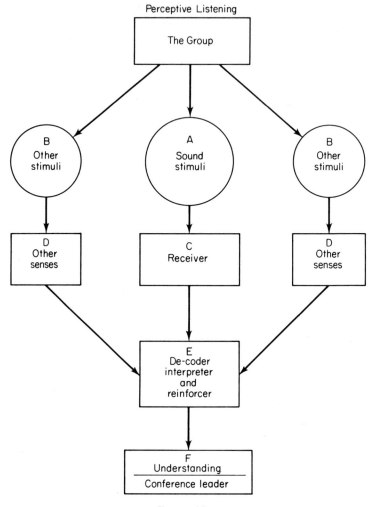

Figure 23

Key: A. The stimulus, primarily sound, originates from some member of the conference group.

B. Other stimuli, such as bodily movements, facial and manual expressions, and external distractions join, reinforce, or even dilute the sound stimulus.

C. The audible stimuli strike the ear and are auded.

D. The nonaudible stimuli are directed to the other senses, such as sight, smell, touch, taste, fear, pain, balance, and so on.

E. Aided by a conscious effort on the part of the receiver to gain understanding, the various stimuli are conducted to the nervous system of the receiver, where they are decoded, interpreted, and reinforced by experience.

F. Decoded and reinforced, and combining the effects of all senses involved, the communication is completed, resulting in understanding in the terms intended by the sender of the stimuli.

Nathan concludes:

> Perceptive listening is a conscious, cognitive effort involving primarily the sense of hearing reinforced by other senses and leading to understanding. When perceptive listening is inspired by a sincere desire to understand, it becomes more than a sensory process. It is an attitude well expressed as "a listening spirit."[51]

Listening is a difficult process even under the most favorable conditions. One reason is that we think much faster than we talk. The average rate of speech of most Americans is around 125 words per minute, whereas it has been found that people can comprehend speech at more than 300 words per minute without significant loss.[52] The lag between speaking speed and listening speed is probably the cause of much of our listening trouble.

A more important collection of obstacles to listening includes: *prejudging,* or jumping to the conclusion that the other person's meaning is understood before it is fully expressed; *ambiguity,* or the possibility, always present, that the idea expressed is open to more than one interpretation; and related to both of these, the *illusion* that effective communication has taken place. These obstacles are especially insidious because they are difficult to detect, and, in some instances, seem to reinforce the conviction of perceptive listening when, in fact, the opposite is the case.

Nichols expresses it this way:

> If we hear something that opposes our most deeply rooted prejudices, notions, convictions, mores, or complexes, our brains may become overstimulated, and not in a direction that leads to good listening. We mentally plan a rebuttal to what we hear, formulate a question designed to embarrass the talker, or perhaps simply turn to thoughts that support our own feelings on the subject at hand.[53]

However, let us not forget that as a speaker, or sender, we are responsible to a large extent for both the attentive *hearing* and the objective *listening* of the audience. An audience that is inattentive and half-asleep may not be *hearing* very efficiently because of the speaker's dull and

---

[51] Nathan, "The Listening Spirit and the Conference Leader," p. 25.

[52] Nichols and Stevens, *Are You Listening?,* pp. 78–79.

[53] Ralph G. Nichols and Leonard A. Stevens, "Listening to People," *Harvard Business Review,* XXXV, No. 5 (September, 1957), 88.

monotonous voice or delivery pattern, or because the subject itself is dull and monotonous, or both. The audience may not be *listening* for the same reasons; however, *listening* is more closely related to subject, organization of material, interest, and linguistic ability. In terms of critical listening, the speaker has serious ethical responsibilities in regard to *stacking* his organization and evidence, *name-calling,* and using abstract language of the *glittering-generality* variety. These devices might improve hearing or attending, but they make objective listening very difficult.

This distinction between hearing and listening, you will recall, is based on the perception process. *Auditory perception* is the general term and *hearing* is the sensating step, or sensation; *listening* is the interpretation. It behooves the speaker to take all of auditory perception into account when organizing and adapting his material, his mood, and his mode of delivery to a particular group of potential listeners. Those factors thought to play the most important role in listening comprehension were reported by Nichols.[54] They are critical in helping you better analyze your listeners for maximum adaptation. Some are more useful in evaluating your own listening habits.

Intelligence
Reading comprehension
Recognition of correct English usage
Size of the listener's vocabulary
Ability to make inferences
Ability to structuralize a speech (that is, to see the organizational plan and the connection of the main points)
Listening for main ideas, not merely for specific facts
Use of special techniques while listening to improve concentration
Real interest in the subject discussed
Emotional adjustment to the speaker's thesis
Curiosity about the subject discussed
Physical fatigue of the listener
Audibility of the speaker
Speaker effectiveness
Admiration for the speaker
Respect for listening as a method of learning
Susceptibility to distraction
Sex of the listener (males are better listeners, on the average)
Room ventilation and temperature

---

[54] Ralph G. Nichols, "Factors in Listening Comprehension," *Speech Monographs,* XV, No. 2 (1948), 161–62.

Use of only the English language at home

High-school scholastic achievement

High-school speech training

Experience in listening to difficult expository material

The listener, however, also has responsibilities in this matter. All speakers are entitled to some listening effort. In the rare case of a required course, which is notoriously dull and taught by an even duller teacher, you may dramatically discover your listening responsibilities as you fail the midsemester examination!

Understanding language usage and subtle linguistic devices is quite obviously an important part of critical listening; more will be said of this element in relationship to good listening habits in Chapter 3.

Listening, then, may be defined as *a conscious, cognitive effort involving primarily the sense of hearing (reinforced by other senses) and leading to interpretation and understanding.*

Summary

Theoretically, human communication is capable of fantastic speeds. The amount of communication we engage in is tremendous. Practices of business, industry, colleges, and universities reflect the growing importance of speech and communication training. The literature here discussed reflects the growing systematization and interdisciplinary character of the study of communication. The importance of speech training to college students in terms of: (1) work in other courses, (2) learning, (3) study habits, and (4) grades and personality has been demonstrated experimentally. Communication is defined as a process involving the sorting, selecting, and sending of symbols in such a way as to help a listener elicit from his own mind a meaning similar to that contained in the mind of the communicator.

The processes of communication and perception are essential fields of knowledge for people who would meaningfully learn communication skills. The suggested model (Fig. 10) includes: (1) idea or concept; (2) selecting and sorting; (3) encoding; (4) transmission; (5) receiving and decoding; (6) selecting and sorting; (7) idea or concept. The element of feedback, or the return of some of the transmitted energy to the source, is vital to self-correction and audience analysis.

The study of perception as a process gives us much insight into the speech and communication act. Perception may be usefully divided into: (1) sensation and (2) interpretation. The effect of past experience, knowledge, set, expectancy, wish, and desire have intense impact upon perception. Autistic thinking is the cause of much distortion in perception and therefore impedes communication. Perception is a function of internal as well as external signals or forces. Listening is an integral part of the communication and perceptual processes and is the most used of the communication skills. Listening may be defined as *a conscious, cognitive effort involving primarily the sense of hearing (reinforced by other senses) and leading to interpretation and understanding.* The speaker must take all of auditory perception into account when organizing and adapting his material, his mood, and his mode of delivery to a particular group of potential listeners.

The point of view of this book is that communication should not be considered as a simple transfer or transmission of meaning from one mind to another. It is a process intimately related to perceptual processes, and it involves the sorting, selecting, and sending of symbols in such a way as to help a listener elicit from his own mind a meaning similar to that contained in the mind of the communicator.

Emotion
and
Confidence   **2**

Six years of studied
empirical and survey observations at Wayne State University[1] have indicated that beginning speech students consider speech fright (or what is
often called stage fright) a serious problem. More than three-fourths of an
average class indicate concern. One-fourth of the typical class prefers
special treatment in the form of instructor conferences and specific reading
assignments. Baird and Knower reported a survey of various college groups
in which 60 to 75 percent of the students admitted that they were bothered
by nervousness in speaking; 35 percent considered it a severe problem.[2]
E. C. Buehler has reported a survey of 1750 students and 77 speech
teachers. On a scale of factor importance, the students ranked self-confidence first.[3]

When a pattern of fear response extends across all or nearly all interpersonal relationships involving oral communication, it may be referred to

---

[1] R. S. Ross and W. J. Osborne, "Survey of Incidence of Stage Fright" (Unpublished research material, Wayne State University, 1968).

[2] A. C. Baird and F. H. Knower, *Essentials of General Speech* (New York:
McGraw-Hill Book Company, 1968), p. 34.

[3] E. C. Buehler, "Progress Report of Survey of Individual Attitudes and Concepts
Concerning Elements Which Make for Effective Speaking" (Mimeographed report,
University of Kansas, August, 1958).

as *reticence.* According to research at the Pennsylvania State University, this figure could reach 5 percent of a class.[4]

The point of all these surveys is that the vast majority of you will suffer some speech fright of varying intensities. If it is true that "misery loves company" or that there is "safety in numbers," then it may be reassuring to know that you are certainly not alone. Even professional performers report violent emotional reactions before some public performances. In terms of acting and emotional problems, some personal reports are quite vivid:

> It's really not fun, acting. Always that tremendous fear. . . . Do you know that before a performance sometimes Laurence Olivier goes back to the foyer and, to release his tension, swears at the audience? Some actors even stick pins in themselves.
>
> *Jane Fonda*

> Acting is a way to overcome your shyness every night. The writer creates a strong, confident person, and that's what you become—unfortunately, only for the moment.
>
> *Shirley Booth*

> Acting scares me senseless. I hate everything I do. Even if it's a crummy radio show with a script, I throw up. I tell ya—it's the equivalent of going voluntarily to hell.
>
> *Judy Holliday*

> You know, acting makes you feel like a burglar sometimes—taking all that money for all that fun.
>
> *Pat O'Brien*[5]

The fact that audiences do not view your fright as seriously as you do indicates that you do not appear and sound as bad as you feel; this should be reassuring. Whether your fear is readily apparent or not, the result may be the same. The consequences of such emotional involvement are not very different from other fright-producing situations. Internally you may feel a dryness in the mouth, a rapid heartbeat, a sinking feeling in the stomach, even difficulty with visceral control. Generally observable behavior patterns in excessively frightened people are reported in a study by Clevenger and King.[6] They suggest three general factors or categories of symptoms:

---

[4] G. M. Phillips, "Reticence: Pathology of the Normal Speaker," *Speech Monographs,* XXV, No. 1 (March, 1968), 44.

[5] Phyllis Battelle, "Stars Give Their Views on Acting as a Career," *The Detroit News,* December 6, 1961.

[6] Theodore Clevenger, Jr. and Thomas R. King, "A Factor Analysis of the Visible Symptoms of Stage Fright," *Speech Monographs,* XXVIII, No. 4 (November, 1961), 296. Also see T. Clevenger, "A Synthesis of Experimental Research in Stage Fright," *Quarterly Journal of Speech,* 45 (1959), 134–45.

FIDGETINESS	INHIBITION	AUTONOMIA
1. Shuffles feet	1. Deadpan	1. Moistens lips
2. Sways	2. Knees tremble	2. Plays with something
3. Swings arms	3. Hands in pocket	3. Blushes
4. Arms stiff	4. Face pale	4. Breathes heavily
5. Lacks eye contact	5. Returns to seat while speaking	5. Swallows repeatedly
6. Paces back and forth	6. Tense face	
	7. Hands tremble	

A study of other dimensions of the experience, intelligence, and personality of students who suffered from speech fright indicated the following conclusions:

1. They have not engaged in as much platform speaking activity.
2. They have not participated as much in extracurricular and social activities.
3. They have difficulty in always making an adequate social adjustment.
4. They tend to have less linguistic ability.
5. They have less interest in activities which involve verbal self-expression and in work involving the evaluation and supervision of others.[7]

The study further indicated through testing that these same students did not differ significantly from the others in terms of the following:

1. General intelligence.
2. Quantitative reasoning ability.
3. The more important phases of personality.
4. Interest in the fields of science, mechanics, nature, and business.

While you are pondering these symptoms and aspects of fright, you should realize that speech courses do help with this all too common problem. On a 10-point scale of speech-fright intensity, Henrikson discovered that at the end of the course the students made an average gain (more confidence) of 6.67 points.[8] Actual speaking experience was considered a major factor in gaining confidence.

The other common and important question you may ask is, "Even if I overcome this problem in the class, will my speech training carry over and help me in another situation?" Several researchers have explored the problem, and their discoveries are also reassuring. This is the psychological

---

[7] Gordon M Law and Boyd V. Sheets, "The Relations of Psychometric Factors to Stage Fright," *Speech Monographs,* XVIII, No. 4 (November, 1951), 266–71.

[8] E. Henrikson, "Some Effects on Stage Fright of a Course in Speech," *Quarterly Journal of Speech,* XXIX, No. 4 (December, 1943), 491.

and learning problem referred to as *transfer*. In a study by S. F. Paulson, speakers were taken from their regular class and made to speak before a strange class audience. The results of an adjustment inventory test indicated no decrease in confidence scores; it was concluded that a transfer of training did take place.[9]

It is encouraging to note that about three-fourths of a group of students at Penn State defined as *reticent* indicated noticeable positive effects on their out-of-class oral behavior after ten weeks of speech training.[10]

To a great extent man is afraid of what he does not understand. Young children may be paralyzed with fear during a severe electrical storm until their mother or father explains what precisely causes the thunder and lightning. Even afterwards the child will experience fear, but not of a paralyzing nature. Loud noises make all people jump and frighten oldsters and youngsters alike, but knowledge and understanding of what caused the loud noise make it possible for us to stop jumping *between* noises.

Because we are dealing with the symptoms and causes of an emotional reaction, it would follow from the preceding discussion that we will be better able to control emotion if we know in some detail what it is and how it operates.

The Nature of Emotion

In 1884, the famous psychologist William James presented us with a relatively simple and extremely useful theory of emotion. One year later, Carl Lange, who had worked independently of James, derived a strikingly similar thesis. The theory is now referred to as the James-Lange theory of emotion. Although there is controversy over this theory in some academic circles, the theory has great practical value for speakers.

> Our natural way of thinking about . . . emotions is that the mental perception of some fact excites the mental affection called the emotion [e.g., fear] and that this later state of mind gives rise to the bodily expression. My thesis on the contrary is that the bodily changes follow directly the perception of the exciting fact [stimulus] and that our feeling [awareness] of the same changes as they occur *is* the emotion.[11]

[9] Stanley F. Paulson, "Changes in Confidence During a Period of Speech Training: Transfer of Training and Comparison of Improved and Nonimproved Groups on the Bell Adjustment Inventory," *Speech Monographs,* XVIII, No. 4 (November, 1951), 260–65.

[10] G. M. Phillips, "Reticence," *Speech Monographs,* XXXV, 49.

[11] William James and Carl Lange, *The Emotions* (Baltimore: The Williams & Wilkins Co., 1922), I, 12. (Brackets and italics are this author's.)

The gist of the above is that it is awareness of our *reactions* to a frightening situation that is the *real* emotion. James' favorite illustration of this theory was that of a man coming upon a bear in the woods. In a nonscientific way, we might say the bear triggers the emotion of fear. Not so, for according to James, our body reacts almost automatically to the bear. Our natural survival devices take over to prepare us for an emergency. Our muscles tense for better agility, our heartbeat and breathing quicken to provide larger supplies of fuel, our glands secrete fluids to sharpen our senses and give us emergency energy. All of this happens in a blinding instant. Then we become aware of our bodily reactions. We sense our heavy breathing, our muscles tense to the point of trembling, perhaps even a surge of adrenalin into our body system. It is this *awareness* of these reactions that frightens us; in other words, that is the emotion. It follows that the bear still has a lot to do with this story! To tell you that if you understand clearly all the physiological reactions described above you've eliminated the bear is ridiculous. However, this knowledge and understanding, other things being equal, *will* help you better control what action you take and thereby considerably improve your chance for survival. This is what we mean by emotional or speech-fright control, and this is the reason we use the term *control* rather than *eliminate* when speaking of fear.

In the same manner that our fear of the bear is caused not by the bear itself but by our *awareness* of our bodily reactions to the bear, we can say that in speech fright it is our *awareness* of these internal and external signs that provides us with the emotion, or at least a reinforcement of the emotion, and may therefore become the cause of a large part of our trouble. The speech situation, though obviously less dangerous, poses a more difficult problem. Nature's physiological provisions typically prepare us for flight or fight, so that we either flee from the bear or attack him. The speech situation inhibits these natural utilizations of survival-oriented emotions, for you can neither attack the audience nor run for the woods. The problem is to drain off some of this excess energy while holding your ground and facing a fear-provoking stimulus (the audience). In your favor is the fact that there are no recorded instances of an audience eating a speaker!

The point of the bear story is to help you better understand the nature of emotion, for understanding and knowledge almost always promote emotional adjustment. There is a second lesson closely related to the first that may be of even more use to you. It is the principle of *objectification*. Intellectualization, objectification, or detailed explanation may destroy or at least take the edge off emotion. Let us imagine a great lover who, when kissing his beloved, decided to analyze objectively exactly what he was doing. A former student, reporting on one of his own objectification experiments, reported, "You know Doc, it takes all the kick out of it!" By the same reasoning, detailed intellectualization of the speech-fright experiences should help take some of the "kick" out of them. A veteran speech psychologist, Dr. Knower, refers to this phenomenon as a *law* of stage-fright control:

> Anything that increases the efficiency of intellectual control or reduces the intensity of emotional responses helps develop confidence in the speech situation.[12]

Have you ever asked yourself, "Why do my arms and hands tremble? Why do I have that sinking feeling in my stomach?" The issue is not *if* you experience these things, but rather *why?* If you do ask why and answer, "Because I'm scared to death," you probably only add to the emotion. This is the time to apply both the James-Lange theory of emotion and the principle of objectification. Remember that the emotion is primarily the result of your *awareness* of your own bodily reactions and that an objective explanation of the physiological experiences will take the edge off of your awareness.

Let us take the case of the trembling extremities. Skeletal muscles are usually arranged in antagonistic groups, one of which opposes the other. The muscles located on the inside or anterior surface of the arm and forearm are called *flexors;* those located on the back or outside (posterior) surface are called *extensors.* The flexors bend or draw up your arm; the extensors extend or straighten the arm. When either set of muscles contract, the opposing group undergoes relaxation—but not complete relaxation, for there is a *tone* to skeletal muscles, which gives them a certain firmness and maintains a slight, steady pull upon their attachments.[13] Suppose you *will* or direct your forearm to raise (much like the diagram—

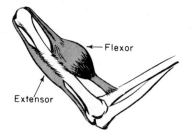

Figure 24. Antagonistic Muscles of the Arm and Forearm

---

[12] Baird and Knower, *Essentials of General Speech,* p. 38.

[13] Diana Clifford Kimber, Carolyn E. Gray, and Caroline E. Stackpole, *Textbook of Anatomy and Physiology,* 11th Ed. (New York: The Macmillan Company, 1946), p. 103.

try it). Your flexor muscles contract and your extensor muscles on the other side of your arm are forced to relax. If you will your arm to straighten out, the antagonistic muscles simply reverse functions. Now try something more interesting. Put your arm in about the position of the picture; will it to stay there and at the same time will both sets of muscles to contract at the same time. If you are really working at it, you will notice a tremble in your arm. If you extend your fingers, the tremble is usually quite evident in the hands. You have just produced a state very similar to the trembling that takes place in speech fright. Your real emotion, acting as it was intended, increases the natural tension of your antagonistic muscles and causes the same kind of trembling. You will still experience some trembling and you will still be aware of it, but theoretically at least, not in exactly the same way as before. You now have increased your intellectual activity about this phenomenon; you now know more about it. Other things being equal, you are better equipped both consciously and subconsciously to adjust to the event when it occurs. Some of the "kick" has been taken out of it. Although the lightning still startles you, you're somewhat better off because science and knowledge have explained *what* it is. Most important, your behavior may change qualitatively in a direction more acceptable to social custom.

A detailed and vivid description of the bodily reaction to threatening situations is provided by W. B. Cannon. These were his conclusions, based upon animal experimentation:

> The adrenalin in the blood is increased . . . which causes strong, rapid heartbeat, suspended activity of the stomach and intestines, wide opening of the air passages in the lungs, release of sugar from the liver, delay of muscle fatigue, free perspiration, dilation of the pupils of the eyes, more red corpuscles to carry oxygen, faster blood coagulation, and increased blood pressure.[14]

The sinking feeling in the stomach which we experience under duress can be physiologically explained in great detail. When faced with a fear-provoking situation, the body calls upon its glandular secretions, notably adrenalin, for emergency energy. These secretions chemically interfere with and literally halt the digestive system. This process tends to make the stomach contract and produces the sensation typically referred to as a "sinking feeling." At the same time, we also become aware of many lesser concomitant reactions, such as a rapidly beating heart (for added circulation) and heavier breathing (for extra oxygen fuel), which help prepare the body for survival. Searching for these rational explanations should help

---

[14] W. B. Cannon, *Bodily Changes in Pain, Hunger, Fear, and Rage* (Boston: Charles T. Branford Co., 1953), p. 368.

you maintain perspective and psychological equilibrium. We are often most afraid of things simply because we do not understand them.

The famous psychologist Edward Titchener was one of the early theorists who suggested that several emotions could not exist together. He believed that although they could follow each other very closely, they could not be mixed. We might say that most people cannot experience two opposite types of emotional reactions at the same time. For example, at that instant when you are boiling mad you are probably not afraid. This is not to suggest that you freely substitute anger for your fright, but you may already have observed that when a speaker is really wrapped up or immersed in his subject, he will tend to be less frightened by the platform situation. This in part helps explain our almost instinctive compensatory actions to fright situations. This is why we whistle while walking through a dark alley. We are acting "as if" we are unafraid—perhaps happy, indignant, or angry. Acting "as if" has helped all of us through emotionally charged situations. It is healthy to whistle in the dark; it is often the difference between panic and poise. Your choice of a speech topic may therefore be important to you emotionally as well as rhetorically. If you are excited or can become excited about your subject, you are making theory work for you—a kind of natural and intelligent whistling in the dark.

Controlling Emotion

The previous section on the nature of emotion has already indicated some of the principles useful in controlling speech fright. Let us talk about some specific actions you can take to further implement the theory.

Understand Emotion

Remember that emotion is primarily the result of *your awareness* of your own bodily reactions. An analysis of these reactions should help control fright. Emotion loses its intensity under explanation and objectification. Face up to your problems and get the facts straight. It is healthy to talk objectively about your fright; your instructor is a good listener. Let him help you talk it out. Thus you will meet your fright on a conscious level where you have the most control. If your mouth feels dry, find out why. If your knees shake, find out why. If you feel faint, find out why. The *why* is usually rather mundane, dull, and unexciting, but it is extremely logical and objective. Should inordinate speech fright persist, you may find it useful to reread and review this entire chapter at a later date.

Utilize Excess Tension

It should be clear from the previous discussion, particularly the bear story, that we direct our actions more usefully once we break the wall of tension with the first step. Actual physical movement—either away from the bear at full speed or toward him Davy-Crockett style—bursts the dam of tension. In your speech situation you are in no real danger. You have primarily the problem of releasing, burning, or draining off some of the extra energy that your body dutifully provides. Once again, the *first* step is very important. Bodily activity will help you utilize your extra energy or tension. This is evidenced by expectant fathers who pace the floor rather than stay put.

In the speaking situation, you might be concerned about how your activity looks and what it communicates to the audience. The strategy here is very simple—plan and direct some of your gross bodily movement in advance—not in a stereotyped way, but nevertheless systematically, complete with options. For example, at the close of your introduction or perhaps at a transition between points, you might plan on moving a step to the side or raising a book or card for emphasis. You have the option to select the precise time and action, depending upon how natural it seems and how tense you are. Another very natural kind of activity is that associated with visual aids. The communication values of visual aids are almost self-evident, but their value as emotion-controlling devices may not be so obvious. If you comment on a picture, demonstrate an object, or write on a blackboard, you have to make perfectly natural movements in the process. This is an excellent way to utilize excess energy. It is the same reason you will probably be asked to give a demonstration or visual-aid speech early in the semester. The lesson is obvious: use planned and directed activity freely as a means of utilizing excess tension and energy.

There are some pre-speech physical actions that can help you reduce your tension and relax. A brisk walk has helped many an athlete unwind. Even moderate exercises are in order. Of course you cannot do push-ups in the classroom, but deep breathing is possible. Lifting or pressing your chair has been successfully prescribed by speech teachers. Isometric exercises are inconspicuous and should help. A yawn is a natural outlet as long as you do not look *too* relaxed! A certain amount of repetition may also be a useful prespeech exercise. If the journey from your chair to the speaker's platform seems like the last mile, rehearse this activity in an empty class room or in measured distances at home. Keep rehearsing it until you sense a monotony in the repetition. College debaters often inadvertently repeat certain strategies and argument patterns so zealously in practice that they run a very real risk of becoming stale when presenting the same ideas in actual debate. Football teams have had similar experience. The point here is that monotonous repetition may help us drain off that keyed-up feeling.

Good health and a reasonable amount of rest are necessary for almost all sound emotional adjustment; speech and communication demand both because so much energy is involved. Assuming an understanding of and a willingness to utilize the suggestions above, a moderate amount of repression of external behavior may then also be in order to help you get started. By repression we mean a form of mental discipline in which you literally force yourself to get on with the business at hand. This is by no means a form of final adjustment, because continued repression would result in extreme fatigue and possible emotional disintegration. However, it is neither unusual nor abnormal to use moderate repression of external behavior as a first step in reaching adjustment.

Redirect Your Attention

Let your emotions work for you when you can. In moments of strain, redirect your attention to other things and bring more tolerable emotions to focus. It is a form of distraction. You try to become so involved in one thing that you are less aware of the other. Psychologists call this compensation. In a speech situation, one very obvious and natural avenue of distraction from your fright is an absorbing or vital interest in your subject. If you can get excited about your subject or develop a positive desire to communicate, you will often find much of your fright diminishing. If you can find humor in your task or in your reactions to it, you may have found a very healthy distraction.

You can redirect your attention in terms of the audience by concentrating on the smiling and pleasant faces for moral support. Most of your audiences are after all supportive. Research indicates that it is true, at least in persuasive speeches, that unfavorable feedback may result in some deterioration of adequate bodily movement, fluency, and the like.[15] One professor reported that he started to overcome his speech fright when he concentrated on the sleeping faces. He may have been substituting anger or he may have decided his fear was a little ridiculous if he was talking only to himself.

One can overdo this form of compensation. Take care not to so concentrate on redirecting your attention that you lose sight of the real purpose of your total effort—communication.

---

[15] Philip P. Amato and Terry H. Ostermeier, "The Effect of Audience Feedback on the Beginning Public Speaker," *The Speech Teacher,* XVI, No. 1 (January, 1967), 56–60.

Protect Your Memory

Our memory like our perceptions may become less dependable under severe forms of emotional duress.[16] It is also a fact that beginning speakers are often frightened, or the initial cause reinforced, by just the thought of forgetting their speech. It apparently becomes a vicious circle— speech fright becomes a cause of forgetting and the thought of forgetting a cause or reinforcer of speech fright.

As with redirecting attention, your subject or topic may have an important part to play. The more you know about a subject and the more enthused and excited you are, the less likely you are to forget your material. Your attitude toward your subject, your involvement in it, and your eagerness to communicate it are all related to memory.

In terms of preparation, the key word for memory protection is *system*. We remember better, we learn better, we speak better, if the material we're dealing with is systematically or serially arranged. Your organization of material can significantly affect your ability to remember. More will be said about rhetorical organization in later chapters. The point here is simply that it is easier to remember a list of 20 automobile names grouped, according to some system (that is, according to manufacturer, size, horsepower, and so on) than one in a random order. Have you ever noticed how rapidly you can learn the names of baseball players? Obviously it is because of the system of positions; if you do not know the positions, you will be slower at learning the names. Find a natural and meaningful order (to you) of your speech materials, and you will find it much easier to remember what comes next. Your audience, incidentally, will probably find your material easier to follow.

One of the most effective memory aids is a visual aid. If you are explaining how an internal-combustion engine works, it is obviously easier to remember functions and parts if you have the engine to point to. If your speech deals with numbers and statistics, a large card with the numbers listed and identified takes considerable pressure off your memory. An occasional speech note with testimony, statistics, or other details tucked in your pocket as a safety precaution is also helpful, even if it is not used. Just the knowledge that you have such a backstop is often worth more than the material on the cards. Some of the best speeches are delivered from a visual outline. All the major points and supporting statements are put on large cardboard visual aids in much the same way as one might put notes on 3 × 5 file cards. They serve much the same function, except that now

---

[16] James T. Freeman, "Set Versus Perceptual Defense: A Confirmation," *Journal of Abnormal Social Psychology,* LI (1955), 710–12.

you get credit for using visual aids instead of being criticized for being too dependent upon your notes. A visual-outline speech or chalk talk, in which you use the blackboard, is an exercise your instructor may wish to prescribe to help you learn the value of visual aids both as mnemonic devices and as agents for clarity.

Despite all the protection you can give your memory, all speakers occasionally experience the frustration of "blank out" or momentary forgetting. A good question is, "What do I do now?" If you have ever watched youngsters delivering memorized poems or salutations at an elementary school convocation, you have heard the children forget their materials. You probably also noticed that they almost instinctively keep repeating the last line they *do* remember in a frantic effort to go back and rerail their memory. This effort may help, but the prompter often has a busy day also. Word-for-word memorization is really not a very intelligent "system," because it cannot relate so many small, unrelated parts. Where word-for-word memorization is concerned, the lesson for you as a speaker should be obvious. However, the principle of repeating the last thing you do remember is still a useful concept. The practical application here is to *review* the material you have just covered. If your memory failure is toward the end of your speech, you can *summarize* the key points you have made. Practical experience indicates that these techniques do help you reawaken your memory. One student who found these suggestions useful formulated his own rule: "When in doubt, summarize." If you blank-out before you have really said anything, your summary had better not start, "In summary," or "In review"!

Evaluate Your Communication Role

We talked earlier of a professor who felt less speech fright when he discovered that most of his class was asleep. With all due respect to student audiences, an honest appraisal is that they are not eagerly leaning forward, straining with every muscle to record for all time the wisdom you are about to emit. Professors know this and so should you. Audiences may on occasion be lively, but more often than not, this is due to the efforts of the speaker. Experienced speakers and teachers live for those eager audience moments. Be objective about your audience. An analysis of speech-rating charts, particularly the write-in comments, indicates a sympathy toward the speaker in the form of a mild commiseration. This, freely translated, means that if the audience is listening at all, they are rooting for you.

However important your speech message, it will probably not be recorded for posterity. If every speaker in a class of 25 gave 10 speeches, any particular speech is 1 out of 250. If it is reassuring to be part of the crowd, then relax. Be realistic about your speech goals and their effect upon the audience.

Think of your speech in terms of the communication process discussed in Chapter 1 and realize the worthy purpose of speech training. Instead of worrying about what damage your ego may suffer, be afraid of *not* being able to motivate an audience to listen. Commiserate with and attempt a humorous perspective as you read the remarks of Adlai Stevenson about the 1952 Presidential campaign.

You must emerge, bright and bubbling with wisdom and well-being, every morning at 8 o'clock, just in time for a charming and profound breakfast talk, shake hands with hundreds, often literally thousands, of people, make several inspiring, newsworthy speeches during the day, confer with political leaders along the way and with your staff all the time, write at every chance, think if possible, read mail and newspapers, talk on the telephone, talk to everybody, dictate, receive delegations, eat, with decorum—and discretion!—and ride through city after city on the back of an open car, smiling until your mouth is dehydrated by the wind, waving until the blood runs out of your arm.

Then, you bounce gaily, confidently, masterfully into great howling halls, shaved and all made up for television with the right color shirt and tie—I always forgot—and a manuscript so defaced with chicken tracks and last minute jottings that you couldn't follow it, even if the spotlights weren't blinding and even if the still photographers didn't shoot you in the eye every time you looked at them. Then all you have to do is make a great, imperishable speech, get out through the pressing crowds with a few score autographs, your clothes intact, your hands bruised, and back to the hotel—in time to see a few important people.

But the real work has just commenced—two or three, sometimes four, hours of frenzied writing and editing of the next day's immortal mouthings so you can get something to the stenographers, so they can get something to the mimeograph machines, so they can get something to the reporters, so they can get something to their papers by deadline time.

The next day is the same. But I gained weight on it. And it's as tenacious as a campaign deficit!

And, too, there is mirth mingled with the misery all along the way. They shout, "Good old Ad-lie!" If you run for office and have a slightly unusual name, let me advise you either to change it before you start, or be prepared to take other people's word for it. And I shall not soon forget about the woman in the crowd in San Francisco who reached into the car to shake hands with me, and not long after discovered that she had lost her diamond ring. Nor will I forget the warm welcome I received on a whistle stop in Bethlehem, Pa., and my thanks to 'the people of Allentown.' My only hope is that *they* forget it! Again, out West, I warmly endorsed the impressive chairman of a meeting as a candidate for Congress, only to discover that he was not running for Congress or anything else.[19]

---

[19] Bill Adler, "Adlai Stevenson's Wit," *THIS WEEK Magazine,* September 12, 1965, p. 5. Reprinted from *THIS WEEK* magazine. Copyrighted 1965 by the United Newspaper Corporation. Reprinted with the permission of the author and his agents, Scott Meredith Literary Agency, Inc., 580 Fifth Ave., New York, New York 10036.

Finally, evaluate your communication role in a total sense. Your speeches will be lost in hundreds of other speeches; your audience is generally sympathetic; your instructor is trained to be alert to your problem; and the rhetorical and psychological research in speech has given us reliable methods and knowledge to help you learn. Have faith in hard-earned experience and knowledge; have faith in the goodness of people; have faith in yourself.

Summary

Most beginning speech students (60 to 75 percent) admit that they are bothered by nervousness. About 35 percent consider it a severe problem. Professional performers report similar feelings of tensions. It is significant that reports indicate you do not *appear* and *sound* as bad as you *feel*. Research also indicates that the frightened people do not differ from the confident minority in very basic ways such as intelligence and the important phases of personality and that students do gain confidence during a course in speech and are able to transfer this learning to other situations.

Understanding the nature of emotion is useful because it helps us objectify our feelings and reactions. The James-Lange theory of emotion suggests essentially that it is our awareness of our *reactions* to a frightening situation that is the *real* emotion. Emotion is a good and necessary phenomenon. The problem is one of control. An understanding of the physiological reactions helps us to control our emotions. Objectification of the emotional reactions tends to take the edge off emotion, making it easier to control. An increase in intellectual activity helps reduce emotional intensity. We are afraid of what we do not understand.

Most people cannot experience two opposite types of emotional reactions at the same time. If you are excited or can become excited about your subject, you are making theory work for you—a kind of natural and intelligent whistling in the dark.

Some specific suggestions for controlling emotion involve:

1. Understanding emotion and the principle that objectification and intellectualization reduce tension.
2. The utilization of excess tension by planning and directing some of your gross bodily activity in advance of the speech situation.
3. The redirecting of your attention to more pleasant emotions to let your emotions work for you.

4. The protecting of your memory through logical systems of organization, visual aids, and pre-set psychological options or alternatives.

5. An honest evaluation of your communication role and situation and a faith in knowledge, the goodness of people, your creator, and yourself.

6. Concentrate on the message more than yourself.

There is no recorded experience of an audience having eaten a speaker!

Language:
Meaning
and Use **3**

Language As Code and Symbol

We will consider language in the light of previous discussions of the communication and perceptual processes, namely as code and symbol. In many respects, it is in the use of oral language that we need our most rigorous training, for there is an infinitely larger number of meanings available to the communicatee (the listener) in the oral situation than in the reader situation, due to the concomitant or simultaneous signals that are operative over and above words. Your voice, for example, is a wonderfully sensitive instrument, which has a powerful influence upon the meaning the listener attaches both to the words and to the speaker himself. The correct use of voice is thus very important. The appearance of the speaker—his dress, movement, facial expressions, and use of gestures—represents another concomitant signal that obviously affects the decoding mechanism of the listener; this general category of visible codes will be referred to as *action*. Another less obvious point to be made is that these codes and signals are related in such a way as to seriously and fundamentally affect each other. Sometimes they work together and strengthen or reinforce the meaning intended by the speaker. Sometimes, however, they conflict with each other and distort the intended meaning to a point of confusion, suspicion, or frustration on the part of the listener. Consider the sloppy student giving a speech on the value of personal neatness, or a professor speaking through a frozen grin while discussing the possibility of a student failing his course. We often express actions contrary to what we really intend. The cause may be tension, emotion involvement, or simply poor speech training.

Let us now turn to the all-important symbols we call *words,* remembering that the concomitant codes and symbols previously discussed will affect their intended meaning over and above what is said here. Words are symbols that are conventionally agreed upon to represent certain things. They are convenient labels, which help us to classify things. It is obvious that there are more things and concepts in the world than there are words. So you think a dog is a dog! Try these definitions.

Dog: a canine animal
Dog: a clamp used on a lathe
Dog: an andiron used in a fireplace
Dog: a worthless person
Dog: a kind of sandwich
Dog: to follow closely
Dog: to loaf on the job
Dogged: persistent
Dog-tired: exhausted
Dog days: hot, sultry weather

By way of further example, if each and every chair in the world had its own label, we would have nothing but dictionaries related to chairs.

Even with the general abstraction or classifying word *chair,* we have developed a large vocabulary of chair-words (for example, Windsor, Hitchcock, stuffed, swivel, rocking). In short, we must use a limited number of words to represent an infinite number of things or we could hardly communicate at all. Despite our useful and necessary dictionaries, no word has real meaning except in the particular context in which it is used. Although the variation in meaning may not always be a serious one, the meaning will never be quite the same from one situation to another. This is because words do represent different meanings in different situations and because they do change when we take words for granted and think of them as actual things rather than as what they really are—representations of things. A good speaker must always ask himself, "What does *this* word mean to *this* audience in *this* situation, in *this* context, as used by *this* speaker at *this* time?"

A word may then be thought of as a representation or generalization having meaning according to its context. When we arrange words into the context (or syntax) of a sentence, we are really fitting generalizations together. The meaning of an English sentence is determined not by words alone, but primarily by the total arrangement and sequence of the words within it. Even this meaning may be vague if its context within the larger paragraph or chapter is not known.

In one sense the communication pattern of a sentence is the systematic exclusion from the listener's attention of meanings he might attach that are *not* intended by the speaker. In short, it may define meanings *not* intended.

Two forward-looking linguists, Donald J. Lloyd and Harry R. Warfel, illustrate this function clearly and simply. Let us use their sentence:

THE YOUNG MAN AT THE CORNER WHO SEEMS VERY MILD BEATS HIS WIFE.

Beginning with *man,* let us use a circle to indicate all the possible meanings of *man* in all potential utterances:

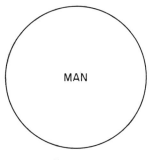

Figure 25

We will take *the* as pointing out one instance of *man*—whatever *man* means. We put a dot in the circle to stand for this one instance.

Figure 26

The word *young*—whatever it means—has the force of cutting out of consideration all meanings of *man* that cannot accept the description *young:*

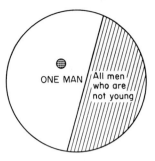

Figure 27

The group *at the corner* cuts out of consideration all meanings of *man* that cannot be located in that bit of space:

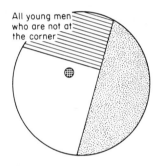

Figure 28

The group *who seems very mild* cuts out all *young men* who do not *seem mild:*

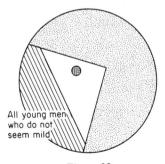

Figure 29

The word *beats* cuts out all such men who *do not beat*—whatever *beat* means:

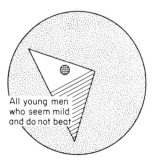

Figure 30

The group *his wife* limits *beats* and by doing so puts a further limitation on *man*. It excludes all other objects of beating, such as *dogs, opponents* or *rugs.*

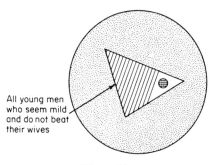

Figure 31

This analysis of a sentence[1] shows how a writer or speaker utilizes arrangement and listener or reader attention to delimit meaning.

> The force of the pattern is to cut away meanings not intended. . . . Each word or word-group removes from consideration all instances of the key word that do not accept the qualification expressed in the word or in the group. The utterance reveals a successive removal from attention of the instances of the key word that are not affirmed by the successive elements in the sentence. It cuts a large and unmanageable area of meaning down to size. The whole sentence becomes the equivalent of what has tradi-

[1] Reprinted by permission of Alfred A. Knopf, Inc., from *American English in Its Cultural Setting* by Donald J. Lloyd and Harry R. Warfel. Copyright 1956 by Donald J. Lloyd and Harry R. Warfel.

tionally been called a proper noun: a noun "used to designate a specific individual, place, etc." It is a marvelous operation.[2]

Long-standing language and word habits may lead to rigid and consistent emotional responses that appear to hold almost regardless of context. A study of racially offensive words[3] found that at least some of the 223 Negroes surveyed in 1964 viewed the following words as derogatory in almost any "Negro–non-Negro" situation. The words asterisked indicate that the non-Negro sample (251 non-Negroes) viewed the words as significantly less derogatory than did the Negro.[4]

RACIALLY POTENT WORDS

Word	% Offensiveness (Negro)	% Offensiveness (Non-Negro)
nigger	95	92
darkie *	87	75
Sambo *	85	74
spook *	83	70
mammy *	78	52
inkspot *	73	38
nappy *	72	43
Aunt Jemima*	70	21
kinky *	69	53
nigra *	67	43
shine *	65	43
you-people *	65	43
pickaninny *	65	39
black *	59	40
Sammie *	58	33
gal *	53	15
boy *	42	8
Charley *	39	8
colored	27	31
Negro	15	15

* Significantly different responses.

But word habits do change! The *New York Amsterdam News,* one of the largest Afro-American newspapers, announced that it would no longer use the word "Negro." They now identify Americans of African descent as Afro-Americans. The Negro Teachers Association of New York City has become the African-American Teachers Association.[5] *Ebony* magazine

---

[2] Lloyd and Warfel, *American English in Its Cultural Setting,* p. 109.

[3] Reprinted by permission of the authors and the Association for Childhood Education International, 3615 Wisconsin Avenue, N.W., Washington, D.C. G. A. Maddox and R. S. Ross, "Strong Words," *Childhood Education,* XLV, No. 5 (January, 1969), 260–64.

[4] The 0.02 level of significance.

[5] Lerone Bennett Jr., "What's In A Name?" *Ebony Magazine,* XXIII, No. 1, (November 1967), 46–54.

surveyed its readers on the potent question of names or labels by asking them to indicate their preferences for the names *Afram, African-American, Afro-American, Black, Colored, Overseas African* or *Negro.* The survey results are not reported as of this writing.[6] However, a study by *The Michigan Chronicle* found in the Detroit area the word "Afro-American" preferred by its respondents.

A poll of 218 registered Negro voters in metropolitan Detroit in late August, 1968 produced the following results in order of preference:

	Total Sample 218	Age 21–40 Sample 98	Age 40+ Sample 120
Negro	32%	24%	36%
Afro-American	24%	22%	26%
Black	16%	19%	13%
Colored	16%	19%	14%
Other	12%	16%	11%

The "other" included replies such as "I'd rather be thought of just as a person," or "As an American."[7]

The word "black" indicates that time and context do make a difference. In the 1964 study by Ross and Maddox, "black" was offensive to 59 percent of the Negroes surveyed. In 1967 the youth section at the Black Power Conference in Newark led the debate against use of the word "Negro." Negro in the 1964 study was offensive to only 15 percent of the Blacks sampled. In the early 1950s, sensitive teachers found "African" was discriminatory to many Afro-American students.

> The reasons for some of the racial potency attached to some words by Negroes are often difficult to understand, and perhaps it is even more difficult for the Negro to understand *why* the non-Negro should find them so difficult. In part this difficulty may be attributed to the fact that there was an almost complete lack of Negroes in some sections of the country previous to the migrations begun after World War I. Besides this, an outright discrimination for many years thereafter allowed for little feedback on Negro reaction to communications. For example, in 1913 a New York department store advertised shoes as "nigger brown," and right up to the 40s, we sold "Nigger-Hair Tobacco."[8]

In the light of the above, it is not difficult to understand why certain sensitivities exist and why the Negro may appear to be overly sensitive in reacting to words not intended to be derogatory. If all Americans were more aware of these words and language segments, which may unneces-

---

[6] *Ibid.,* p. 54.

[7] "Negro, Colored or Black?" *The Detroit News,* Sept. 8, 1968, p. 1.

[8] G. A. Maddox and R. S. Ross, "Strong Words," *Childhood Education,* Vol. 45, p. 260.

sarily provoke hostility, perhaps we could foster better communication between us.

W. W. Bauer, a physician, put it well: "Words can be many things. They can be weapons. They can be messengers of peace. The right word can soothe like the soft touch of a gentle hand. The wrong word can lacerate like a sword. Even truth, unkindly or unskillfully spoken, can be as deadly as any poison."[9]

The emotional interpretations attached to language demand careful audience analysis and word selection on the part of the speaker. Words are not things or emotions, but we often act as if they were. Language is by nature abstract and involves generalizations about concrete or real things.

Abstraction

Abstracting is a process of thinking in which we selectively leave out details about concrete or real things. The nature of perception indicates that we are dealing with at least two factors, namely (1) sensation and (2) interpretation of the stimuli impinging upon our senses. This interpretation is heavily controlled by our individual knowledge, experience, and emotional set. For this reason, as well as the limitations of our language system discussed previously, all language involves an element of abstraction.

The process of abstraction may be classified into levels. For example, Bambi may be considered a first-order verbal abstraction; that is, Bambi is a very specific form and kind of deer. A deer in turn is a special kind of animal and so on. As we move from lower- to higher-order abstractions, we tend to consider fewer and fewer details of the specific or original object. Another way of looking at abstracting is to consider first-hand observations as facts, but facts which may never be described in an absolutely complete way. If we become divorced from firsthand descriptions, we are in a different order of abstraction—inference. Most simply, an inference goes beyond what is observed. If an ambulance is in your driveway when you return home, you may say, "One of my family has been seriously hurt." This is an inference. You must go into the house to see if it is valid. Upon entering the house, you may find a close friend excitedly telling your healthy family about his new business venture of converting station wagons into ambulances. Suppose you have been told by a resort owner that the fishing is great on the edge of some weeds. If you are a veteran fisherman, you will ask, "What does 'great' mean?" You will want more than infer-

[9] W. W. Bauer, "The Bloodless Emergency," *This Week Magazine*, Oct. 23, 1966, p. 25.

ences, namely descriptions of this great fishing ("Just this morning a fellow took five bass in two hours"). Of course, in dealing with fishermen one might be just a little suspicious of the reliability of the description (another inference). One scholar put it this way: "The reliability of inferences depends on the reliability of the descriptive premises, and description is more reliable than inference."[10] When we are in the realm of inference, then, we are dealing with probability rather than certainty.

Specificity

When we support our inferential statements with specific, descriptive statements and examples, we will not only be using more accurate, but probably more interesting language. The question of how much specificity to use is not always an easy one. For example, a physicist, in explaining atomic fission to us, might choose only terms that are closely related to their referents—that is, highly specific, technical, and scientific. He is in one sense using accurate language, but his message (because of the detail) may be very long and for non-physicists very difficult to understand. Should he decide to eliminate detail in an effort to use less time and to avoid technical language in an effort to sustain interest, he will then lose precision of meaning; his listeners may attach a wider range of meanings from their own experiences than he had intended, and this might lead to serious distortion, confusion, or contradiction.

For the speaker, the answer to this dilemma is typically found in the interest and previous knowledge of the audience. Just how important is precision in relation to this subject and this audience? Is there a potential danger involved, such as in a drug prescription or in a speech on hypodermic injections to an audience of student nurses? Time is another factor in resolving this problem. Classroom speeches will tend to be short, and this fact alone may foster the problems of overgeneralization, lack of specificity, and inaccuracy of meaning. It is probably true that it is easier to give a long speech than a short one.

Language and Personality

Language and the particular character you give it through usage has obvious importance in terms of your message. However, language habits alone often convey our

---

[10] Alfred Korzybski, *Science and Sanity* (Lancaster, Pa.: The Science Press Printing Co., 1933), p. 479.

personality (or assumed personality) to the listener. For example, extreme cases of talkativeness or undertalkativeness are often indications of emotional maladjustment. This pattern may afflict all of us in moments of distress, peril, or unhappiness, but a consistent pattern may call for professional help. As was indicated in Chapter 1, the problem of autistic thinking, or interpreting communication only in terms of your desires, is a serious problem; when practiced consistently, it is thought to be indicative of what the psychiatrist calls paranoia. One of the most characteristic language patterns of schizophrenics is an apparent confusion between words and things. The words are not representations of reality, but reality itself. For the schizophrenic, objective systematic abstraction is difficult, and he is extremely one-sided and opinionated. The sobering thought in discussing the extreme language habits of maladjusted people is that we are all guilty to some degree of doing all these things. It behooves us to be aware of our patterns lest we too represent a one-value world of words without referents. All "normal" speakers should ponder Wendell Johnson's compelling description of the linguistically irresponsible behavior of schizophrenics:

> (1) An "emotional flatness," an unresponsive, poker-faced air of detachment; (2) a grotesque confusion of sense and nonsense, essentially the same tone of voice, facial expression, and general manner being employed in making sensible remarks as in uttering the purest gibberish; (3) an apparent lack of self-criticism, a striking failure to show any glimmer of curiosity about whether the listener understands or agrees; and (4) a general confusion or identification of level of abstraction, as though all levels were one and the same, there being no apparent differentiation between higher and lower orders of inference and between inference and description.[11]

If the last paragraph frightened you just a little, this is a healthy sign, for your powers of evaluation had to go beyond just the words. Remember that your language habits bespeak your personality. We shall now examine some practical suggestions for improving your language and avoiding linguistic behavior patterns that convey unintended and undesirable meanings.

Improving Your Language Habits

Almost any good course in speech, whatever its context (radio, television, public speaking, persuasion, semantics, rhetoric, correction, theater, communication, discus-

---

[11] Wendell Johnson, *People in Quandaries* (New York: Harper & Row, Publishers, 1946), p. 275.

sion, or debate), puts a high premium on language habits. The instructor will criticize you diligently, for he knows that proper language habits will make it easier for you to adjust to the linguistic demands of college life.

Reading and listening, when done systematically, will help improve your language behavior. In both reading and listening, you are essentially involved in the receiving and decoding function of communication. Critical, objective listening and reading habits have been an intimate part in the training of almost all famous speakers.[12]

When reading or listening to a speech, try to determine what the words mean to the speaker and how the time of the communication might alter the meaning. All the communication signals and cues have to be considered in critical listening; as was discussed earlier, the nonword signals (gestures, visual aids, vocal emphasis, and others) are an intimate part of the message. The way in which an idea is stated cannot really be divorced from the idea itself. Perhaps the most important aspect of listening, as well as reading, pertains to the listener's awareness of his own beliefs, prejudices, or lack of knowledge; *what* we believe profoundly influences our ability to perceive objectively. This is not to suggest that one should not believe anything. Were this the case, we might never make any kind of a necessary decision. The point is simply to know more precisely *what* you believe and be aware of its role in your listening and reading habits.

It should be evident to you by this time that it is literally impossible for a person to "say exactly what he means." Much of our language behavior is what S. I. Hayakawa calls presymbolic[13]—that is, it may function even without recognizable speech or perhaps with symbols that approach the character of an idiom. A grunt from my office partner at 8:00 A.M. means, "Good morning, it's good to see you." When you pass a friend on the street and he says "Hi," how does this really differ from "How are you?" Does "Nice day" mean just that and no more?

A favorite illustration of many teachers regarding this point concerns a man staring dejectedly at a very flat tire. A smiling farmer comes up and asks, "Got a flat tire?" If we take his words in an absolutely literal sense his communication appears stupid indeed and we might answer, "Can't you see, birdbrain?" A famous psychiatrist interprets the words, "Got a flat tire?" as follows:

Hello—I see you are in trouble. I'm a stranger to you but I might be your friend now that I have a chance to be if I had any assurance that my friendship would be welcomed. Are you approachable? Are you a decent

12 See W. N. Brigance, ed., *History and Criticism of American Public Address* (New York: McGraw-Hill Book Company, 1943), p. vii.
13 S. I. Hayakawa, *Language in Thought and Action* (New York: Harcourt, Brace & World, Inc., 1949), p. 77.

fellow? Would you appreciate it if I helped you? I would like to do so but I don't want to be rebuffed. This is what my voice sounds like. What does your voice sound like?[14]

When language is used in a presymbolic sense, we have to look considerably beyond the actual words to get the real meaning intended. We must take precautions to see that in our efforts to become alert, critical listeners, we do not become so literal-minded that we mistake tact and social grace for inaneness, hypocrisy, or stupidity. Much of what we refer to as small talk is in part presymbolic language. In the interest of being an objective and honest receiver or listener, we must strive to distinguish presymbolic from symbolic language.

Let us now look at some specific actions you might take as a communicative and responsible speaker to improve your use of language.

One of the most prevalent communication faults on the part of student speakers is faulty or inadequate generalization. This is the problem of selectively leaving out details and arriving at an overstatement or concluding after only a modest search that a thing is true beyond any shadow of doubt. If upon driving into Detroit for the first time you (1) witness a serious accident, (2) observe a truck exceeding the speed limit, and (3) get a dented fender in a busy intersection, it might be very easy to conclude absolutely and speak absolutely about the character of Detroit drivers. However, a search of comparative safety records, driver education programs, and driver insurance rates would be minimal prerequisites for any intelligent deduction about Detroit drivers. Then you might want to qualify specifically your generalization by noting that Detroit has more cars per capita than any other city in the world.

A violently antiunion student speaker opened one of his class speeches with the words, "Unions are ruining this country. I am going to prove to you that they are entirely corrupt and more dangerous than the Communist Party." The sound of this language was enough for his opponents to throw up an emotional communication barrier so that not much useful speaking took place. The most interesting part of this story is that it was the pro-management people who were most critical of his speech. Even when a sophisticated audience agrees essentially with your point of view, they are offended by extreme overstatement and overgeneralization, for it is an indication of immaturity, emotional insecurity, or stupidity. Certain persons (for example, Hitler) have successfully disregarded this rule, but as history records and evaluates these complicated situations one finds that the wages of extreme and unethical generalization are almost always the same.

---

[14] Karl Menninger, *Love Against Hate* (New York: Harcourt, Brace & World, Inc., 1942), pp. 268–69.

The irony and tyranny of overgeneralization is that it is usually not intended—it seems so obvious that all Detroit drivers are crazy! When a person speaks from firsthand experience in a sincere and friendly voice without being aware or conscious of his faulty abstracting or generalizing, we are faced with a serious problem. The speaker obviously carries an ethical responsibility proportionate to his reputation. Perhaps this is why sophisticated men of high ethical qualities are often accused of qualifying things to the point of vagueness—which itself raises the ethical question as to how much you can qualify before you in effect completely dodge your obligations and responsibilities. The communication problems of generalization are complicated, frustrating, and often dangerous for the speaker. Once this fact is clearly understood, you have already solved much of the practical problem, for it is in being *aware* or conscious of abstracting and generalizing that we find the beginnings of the checks and balances that inhibit overstatement and reckless generalization.

A practical way of implementing this awareness is to qualify statements with great care. The date of an event often seriously affects the meaning a listener will attach to it. The following hypothetical statement by the Emperor of Japan might have a different meaning according to the date:

> At last the Japanese people have taken the actions which will restore their rightful dignity.
>
> January 7, 1925
> December 7, 1941
> June 23, 1945
> July 1, 1968

A favorite exam question of one psychology professor was, "What are Thorndike's laws of learning?" The devastating character of this question is that Thorndike had changed his mind about some of his laws of learning and had made this clear in his writings after 1930. If you had read only his pre-1930 writings, you would not have known this.

Another practical implementation is to leave your listeners with the impression that you have not said the last word on the subject. In this case you might consider adding some form of verbal *et cetera* to your qualifying terms; you thereby avoid alienating your listeners by seeming a naïve know-it-all, blinded by zeal, bias, or prejudice.

Finally (and that itself is a dangerous word), try to think like the listener; try to understand your subject and position from *his* point of view. Audience analysis is a critical part of public speaking and will be covered in more detail in Chapter 4. Knowing what you think is equally important. If you do not care what the audience thinks, are not very sure of your own purpose, and are unaware of your preferences, your beliefs, and your word meanings, you are in for a difficult and frustrating series of speeches. The meaning of any speech is really in the mind of the listener. You must so manipulate your language to help him select and sort from his word-representations something approximating your purpose.

> Humpty-Dumpty said: "There's glory for you." "I don't know what you mean by 'glory,'" Alice said. Humpty-Dumpty smiled contemptuously. "Of course you don't—till I tell you." "But 'glory' doesn't mean 'a nice knock-down argument,'" Alice objected. "When I use a word," Humpty-Dumpty said in a rather scornful tone, "It means just what I choose it to mean, neither more nor less."[15]

Summary

Language has been discussed primarily in the context of code and symbol. Oral language calls for more rigorous training than other forms because of the larger number of concomitant signals. Voice, for example, has a powerful influence upon meaning. A speaker's appearance and gestures represent still another concomitant signal which affects the listeners.

Words are a form of symbol. A word is a generally agreed upon representation of a thing. There are obviously more things and concepts in the world than there are words, so a word may be thought of as a representation or generalization having meaning according to its context. A speaker should ask himself, "What does *this* word mean to *this* audience in *this* situation, in *this* context, as used by *this* speaker at *this* time?" A good sentence systematically excludes from the listener's attention meanings he might attach that are not intended by the speaker—in short, to qualify by defining meanings *not* intended.

Abstraction is that process of thinking in which we selectively leave out details about concrete or real things. Short speeches may foster overgeneralization. This is why short speeches often call for more preparation than long ones.

Language habits bespeak your personality. Seriously maladjusted people can often be identified by their language habits. Speech courses, together with attentive reading and listening, will help you learn proper language behavior.

The *way* in which you say a thing is often as important as *what* you say. The listener as well as the speaker should be aware of his own beliefs,

---

[15] Lewis Carroll, *Through the Looking-Glass* (Cleveland: The World Publishing Company, 1946), p. 245.

prejudices, or lack of knowledge. It is almost impossible to say *exactly* what you mean. We must take precautions not to become so literal-minded that we mistake tact and social grace for hypocrisy or stupidity. We must strive to distinguish presymbolic from symbolic language.

Sophisticated audiences are offended by extreme overgeneralization even when they agree with your general point of view. The speaker carries a tremendous ethical responsibility. It is in being conscious of abstraction and generalization that we begin to meet our ethical responsibilities. Qualify your statements in terms of date and time and verbal *et ceteras*. Try to think like the listener. Manipulate your language so as to help the listener select and sort from his word-representations something approximating your purpose.

Purpose
and Delivery
in
Speaking **4**

General Purposes for Speaking

In the previous three chapters, we have discussed some general theory and knowledge essential to intelligent, objective speech and communication, namely: the process of communication, the nature of emotion and its relation to confidence, and the use of language. In this chapter, we will study the general purposes for speaking and the various ways of delivering a speech. The specific ways of preparing and outlining a speech will be explained and illustrated in a later chapter.

The insurance agent who comes to your door with policy in hand is primarily interested in selling you the policy. Even though he may present an armload of objective and practical information to indicate the risks of not having insurance and to describe how the policy works, his general purpose is to persuade. A speech billed as an "Informative Talk on the Arts" may turn out to be a highly derogatory piece of persuasion on abstraction or abstract painting, although most of the material may be truly informative and perhaps very entertaining. These examples illustrate the difficulty of intelligently dividing the purposes for speaking into even the apparently obvious ones of informing, persuading, and entertaining. It is probably true that there is no such thing as a purely informative, purely persuasive, or even purely entertaining speech. Even the most overgeneralized, flamboyant oratory probably involves at least a smidgeon of information. Entertainment, from court jesters to comedy players, has for ages been the vehicle of subtle and effective persuasion. And some very effective persuasive speeches have had the sound or ring of informative talks; some in fact, were compositionally almost all information.

The sheer amount of informative, entertaining, or persuasive elements does not alone indicate the kind of speech or speaker purpose with which we are dealing. The arrangement of the material, the information level of the audience, the speaker's style and vocal adaptation, and many more factors must be taken into consideration.

With the above paragraphs as qualifiers, let us become a little more arbitrary. Educationally, it is practical and useful to take these intermixed purposes one at a time. If your instructor asks you to prepare an informative speech for the next class and you state your purpose as, "To inform the class why they should join the Republican party," you had better be prepared for criticism. He will probably suggest that you save the subject for the persuasive speech assignment and that you then more accurately state your purpose as, "To persuade the class to join the Republican party." You might use as your purpose, "To inform the class about the history of the Republican party." The speech then becomes essentially or primarily either informative or persuasive depending upon the treatment and emphasis you use. Certainly this *could* be an excellent, *essentially* informative speech subject.

It might be said that your real purpose is known in terms of the primary reaction you want from your audience. The general purposes for speaking may be stated as follows:

THE GENERAL PURPOSES FOR SPEAKING

Purpose	Goals
To inform	Clarity
	Interest
	Understanding
To persuade	Belief
	Action
	Stimulation
To entertain	Interest
	Enjoyment
	Humor

To Inform

One of the most frequent purposes for speaking is to inform people of something about which you either have more knowledge than they do or know in a different or more specific way. This is the purpose of a typing teacher who is showing students how to approach the keyboard. The teacher or instructor also lectures primarily to inform. The speaker who would inform has the obligation of making his information or instruction clear and interesting as well as easy for the audience to learn, remember, and apply. To achieve these goals, a speaker should know something of how man learns (this will be discussed in detail in Chapter 8). Briefly, a man learns through his previous knowledge and experience, and he learns more easily when material is arranged in some meaningful sequence or serial order. He remembers better because of reinforcement (enhancing the message through repetition), verbal emphasis, organization, effective use of voice, and similar techniques. The primary goal in informative speaking is *audience understanding;* the key principles involved are *clarity, interest,* and *organization of material.*

To Persuade

The general goals of a speech to persuade involve getting people to believe something, getting people to do something, and stimulating or in-spiring people to a higher level of enthusiasm and devotion.

These divisions (belief, action, and stimulation), like the general pur-poses for speaking, often overlap and are not easily discernible at first glance. When no immediate or relatively immediate action is being called for, the speaker may be attempting to convince or to induce *belief.* This might be illustrated by persuasive speeches, such as "Foreign Policy," "The Threat of Communism," or "Uphold the United Nations." No specific and immediate action or performance is asked of the audience. Rather, the audience is asked to agree with the speaker and to believe and be con-vinced. This assumes that the audience does not typically have the power to act except in some remote or distantly related way. If the audience were the Congress of the United States, these could become action purposes.

When the audience is asked to do something specific and immediately following the speech, the purpose is one of *action.* A speech asking for donations to the Red Cross, which is concluded by passing a container for contributions among the audience, is an obvious example. Electioneering speeches asking people to vote or to sign petitions are further examples. Most sales talks are action speeches—even though the TV announcer does not really expect you to run out and buy a Chevrolet at 11:30 P.M. Nevertheless, the action is typically specific and typically available in the very near future.

When a speaker is seeking a higher degree of audience involvement, enthusiasm, or devotion on issues and beliefs that the audience already holds, his purpose is one of *inspiration* or *stimulation.* For example, a speech for party unity at a political convention after the nominee has been selected. In short, the purpose of stimulation is found in those situations where the speaker is: (1) not trying to change any basic attitudes, but rather to reinforce them; (2) not trying to prove anything, but rather to remind them; (3) not calling for any special or unique action, but inspiring them to a more enthusiastic fulfillment of the actions to which they are already committed.

To Entertain

When your purpose in speaking is to help people escape from reality, and you sincerely desire that they enjoy themselves, your general purpose is to entertain. The "fun," after-dinner, or radio-television speeches are the most typical examples. These speeches involve jokes, stories, and a variety of humor depending upon the experience, skill, and personality of both the speaker and his audience. In a speech solely to entertain, the audience should preferably understand that purpose and be genuinely encouraged to relax and enjoy themselves.

A word of warning is in order for both beginning speakers and experienced speakers. Other things being equal, the speech to entertain is the most difficult kind of speech to give! The feedback is more rapid and far less subtle. There is little doubt when a funny story or joke does not succeed. The effect on the speaker is often demoralizing and the presentation and adaptation of the rest of the speech may suffer. Practice is critical.

Types of Delivery

The four principal ways of delivering a speech are: (1) by reading from a manuscript, (2) by memorization, (3) by impromptu delivery, and (4) by speaking extemporaneously. The subject and the occasion are the primary determinants of which one or which combination of types should be used at a given time.

Reading from Manuscript

In this type of delivery, the speaker presents his subject by reading a completely written out, verbatim manuscript to the audience. Fortunately, the subjects and occasions that demand this method of delivery and preparation are few, for this is probably the most difficult of all the types of delivery; however, such occasions are on the increase. An important policy speech by the United States Secretary of State may be dissected word by word by foreign governments; therefore, it will call for maximum accuracy in wording and a minimum of opportunity for misstatement. Our mass media make further demands on speaker inflexibility. Very often a copy of the manuscript is obtained in advance of the speech so that the newspapers can print or quote the speech almost before it has been delivered. When such a speaker deviates from his manuscript, he invites trouble and confusion. Certain highly complicated and technical subjects demanding absolute accuracy may call for manuscript reading. Very rigid and inflexible time limits may also necessitate reading from a manuscript so that the speech does not exceed the allotted time; this is especially important in radio and television broadcasts.

The problems of this type of delivery, even for a classroom speech, should be obvious. The preparation must be painfully accurate, but worse, there is little chance for spontaneity or for momentary adaptation or adjustment of the material to the ever changing demands of the audience. The actual delivery, except for very exceptional readers, is hamstrung by a lack of eye-contact and directness; the speaker's eyes are typically glued to his manuscript, except for furtive glances into outer space, which only cause him to lose his place. This embarrassment may cause him to retrench, by which he loses emphasis and vocal variety. A lively sense of communication is almost impossible to maintain in this situation—and for some the word is *dull!*

One of the real ironies in speech training is that the beginner, apparently in an effort to avoid the inevitable confrontation with the audience, may use the manuscript as something to hide behind. This only delays his self-development, because it usually results in an unsuccessful audience experience, which is extremely frustrating to the beginner.

Yet even with all the problems attendant upon this type of delivery, we find ourselves in a world demanding more and more dependence on manuscripts.

When writing a manuscript to be read orally to an audience, we have to make some fundamental, stylistic changes in the actual writing. The language of a writer, for example, is less direct. He uses *a person, people, the reader;* a speaker uses *I, you, they,* and the like. The other differences are not as obvious at first glance. Although we might remember to extemporize in short, simple sentences, our tendency is to write in longer, more complex ones. When we are doing literary writing (that is, material that will be read silently by the receiver), we have less problem with this style, for the receiver can go back and reread and review. But in a speech, the necessity of shorter, less complex sentences is critical, as is the use of more repetition, restatement, and reinforcement. Remember, the listener cannot stop and go back over the material or use a dictionary like a reader can. The style of the spoken word must be, as Professor Brigance said, "instantly intelligible"[1] to the listener. This requires more illustrations, examples, analogies, contrasts, and vividness than style of the written essay. The secret is to write "out loud."[2]

The actual delivery of the speech from a manuscript is equally special. Normal eye-contact and vocal patterns are often disrupted. In addition, the manuscript itself may be a problem if the lighting is bad or your vision otherwise impaired. A fan has been known to foul up a speaker. The position of the manuscript also creates problems. You may either hold your manuscript in your hand at about waist level or put it on a lectern. In one case, you inhibit your hand gestures; in the other, you hide most of your body. In either method, the problem is to let your eyes drop to the paper while keeping the head erect.

Most good manuscript reading involves a generous amount of memorization, but partial memorization only—that is, language groups held together for you by meaning. This permits you more time to look at the audience. When your memory gives out, you refer back to the manuscript for the cue that allows you to move on to the next memorized language group. The problem is trying to find your place! Marginal notes, underlinings, and various markings can assist you here. The real insurance is an intimate understanding of your message and practice, practice, practice. To affect real oral communication, you must learn to spend considerably more time looking at your audience than at your manuscript.

The problems of voice may also be acute. Most people do not read well without practice and training; that is why we have courses in interpretative reading. Beginners may singsong, use stress and inflection separate from meaning, or project a withdrawal tendency in a sonorous, unbroken monotone. The varying of rate, loudness, pitch, and quality, along with judicious use of pauses, are essential in manuscript reading. It is most critical to keep these vocal variations closely coupled to the meanings involved. The secret is to try to develop a *wide eye-voice span*. (For a more extensive discussion of voice, see Chapter 6.)

Memorization

Occasionally an effective speech is delivered from memory (that is, a carefully written speech, every single word of which is committed to memory). Excluding the actor, who works so hard at sounding sponta-

---

[1] W. N. Brigance, *The Spoken Word* (New York: Appleton-Century-Crofts, 1931), p. 189.

[2] Terminology is taken from the lectures of Mrs. C. Youngjohn, Wayne State University, 1970.

neous despite exact memorization, there is little justification for a completely memorized speech. The effort required in a word-for-word memorization is enormous. The delivery, except by professional actors, is typically stilted, rhythmical, and impersonal, and the method allows for no easy adaptation of material to the audience. However, just as in reading from a manuscript, many frightened beginners will undertake this enormous task. This method can induce real panic if memory does fail. There is literally neither a place to go nor a specific thing to do. The gradeschooler with a memorized poem is in far better shape than most speakers, for he has a prompter. Moreover, it is only a poem, not his own personal message that is in jeopardy.

This is not to say that you should not memorize *parts* of your speech. A dramatic introduction, a conclusion making use of poetry, a piece of testimony, a complicated group of statistics (when visual aids are unavailable or awkward) are all likely things for memorization.

Impromptu Delivery

When you are asked to speak on the spur of the moment, without advance notice or time for specific preparation, this type of speaking is called impromptu. Typically, however, you will not be asked to make even an impromptu speech unless you have some general subject-matter preparation, if only by reason of your special knowledge, experience, or training. If you have some special experience or expertise that makes you vulnerable to momentary requests for a "few words," you had better carry at least a mental outline with you at all times. In this way you cut the risks of being caught completely off guard. An African student from Kenya explained that even in the most informal gatherings he was routinely asked to explain something about Kenya, his reaction to America, and the like. In these situations, he eventually found himself in a true speaking situation as more people gathered around and he did more and more of the talking. To protect himself, he prepared several highly adaptable speech outlines, committed the outlines to memory, and then tried to second guess each situation and group in which he was apt to find himself. He explained that he has become so adept at this that he is now disappointed if he *isn't* asked to say a few words. People are amazed at his fluent and well organized "impromptu" remarks!

Your instructor may give you some experience in impromptu speaking by simply stating two or three speech topics, telling you to choose one topic, take a minute to collect your wits, and then start talking. If you find yourself in this or any other impromptu or potentially impromptu situation, here are some general rules which may keep you from looking completely ridiculous:

1. Second-guess the situation. Try to avoid a true impromptu speech by figuring the odds on the likelihood of your being called upon and on what topic you will be speaking.
2. Relate the topic under consideration to your experience. You will tend to speak more easily and confidently about that with which you have had specific experience.
3. When in doubt, summarize. There may be moments when you lose the thread of what you were saying or where you were going. At this moment, a quick review or summary often restores perspective and allows your mind to retrack.
4. Be brief! The less impromptu exposure, the less chance for you to become incoherent.
5. Quit when you are ahead! All too often a man makes a good impromptu speech and then, either because he feels he has not said enough or because his momentary success has given him confidence, he continues to ramble on and on until he eventually destroys whatever communication he had achieved.
6. If you really have nothing to say, then don't! Better to be thought a fool than to open your mouth and remove all doubt.

Extemporaneous Delivery

The extemporaneous method of speaking involves the preparation of a thorough but flexible outline, the cataloguing of a wealth of potentially usable material, and the use of a basic or general outline, which is either memorized or carried by the speaker. The language and wording of the speech are adaptable, as are the use of speech materials and details.

In this method, the emphasis is on knowing your subject and knowing your audience. It typically means collecting a lot more material than you will need. Thus, if one illustration or piece of evidence does not satisfy your audience, you will immediately be able to select another. If one strategy of organization is unclear, you will need a predetermined alternate to adapt to the audience confusion of the moment.

The chief and obvious advantage of extemporaneous preparation and delivery is that it gives you the confident flexibility and adaptability essential to an audience- and communication-sensitive speaker. You are able to respond successfully to the communication problems as they develop. You are thinking on your feet in the best sense of the term.

In general, extemporaneous delivery is most effective when given from a brief, but meaningful outline, which is carried either in your head or your hand and supported by a very thorough preparation. This is the type of preparation and delivery expected of you except for those special exercises your instructor may announce.

Characteristics of Good Delivery

In the previous section on extemporaneous delivery, it was indicated that this method gives you potentially a more thorough understanding of your subject and the words you use; that further it gives you a flexibility of thought and adaptability of material and a meaningful sensitivity (or *empathy*) toward the listeners. These are the essential qualities of good conversation and interpersonal communication. These same qualities should be the mood of all good speeches as well. The speaker who seeks to inspire need not sound artificial or take on the style of high elocution. A speaker can be fluently eloquent without sounding like an oracle. On the other hand, the adoption of conversational qualities to public speaking does not mean a matter-of-fact voice, poor preparation, or careless language.

A very great speech teacher, James A. Winans, once put it this way: "It is not true that a public speech to be conversational need sound like conversation. Conventional differences may make it sound very different."[3] We are seeking the best qualities and moods of conversation, not a stylized version of conversation.

Research studies generally reveal that those characteristics most often associated with effective speaking include the following:

1. Clear organization leading to a meaningful conclusion.
2. A definiteness of concept and preciseness in language and wording.
3. Clear, distinct, and pleasant voice and articulation.
4. A forthright sense of communication indicated by some direct eye-contact.
5. An alertness of body and mind, indicating enthusiasm.
6. A controlled yet flexible use of bodily activity, which enhances or reinforces meaning.

Characteristics of Bad Delivery

Speech studies to determine just what specific aspects of delivery are unpleasant, ineffective, or actually annoying to audiences are most useful in helping us recognize effective delivery.[4] Those aspects actually considered annoying include:

---

[3] James A. Winans, *Speech Making* (New York: Appleton-Century-Crofts, 1938), p. 17.

[4] S. R. Toussaint, "A Study of the Annoying Characteristics and Practices of Public Speakers (Ph.D. Dissertation, University of Wisconsin, 1938); also Alan H. Monroe,

1. Evident lack of preparation and knowledge.
2. A dangling conclusion, in which the speaker seems unable or unwilling to close and simply repeats himself.
3. A mumbling of words leading to indistinct speech.
4. A general vagueness, indefiniteness, and lack of clarity.
5. Poor reading or delivery from manuscript. (Monotonous, stiff, indirect.)
6. Superfluous verbalizations of such inserts as "ah," "er," and "uh."
7. Excessive mispronunciation and grammatical mistakes.
8. A loss of temper over relatively routine disturbances or interruptions.

Other aspects of delivery which lead to ineffective speaking include:

1. A stiffness or rigidity of bodily action.
2. An avoidance of the audience by refusing to look at them.
3. A weak, indistinct, or monotonous voice.
4. Excessive nervousness or fidgeting.
5. An evident lack of enthusiasm.

Summary

The general purposes for speaking are to inform, to persuade, and to entertain. Many speeches combine these purposes and are difficult to classify. The degree of information, entertainment, or persuasion in a speech does not alone indicate the speaker's purpose; we must also consider the arrangement of the material, the information level of the audience, and the speaker's style and vocal adaptation. It may be said that the real purpose is known in terms of the primary reaction desired from your audience. The primary goal in informative speaking is audience understanding. The key principles are clarity, interest, and organization of material. In a speech to persuade, the speaker tries to make people *believe* something, urges them to *do* something, or attempts to *stimulate* them to a higher level of enthusiasm. The goals of a speech to entertain are to help people escape from reality and to enjoy themselves without the threat of some hidden agenda or meaning.

The four principal ways of delivering a speech are by reading from a manuscript, by memorization, by impromptu delivery, and by extempora-

---

"Measurement and Analysis of Audience Reaction to Student Speakers Studied in Attitude Changes," *Bulletin of Purdue University Studies in Higher Education,* Vol. 32, 1937.

neous speaking. In manuscript delivery, the speaker presents his subject by reading a completely written speech verbatim to the audience. In memorization, the speaker commits every word of his manuscript to memory. Impromptu delivery involves being asked to speak on the spur of the moment without advance notice or time for specific preparation. In the extemporaneous method, a thorough but flexible outline is prepared, a wealth of potentially usable material is catalogued, and a basic general outline is either memorized or carried by the speaker; the language and wording of such a speech may be specific, but is always adaptable to circumstances, as is the use of speech materials and details.

The characteristics of good delivery include: a conversational quality; a definiteness of concept, wording, and pronunciation; a clear, pleasant voice and articulation; direct eye-contact; enthusiasm; and a controlled yet flexible use of bodily action.

The characteristics of bad delivery include: evident lack of preparation; dangling conclusions; mumbling; vagueness; stiff reading; excess verbalizations; mispronunciation; loss of temper; rigid bodily action; lack of eye-contact; weak voice; fidgeting; and an evident lack of enthusiasm.

Bodily
Action **5**

The Role of Bodily Expression

In Chapter 1, we learned that the receiver decodes the communication in terms of the total stimulus presented to him. What your audience sees may seriously affect what they decode or abstract from what you say. In clever pantomime, the communication is sometimes much more clear and emphatic than if the actor were to speak. Bodily action may therefore play an important part in the total impression made by the speaker.

Unconscious Communication

There is usually much unconscious visible speech accompanying each of us. We constantly use bodily action in our everyday conversation. It is a definite part of our communication system. The way a person walks at a given moment may demonstrate his mood more adequately than do his words.

A speaker deciding to repress all bodily action as a means of trying to avoid looking awkward usually succeeds in communicating even more awkwardness and actually looking more unnatural and ridiculous. In addition, such repression may lead to poor emotional control. A lack of action often makes the message more obtuse. There is no point in trying to avoid

76

or repress bodily action, but rather good reason to understand it, control it, and use it.

Communication by Stereotypes

Our research into portrayal and recognition of emotional states such as anger, love, and fear has shown that we do rely on learned action habits to decode at least these highly abstract messages.[1]

The expression on the face of a person photographed as he is being stuck with a needle may be incorrectly identified as portraying love. If the viewer also sees the needle or stimulus, his chances of identifying the emotion are much better. If a person is asked to portray or act pain in stereotype, the viewers get the message.

Certain cultures and groups have action patterns that are stereotyped in ways different from our own. For the Japanese, a smile does not indicate amusement, but rather politeness.[2] The American Indian had an elaborate sign language that the pioneers had to learn before they could communicate effectively.

These facts lead the speaker to the problem of how much stereotype or formalism to use. One needs enough stereotype to be understood, but not so much as to appear artificial. American speech education in the nineteenth century suffered through a highly mechanistic approach. This was a period of flamboyant language and highly stylized gestures. Delsarte, a French scholar, contributed a system of gesture during this time, which contained some 81 gestures for practically all members of the body, including specific ones for the nose, eyebrows, and feet. In answer to this elocutionary movement, the famous School of Expression of S. S. Curry was born. This view taught that "Every action of face or hand . . . is simply an outward effect of an inward condition. Any motion or tone that is otherwise is not expression."[3] In other words, a speaker should be so saturated with his subject that his expression would be dynamic and spontaneous. At present we recognize that communicative bodily action does rely on certain learned, general stereotypes, which we use in natural and relatively spontaneous ways.

---

[1] See Landis and Felekey in Henry E. Garrett, *Great Experiments in Psychology* (New York: Appleton-Century-Crofts, 1941), pp. 328–30; also see Dusenbury and Knower, "Experimental Studies of the Symbolism of Action and Voice," *Quarterly Journal of Speech*, XXIV, No. 3 (1938), 424–36.

[2] Weston LaBarre, "The Cultural Basis of Emotions and Gestures," *Journal of Personality*, XVI, No. 1 (1947), 49–69.

[3] S. S. Curry, *Foundations of Expression* (Boston: The Expression Co., 1920), p. 10.

Empathy

If your instructor runs his fingernails sharply across the blackboard, you probably cringe and literally grit your teeth. If you have ever seen a youngster take a violent and bruising fall, you probably "felt" the pain as you projected your own consciousness into the youngster's action. This projection of consciousness is the meaning of emphatic response. Empathy therefore involves a muscular reaction, and an audience imitates in part the actions of the speaker. When a speaker appears mortally afraid and tense, the audience dies a little. When he acts tired, the audience feels tired or bored. When he paces the floor like a caged lion, the audience usually tires before he does. The speaker should take the audience into account when considering his bodily action. He should attempt to use that kind and amount of action that will help achieve the speech purpose.

Emotion

In Chapter 2, it was indicated that a prolonged repression of normal physical outlets could result in emotional disintegration. One can drain off pent-up tension by bodily action. That is often why some speakers pace the floor or incessantly fidget. Instead of actions that are distracting, use meaningful bodily action that will help you control your speech fright at the same time it helps communicate your message.

The Elements of Bodily Action

These elements or instruments are the actual physical behavior patterns that make up the total bodily action. Their separation is primarily arbitrary and academic, for they most often occur simultaneously.

General Impression

The general impression you create is a synthesis not only of all the elements that are communicated to your audience but also of the momentary things over which you may not always have control—for example, the lighting, the building, the platform, the person who introduces you, and other such factors. However, there are relatively simple things over which you *do* have some control and which may contribute in a major way to your general impression. The problem of dress is one of these; the watchword is *appropriate*. You do not want to appear conspicuous and yet you do wish to live up to the expectations of dress the audience has for its speakers. Your physical and psychological comfort affect your bodily action. If the audience remembers your leotard instead of your speech, you can draw your own conclusion. It goes without saying that, as with appropriate dress, one's general impression is better if he is personally neat, washed, and combed.

Another problem is whether to address the audience from a sitting or standing position. Some small, informal audiences may prefer that you sit while speaking to them, and you might feel conspicuous standing on a platform with three or four people at your feet. However, some small groups are actually affronted if the speaker sits. The general impression they get, apparently, is one of not being considered important enough for a stand-up speech. A lot depends upon how well you know the group and how well they know you. As a general rule there is less risk in standing, even before a very small group. If people should appear uncomfortable, it is much easier to sit down after a speech has started than to stand up. Through observations made in an "Effective Supervision" course (in which 8 to 12 students, typically foremen, formally rate the teachers), the evaluations of the otherwise generally equal instructors were in favor of those who stood while communicating.

All bodily action elements contribute to general impression. The more important of these elements are discussed below.

Posture

Posture is an integral and important part of your general impression not only from the point of view of empathy and what the audience infers, but also in terms of your own reactions to yourself. Whether you slouch and cower or whether you stand with military bearing momentarily affects your outlook and sense of power or control over yourself. Acting "as if" can affect your actions. The previous discussion of empathy indicated how seriously posture can affect the audience.

In general, good posture involves the distribution of body weight in a comfortable and poised way consistent with the impression desired by the speaker. You should be erect without looking stiff, comfortable without appearing limp. Your bearing should be alert, self-possessed, and communicative. Good posture and poise are a kind of studied nonchalance. The great danger, as with all studied bodily action, is one of appearing artificial, conspicuous, or out of phase.

A satisfactory standing position should be a balanced one in which, for example, a sudden push would allow you to recover quickly. Your feet should be fairly close together, with one foot slightly ahead of the other. Keep your hips straight, shoulders back, and chin in. Experiment in looking for a poised, natural speaking stance. There is no one way that is right for every speech! The stance you finally select will have to be modified to meet changing speech circumstances, such as the size and nature of the audience, the formality of the occasion, and so on.

Walking

Actors have long known the importance of gait and walk in expressing various moods and degrees of emphasis. The *femme fatale* has a walk that clearly communicates her role; the sneaky villain also has a stereotyped walk. The child about to be spanked has a considerably different walk than the same child on his way to the movies.

Walking may serve as a form of physical punctuation. Transitions and pauses may be reinforced with a few steps to the side, emphasis with a step forward. As does the actor, the speaker wishes to appear natural, not awkward. If your walking is inept, ungraceful, or mechanical, it will distract from its intended purpose; if it is random, it will distract from the general speech purpose.

Walking also has empathic qualities for the audience. It can afford physical relief to a suffering audience. By the same token, too much walking can literally wear an audience out. A certain amount of devised, purposeful walking is often helpful in affording an outlet for muscular tension for both the speaker and the audience.

The question of the amount and kind of walking desirable involves the same considerations that affect all bodily action: the subject, the speaker, the size of the audience, the formality of the situation, and so on. In general, the more formal the situation, the less pronounced your walking should be. The larger the audience, the more definite your steps may be.

One should also remember that walking, like all bodily action, starts before you actually start to speak. When you leave your chair to approach the speaker's stand, your communication has already begun; nor are you finished until you have walked off the platform.

Facial Expression

In the studies on the portrayal and recognition of emotion already discussed, most of the pictures taken were of the facial expressions of the people involved in the experiments. This was because the researchers thought the face was the most expressive and quickly altered part of our anatomy. This may very well be the case. We have all heard of "The face that launched a thousand ships," or that "The eyes are the mirror of the soul."

The problem is that the speaker may inadvertently use stereotyped facial expressions or those unmatched with the subject. A girl in a speech class once had a temporary facial tick so that her eye uncontrollably winked at about 60-second intervals when she was speaking. Even after the class discovered that it was a tick, the signal confusion was alarming. Once she learned to blink both eyes, part of the problem was solved. The blink of one eye (wink) has a highly specialized, stereotyped meaning. The wink of two eyes simultaneously (blink) has no stereotyped meaning (unless done in rapid succession) and was not confusing or particularly distracting. An emotionally tense person may tighten his jaw and unconsciously assume a crocodile grin. This usually passes as he relaxes, but the first few moments of a serious speech by a grinning speaker can be most perplexing.

The eyes, at least in relatively small audiences, are vehicles of much communication, as was indicated with the wink example. Right or wrong, audiences are wary of shifty eyes. "He avoids my eye." They expect to be looked at—not incessantly stared at, but occasionally looked at. Direct, forthright delivery (directness) is defined by many, and not unrealistically, as based on "eye-contact."

Simply stated, the lessons to be learned are: (1) avoid inadvertent or mismatched facial stereotypes; (2) use some eye-contact with the audience; (3) free your natural and spontaneous facial expressions so that they may reinforce your message.

Gesture

In discussing gesture, we shall be concerned primarily with the hands and arms, but always keep in mind that you gesture with your entire body and personality. In a very general way, all people use gestures for two rhetorical purposes—to reinforce a concept or to help describe something.

(a) REINFORCING GESTURES. It seems natural to clench your fist or perhaps even pound the lectern when trying to communicate a strong feeling. This reinforces and gives emphasis to your words. In rejecting or disagreeing verbally, one might routinely turn his palms down or out. In pleading or appealing, one might naturally turn his palms up or in. These types of gestures reinforce through emphasis; others reinforce through a kind of suggestion. In communicating a scolding attitude toward the other political party, one might wag his finger in much the same way that the stereotyped teacher does. Speakers may reinforce a division or separation of points by using first one hand ("On the one hand it can be said . . .") and then the other. Or it may be that only one hand is used, and the speaker may with a vertical palm suggest several divisions or categories as he slices the air, moving his hand on a level plane from left to right. No two people use these reinforcing gestures exactly alike, but the general stereotype is usually recognizable.

(b) DESCRIPTIVE GESTURES. When asked to describe the size or shape of something, it is natural to use your hands to indicate the dimensions. A circular staircase would be difficult to describe to a person who had never seen one if you could not use your hands. All descriptive gestures are in some part also reinforcing and emphatic. The fellow describing his blind date communicates more than just size and shape with his gestures. We might, for example, quickly infer his approval or disapproval.

Standards of Good Bodily Action

Appropriateness

Your subject, your particular physiology and personality, and most important, the size and nature of the audience are the measures of appropriate bodily action. A very formal subject, particularly if connected with a formal occasion and a small, older audience, would generally call for a poised, but relatively restricted bodily action. The grandiose movement and the grand sweep of the arms would be out of place. Other things being equal, the larger the audience the more gross and unrestricted your bodily action may become.

For most speakers the problem is one of too little bodily action, whatever the speech occasion. When you are finally free of your inhibitions, however, remember to match your bodily actions to the best expectations of the audience.

Variety

Any bodily action, but particularly gestures, should be varied occasionally; otherwise the routineness may call attention to itself and not only cease to carry meaning, but also become a distraction. A speaker who pounds the table for *every* point he makes, regardless of its importance, soon loses the reinforcing effect of such a gesture. A random or meaningful gesture used in moderation does not harm your communication, but if it is repeated again and again, even though not really a reinforcing or descriptive gesture, it is no longer a random gesture and may interfere with the message. Monotony of action, whether meaningful or not, is usually distracting. All of us tend to repeat our favorite gestures, and these mannerisms often reflect our personalities. We must periodically ask ourselves if we are overworking some gesture and if our bodily actions really reflect the kind of personality we would like to project. Part of the problem is that we are typically unaware of overdoing a favorite gesture, particularly if it is used primarily as a tension release. Your instructor will feedback this information so that you can correct this distracting monotony.

Physical Coordination

Physical coordination means the integration of all parts of the body in expressing yourself. You can appear quite ridiculous by locking your elbows to your sides and moving only your forearms and hands. The whole body is always involved in any bodily action. A literal detachment will make you appear mechanical.

Verbal Coordination

By verbal coordination is meant the concomitant synchronization of words and action to achieve maximum reinforcement of the message. This is a timing problem, which is primarily related to rehearsed or "canned" bodily action. A lack of coordination can be quite humorous. Try "Uncle Sam needs *you,*" but instead of pointing on the word *you,* wait three seconds more and then point!

Dynamic Bodily Action

By dynamic bodily action is meant the projection of a lively, animated, vigorous sense of communication. The use of bodily action should be essentially spontaneous; that is, the mechanics of bodily action should be at the momentary call and disposal of your best extemporaneous thoughts and impulses. Sometimes to become dynamic and spontaneous in your bodily action, you have to prime the pump by including some speech details that require bodily action, such as visual aids, demonstrations, and concepts, which require description of shape or size and imitations of people of animals.

Summary

What your audience sees profoundly affects what they decode or abstract from what you say. There is usually much unconscious visible speech accompanying all of us. A lack of action often makes the message more obtuse. There is therefore no point in trying to avoid or repress bodily action, but rather good reason to understand it, control it, and use it.

In general, a speaker should be so saturated with his subject that his bodily action will be both dynamic and spontaneous. It is also evident that we communicate through many learned action stereotypes which a speaker must utilize.

Empathy involves a muscular reaction in which the audience imitates in part the actions of the speaker. A speaker should adapt his bodily action to the emphatic requirements and expectations of his audience.

Prolonged repression of normal bodily action can result in emotional disintegration. One should use meaningful bodily action to help control speech fright as well as to communicate the message.

General impression is a synthesis of all the action elements that are communicated to an audience. Your dress should be appropriate for the occasion and in keeping with the expectations of the audience. If there is any question about the advisability of standing or sitting, you should probably stand.

Posture is an integral part of your impression not only in terms of what the audience infers cognitively and empathically but also in terms of your own perceptions and reactions to yourself. Good posture and poise are a kind of studied nonchalance. The great danger is in appearing artificial, conspicuous, or out of phase.

Walking is an important method in expressing various moods and degrees of emphasis. It serves as a form of physical punctuation for the speaker. Walking also has empathic aspects for the audience. It can afford physical relief to a cramped or suffering audience.

The lessons for good facial expression are: (1) avoid inadvertent or mismatched facial stereotypes; (2) make eye-contact with the audience; (3) free your natural and spontaneous expressions so that they may reinforce your message.

Some gestures are used primarily as a concomitant emphasis or as a further suggestion to help reinforce the message. These are the *reinforcing* gestures. Others are used primarily to describe the shape or size of objects and are called *descriptive* gestures.

The standards of good bodily action call for: (1) *appropriateness* to your subject, your particular physiology and personality, and the size and nature of the audience; (2) *variety* of bodily action, so that monotony does not cause a loss of the reinforcing effect; (3) *physical* and (4) *verbal* coordination, which involve correct timing and the use of the entire body in an integrated way; and (5) *dynamic* and spontaneous projection of a lively, animated sense of communication.

Voice
and
Articulation **6**

Voice and Personality

An expert in voice and diction training once said, "Bluntly stated, one may have a dull, uninteresting, or unpleasant voice because his voice is defective or improperly used; but he may also have such a voice because he is a dull, uninteresting, or unpleasant person."[1] He goes on to point out that vocal training, like all speech training, cannot take place in a vacuum, that it proceeds in intimate relationship with one's total personality. Just as personality affects voice, voice improvement may affect personality.

In any event, the voice contributes much to the total communication signal. It may be that it is the single most important code we emit. Just as with pantomime, we have certain long-standing stereotypes that we take for granted. We recognize certain radio roles as voice stereotypes—"mean character," "hero," "sissy," "stupid." The very great danger is that one might assume an artificial or affected voice on a permanent basis. Of course we all occasionally fail to match the voice we "put on" with the situation in which we find ourselves. Listen to yourself on occasion. If you sound "arty" when talking about fertilizer, it may just be that your voice habits are altering your personality in ways that will seriously affect your communication.

---

[1] Virgil A. Anderson, *Training the Speaking Voice* (New York: Oxford University Press, Inc., 1942), p. *xvii*.

86

The discussion above leads to the question of what is abnormal or defective speech. Charles Van Riper, a highly respected speech clinician, put it quite clearly: "Speech is defective when it deviates so far from the speech of other people that it calls attention to itself, interferes with communication, or causes its possessor to be maladjusted."[2] Some of Dr. Van Riper's experiences indicate that all deviations do not constitute defects:

> A successful auctioneer became worried and came to our clinic when a public school dramatics teacher told him his voice was too nasal. After examining his speech we offered our congratulations and sent him home contented with the same timbre he had brought.

> One week after a student in an introductory college class in speech correction had first listened to the repetitions of a severe stutterer, she came, agitated and aghast, to tell us that she had repeated three times that very day and had discovered that she stuttered too. We reassured her and told her that many students in abnormal psychology classes experienced parallel misgivings as to their sanity.[3]

We are not totally consistent in our voice and articulation patterns; we vary, adjust, and adapt to moods, subjects, and people, as indeed we should. It is when our deviations become conspicuous in ways damaging to our intended communication that we have problems.

We do have many deviations that are not defects in a clinical sense yet do call for some personal remedial action. Some common problems that are usually quickly adjusted through normal speech training are fast rate, wrong pitch, loudness, and certain functional articulation disorders such as the substitution of a *d* sound for a *th* sound (*d*ese for *th*ese). However, there are physiological and functional disorders that may call for the services of a qualified speech correctionist. Your instructor is in a position to determine your needs. The physiological aspects refer to any uncorrected organic conditions such as cleft palate, malocclusion of the teeth, or enlarged tonsils, which *may* cause conspicuous deviations. The functional disorders are those caused by habitual misuse of all or part of the voice and articulation mechanisms—poor breathing, tight jaw, lazy lips. The majority of articulation problems are functional—that is, they are simply bad habits.

---

[2] Charles Van Riper, *Speech Correction* (Englewood Cliffs, N.J.: Prentice-Hall, Inc., 1947), p. 15.
[3] *Ibid.*

The Vocal Process

The vocal process involves organs of the body whose primary function is physiological. We use muscles and bones that have as their first responsibility respiration, mastication, and swallowing. In using or retraining these organs for speech, therefore, we must take care not to create a radical perversion of the physiological functions. That physical moods or states such as exhaustion or inebriation cause noticeable physical variations is obvious. That these same and related states affect the sound of the noise and notes produced is also obvious. This combination of noise and musical notes is voice, and voice is a large part of the stuff of which communication is made. For these reasons, a brief physiological description of the speech organs is necessary.

In order to produce modifiable sound, a mechanism with certain functions and characteristics is necessary. In almost any musical instrument, an *energy source* is the first prerequisite, whether it be a violin bow or a saxophone player's lungs. The second requisite is a *vibrator,* such as the violin string or the saxophone reed. The third function involves strengthening or building up the resultant sound; this is called *resonation.* The resonators of the violin are the hollow body and the texture of the materials, whereas the primarily metal texture of the saxophone produces a sound easily distinguishable from a violin. When one alters or modifies the size, shape, and texture of the resonating agents in some recognizable, consistent, or pleasing way, we call it music. Let us now analyze the human vocal process in the same terms.

The Energy Source

The breathing machinery is our energy source for voice production (phonation). The primary purpose of this machinery is to bring oxygen into the lungs as a source of fuel for the body and also to expel the waste gases. The various physical demands of the body noticeably affect this machinery. When running we need more energy (oxygen), and therefore our breathing becomes harder or faster. Speech after running the hundred-yard dash is difficult.

We normally speak on exhalation rather than inhalation. Thus we are quite apt to notice a heavier than usual inhalation cycle, particularly if it is public speech and we are under some emotional load. According to the

James-Lange theory (see p. 38), the awareness of an unexplained physical reaction such as this one might lead to speech fright and may in fact *be* emotion. It is normal for the inhalation effort to be different in public speaking for the reasons indicated. We should of course make every effort for our breathing machinery or energy source to operate as efficiently as possible. This involves good posture, comfortable clothes, ventilation, bodily rest, and an understanding of the unexpected inhalation variations that are the source of much speech fright.

The Vibrator

The vocal cords within the larynx or Adam's apple are the vibrating agents. The larynx, located on top of the trachea or windpipe, has a flap called the epiglottis, which closes when you swallow. The air is forced up the trachea through the vocal cords in the larynx and causes them to vibrate, producing sound. Figure 32 shows clearly the trachea and the esophagus. Probably all of us have had the experience of food going down the "wrong throat," which is usually the result of swallowing food at the instant of starting phonation. Because speech is an overlaid function, it is not too unusual for this to happen. You are really asking the epiglottis to be both opened and closed at the same time. A physical problem such as this is normally taken care of naturally by the body's defense systems. You automatically cough and expel the food or liquid from your windpipe. However, if this happens during a speech, the psychological impact may be quite frightening. The dangers of chewing gum or throat lozenges while speaking are evident. The embarrassment is not worth whatever relaxation the chewing affords.

The Resonators

The sound produced by the action of the energy source and the vibrator now permeates the entire head, so that the head then becomes an agent of resonation. We said earlier that sound changes as the resonators vary in size, shape, and texture. The cavities in your head are quite readily altered. For example, the size and shape of your aural cavity is changed as you open your mouth or shift your tongue position. If you hold your nose, you immediately notice a change in vocal quality. This is because a certain amount of sound escapes through your nose when you speak. The nasal cavity is controlled and changed by the action of the tongue and soft palate. The sinuses in your head also are resonators; when their texture and

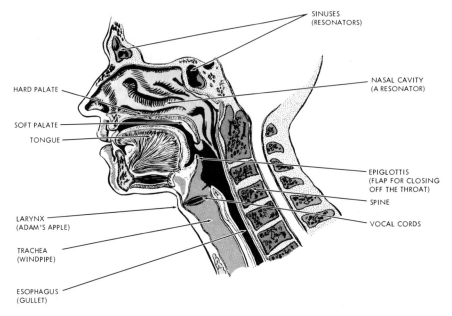

SINUSES
(RESONATORS)

NASAL CAVITY
(A RESONATOR)

HARD PALATE

SOFT PALATE

TONGUE

EPIGLOTTIS
(FLAP FOR CLOSING
OFF THE THROAT)

SPINE

LARYNX
(ADAM'S APPLE)

VOCAL CORDS

TRACHEA
(WINDPIPE)

ESOPHAGUS
(GULLET)

Figure 32.   Where Speech Sounds Are Formed.

size is changed, as during a head cold, you are quickly aware of voice changes. We recognize people by their voices in a large part because of the inherent qualities of their resonators, but it is also evident that we have considerable control over resonation if we work at it. This is demonstrated by people who make a living at imitating other people's voices.

The Modifiers

The resonated sound is now more precisely modified, interrupted, and delineated in conventionalized segments, which we may call speech. The modifying agents are the lips, teeth, tongue, jaw, and soft palate. Their function is most recognizable in the consonant interruptions. Try to say the word pill without bringing your lips together. The *p* demands a specific kind of labial modification; so do others like *b* or *m*. The consonants are really voiceless except for certain mechanical noises that may go with them, such as the hissing of an *s*. The vowels carry the voice. The consonants are known through the alteration and specific interruptions of those vowels by the modifying agents, namely the lips, teeth, tongue, jaw, and palate. The importance of the modifiers to articulation is self-evident. If there are physiological defects, such as defective teeth or cleft palate, acceptable enunciation may be difficult until one has surgery or has been taught to compensate by a qualified speech pathologist. Faulty enunciation is more commonly caused by lack of knowledge, lazy speech habits, or on occasion, overly precise habits.

Variable Characteristics of Voice

There are certain attributes of voice that you can vary in easily distinguished ways and over which you have considerable control. You can change your *rate* or speed of utterance; you can adjust your *loudness* almost as you would that of a radio; you can speak at different *pitch* levels; and you can alter the overtones or partial tones, which represent a kind of *quality* control often referred to as *timbre* or *vocal color*.

Rate

There are test passages devised for actually measuring your verbal speed in WPM's (words per minute).[4] In general, a rate in excess of 185 WPM is too rapid for a normal speaking situation, and a rate of less than 140 WPM is too slow.[5,6] The problem of measurement is complex, for certain communications utilize a very rapid rate and others a slow or mixed rate. A further problem is that words and sounds are not truly separately formed units, but tend to flow from one sound to another; this affects both articulation and pronunciation. Take the phrase, "Did you eat?" If really speeded up, it becomes, "Jeet." This process is called *assimilation*. The length of sound or tones is also a factor, as are pauses, phrasing, and general rhythm patterns.

The duration of sounds and words normally varies with emotional moods. We typically use tones of relatively short or even staccato duration when expressing anger and more prolonged tones for expressing love. Good speakers tend to have a longer average duration of words than do poor speakers. A poor speaker is more apt to use staccato speech consistently.

---

[4] F. L. Darley, "A Normative Study of Oral Reading Rate" (Master's thesis, State University of Iowa, 1940).

[5] Grant Fairbanks, *Voice and Articulation Drillbook* (New York: Harper & Row, Publishers, 1960), p. 115.

[6] Some authorities argue that since listening rates may be 400–800 WPM, a speaking rate of 200 WPM is not unrealistic.

A person's use of pauses and phrases is also a factor in his rate of speaking. The "meaningful pause" is no idle jest; it has much to do with our communication. Phrases are selected groups of words that typically form a fragmentary thought unit. In oral speech you have much more flexibility than grammar permits in written communication. You should be guided by the fine shades of meaning you wish to express, rather than by mechanical rules. The pauses occur between the words and phrases, and the number and duration of pauses seriously alter the expression of meaning. The complexity and nature of your speech material should also affect your decisions on phrases and pauses. If you were to use a long pause after a phrase for emphasis, fine, but if the phrase were relatively inane you might appear ridiculous. If you were to use long pauses in a random manner not related to meaning (not an uncommon error), you then *confuse* your audience. The short pauses generally indicate that there is more to come. If you routinely use a rather intermediate length pause without consistently relating it to what you are saying, you run the added danger of monotony. Be sure that your speech pattern of pauses and phrases does not take on a fixed pattern or rhythm that interferes with your communication.

Rhythm patterns really involve all the variable characteristics of voice. Excessively recurring pitch and volume patterns also contribute to the singsong, pause-phrase problem so prevalent among improperly trained speakers.

Loudness

A very common fault among beginning speakers is an improper projecting of the voice to the audience. They either project more volume than the situation calls for, or even more typically, they do not project enough. It is essential that your audience be able to hear you. Loudness refers to the magnitude of the total signal. You may think of this generally as volume, but speech science indicates that volume is so intimately related to pitch that the term may be misleading. Your volume is easier to raise as your pitch goes up. Furthermore, it is possible to speak with more force or intensity without proportionately altering your volume. If your duration of tones is too short, you may not be getting adequate loudness simply because the mechanism has not been given a chance to produce for you; this may be caused by a restricted energy source or breathing apparatus, but most likely it is related to your pitch selection. More will be said of this in the following discussion on pitch.

The psychological reasons for this common lack of projection involve a form of avoidance of the speech situation. You tend to *withdraw* from threatening situations. Poor projection is a logical and normal device when you cannot really run away. It may also be a form of *repression;* you hold yourself in check emotionally to get through the ordeal. Once again, loudness suffers. It is almost as if speaking with a soft, barely audible voice is the next best thing to not being in the speech situation at all.

Your audience will help you adjust your loudness. Look at them for feedback signs. Are they straining to hear? Are they withdrawing?

Much of what we call vocal variety is related to loudness. The force with which you utter certain phrases or words is a form of oral punctuation and can add much to understanding. The manner in which force is applied is also a factor. You may use a lot of oral exclamation marks or you may, through intensity, figuratively underline many words. In the latter case the intensity could go either way; that is, the contrast or variety is important. An audible whisper can be powerful emphasis under some speech situations. These are some of the loudness dimensions of vocal variety.

Pitch

The frequency of vibration of the vocal cords determines the measurements of the sound wave. The frequency of vibrations in a sound wave is *pitch.* More simply, pitch refers to a tonal position on a musical scale. When we speak, we typically range through a variety of pitches, which are normally distributed in terms of usage. That is, if we were to plot the number, we would find a central pitch about which the others vary in relatively predictable frequencies. The typical musical range may include two octaves. The problem of *optimum* pitch level for a given person is a complex one. To locate your best general pitch level often involves a compromise between mechanical vocal efficiency and what is generally accepted as being pleasing or appropriate. For example, if your *optimum* pitch is exceptionally high for a man in our culture, you may wish to lower your *habitual* pitch level even though you may lose some vocal efficiency. If you lower your pitch unreasonably, this loss of vocal efficiency shows up as inflexible pitch or lack of variety and may also result in an impairment of loudness.

For most people, optimum pitch should be the habitual or central pitch. Our optimum pitch is not infrequently found a little below the habitual or normal pitch due to tensions that restrict the apparatus. Young men may so deliberately strive for very low voices that the reverse is occasionally true.

Trying to locate your optimum pitch from the viewpoint of vocal efficiency alone is fun (if not always entirely reliable). With the aid of a piano, determine in relation to middle C the lowest and highest note you can sing without a complete loss of quality. This interval is your singing *range*. "The average[7] voice will be found to perform best when the speaking level is at approximately the midpoint of the lowest octave of the singing range."[8] The next step is to try to locate your habitual or most frequently used pitch by a sample of normal speech. Hit the piano keys in the vicinity of the optimum pitch already located as you speak or read until you get a kind of blend or synthesis. You will then have a rough idea as to whether or not your present general pitch level is adequate.

It is obvious that you could speak at your best all-around pitch and be terribly monotonous if you became a "Johnny-one-note" who lacked pitch variety in the form of *shifts* or *inflections*. A shift is a pitch change that occurs between independent sounds or phonations; an inflection is a pitch change without interruption of a given phonation.

Quality

Voice quality is a product modification and modulation of the vocal cord tone by the resonators. It is that attribute of tone and sound waves which enables us to discriminate between two sounds that are otherwise alike in pitch, duration, and loudness.[9]

Other things being equal, we can still easily distinguish the excessively nasal, breathy, or harsh voice. In addition to these, we are able to make distinctions of a much more subtle nature: for example, we recognize the voice of a person sincerely touched by a tribute or the voice of a person who is suppressing anger. Emotional moods affect voice quality and may have a profound effect upon emphasis and meaning. In this context, voice quality is often referred to as *timbre*.

Quality is considered defective when it is routinely deviate and when the deviations detract from the message or meaning. Certain organic disorders, such as a cleft palate, or nasal obstructions, can cause these defects. Emotional moods may also result in quality deviations which, even if temporary, appear as defects. There are, in addition, the strictly temporary, organic insufficiencies caused by head colds, sore throats and the like. However, we are primarily interested here in nonorganic, functional defects —in other words, with faulty habits.

Some of the more common voice-quality problems are nasality, breathiness, and harshness.

---

[7] Women just under middle C; men one octave lower.

[8] Anderson, *Training the Speaking Voice*, p. 368.

[9] Fairbanks, *Voice and Articulation Drillbook,* Chs. 1 and 15.

(a) *Nasality*. This problem is caused by an excess of nasal resonance particularly for nonnasal voiced sounds. The vowels are most noticeably deviate. Aside from other organic defects, the problem is typically caused by not opening the mouth wide enough or by improper use of the soft palate or tongue. The factor of assimilation also plays a role here. A person may excessively run the nasal sounds right into following vowels, or when the vowel precedes the nasal consonant, he may have initiated the nasal resonance too early, that is, during the phonation of the vowel. This is called assimilated nasality and is one of the more frequent bad habits to guard against. Opening the mouth wider and a firmer tongue action help control the initiation and termination of nasal resonance.

(b) *Breathiness*. If your vocal cords do not draw close enough together during phonation, an excess of unvocalized air escapes, giving your voice a breathy or aspirate quality. Functional reasons for this phenomenon may be related to faulty breathing habits (see p. 88), insufficient loudness, or too low a pitch level. Improper or too-frequent inhalation, often caused by deviate-rate characteristics, may be at fault. Insufficient loudness automatically causes more unvocalized air to escape. A whisper is obviously breathy; on the other hand, it is practically impossible to emit a really loud tone that is breathy. The role of pitch is related in that if you are straining for an unusually low pitch, you may affect both loudness and larynx control, either of which can cause breathiness.

Frequent temporary causes of breathiness are overexertion, emotional strain, illness, and on occasion, certain affectations thought to be desirable.

(c) *Harshness*. Harshness is meant here to include also huskiness, hoarseness, and throatiness. These terms and more are specifically defined by voice scientists, but for our purposes, we may think of all these as describing a rasping, unmusical quality. We all do it frequently when grunting, growling, or when suffering from a sore throat after cheering at a football game.

A chronic harshness is often organically caused and should call for diagnosis by both a qualified speech pathologist and a physician. The most frequent functional cause is a routine misuse of voice, which, if serious enough, can lead to organic pathologies. This misuse is typically accompanied by tension in the laryngeal muscles, which may be caused by general tension and emotional load (see Chapter 2) or by a speaker's too frequent attempts to show strain, emotion, or earnestness in his communication. He actually constricts his throat while attempting to project loudness (particularly at low pitches) at the same time. This results in a stridently harsh quality often referred to as "clergyman's throat." General tenseness is probably the most common functional cause of a consistently harsh vocal quality.

The Articulatory Process

The Organs of Articulation

The word *articulation* refers in general to a mobile joining or fitting of things together. For example, the bones and cartilages in your elbow are said to articulate. The word is well suited to the action of the speech organs as they interact with one another and help fit or join the various sound units into agreed-upon patterns that we call speech. This articulating of bones, muscles, teeth and so on is obviously amenable to training. Just as the musician, typist, and surgeon must learn certain motor skills and habits pertinent to the articulating of the knuckles, bones, and cartilages in their hands, so too must the speaker develop good skills and habits with his articulating mechanisms. If a musician is lazy with his fingers, it qualitatively decreases the beauty or acceptability of his effort. If a typist is careless about the use or consistent placement of her fingers, it may cost her a job. Your habits and training in articulation of such organs as teeth, tongue, lips, palate, and jaw are of great importance to you also.

Articulation where dialect related should be adapted to groups and situations to some extent particularly if you are a part of those groups. Many students have developed two dialects to facilitate communication. Whatever the utility of such adaptation, take care that you don't develop poor, unplanned articulations of a primarily mechanical nature. These might call adverse attention to yourself regardless of the situation. You may wish on occasion to test or make an inventory of your articulation habits to be sure you are not becoming careless. A short articulation test is supplied at the close of this chapter.

Common Articulatory Faults

Some of the more common causes of slovenly articulation in a mechanical sense are: (a) locked jaw, (b) lazy lips, and (c) mushy mouth.

LOCKED JAW. The speaker simply will not open his mouth wide enough. His jaw is tight and seems locked in position. He talks through his teeth and nose because the sound has to get out somehow. His projection is curtailed; his resonance is mismatched; his vowel quality is particularly impaired. This may in part be caused by tension and speech fright, but the admonition is the same—unlock your jaw, open your mouth!

LAZY LIPS. In this case the lips are so tight or so slack that in either condition they do not adequately shape the mouth opening for proper vowel resonation or for the proper articulation of the labial or lip consonants (*p, b, m, w, f,* and *v*). The rule is simple: allow your lips to perform their necessary functions. The visual lack of lip action is also disconcerting to many listeners. Unless you are a ventriloquist, free your lips.

MUSHY MOUTH. This problem is caused primarily by feeble or sluggish tongue activity. Because the tongue is our most important articulation organ, you may foul up a large part of your speech if you are guilty of this fault. The fine shades of tone between vowels are obviously in jeopardy, since the tongue position in large part decides the shape and size of the aural cavity. Many consonants also depend heavily upon vigorous and precise tongue action. A *th* sound (*th*ese) easily becomes a *d* sound (*d*ese) if the tongue is lazy and does not move forward far enough to actually articulate with the teeth. Other consonants such as d, l, r and s also call for vigorous and specific tongue action. If your tongue action is slack, languid, drooping, and feeble, you will be afflicted with mushy mouth. A vigorous and firm tongue action where you can feel your tongue articulate with your teeth on the appropriate sounds is your best safeguard against this problem.

Articulation Inventory

The following phonetic inventory and diagnostic sentences are taken from a drill book by the late Grant Fairbanks, an outstanding voice scientist.[10] Each sentence tests a particular sound as listed on the phonetic inventory.

PHONETIC INVENTORY

TYPE OF ERROR

	Substitution	Omission	Distortion	Slighting
1. [i]	. . .	. . .	. . .	. . .
2. [ɪ]	. . .	. . .	. . .	. . .
3. [eɪ]	. . .	. . .	. . .	. . .
4. [ɛ]	. . .	. . .	. . .	. . .
5. [æ]	. . .	. . .	. . .	. . .
6. [ʌ]	. . .	. . .	. . .	. . .
7. [ɑ]	. . .	. . .	. . .	. . .

[10] Form 2, "Phonetic Inventory—Sentences for Phonetic Inventory" from *Voice and Articulation Drillbook*, Second Edition, by Grant Fairbanks. Copyright © 1960 by Grant Fairbanks. By permission of Harper & Row, Publishers, Incorporated.

PHONETIC INVENTORY

TYPE OF ERROR

	Substitution	Omission	Distortion	Slighting
8. [ɔ]	...	...	...	...
9. [oʊ]	...	...	...	...
10. [ʊ]	...	...	...	...
11. [u]	...	...	...	...
12. [ju]	...	...	...	...
13. [aʊ]	...	...	...	...
14. [aɪ]	...	...	...	...
15. [ɔɪ]	...	...	...	...
16. [ɝ]	...	...	...	...
17. [ɚ]	...	...	...	...
18. [r]	...	...	...	...
19. [l]	...	...	...	...
20. [m]	...	...	...	...
21. [n]	...	...	...	...
22. [ŋ]	...	...	...	...
23. [j]	...	...	...	...
24. [w]	...	...	...	...
25. [hw]	...	...	...	...
26. [h]	...	...	...	...
27. [p]	...	...	...	...
28. [b]	...	...	...	...
29. [t]	...	...	...	...
30. [d]	...	...	...	...
31. [k]	...	...	...	...
32. [g]	...	...	...	...
33. [f]	...	...	...	...
34. [v]	...	...	...	...
35. [θ]	...	...	...	...
36. [ð]	...	...	...	...
37. [s]	...	...	...	...
38. [z]	...	...	...	...
39. [ʃ]	...	...	...	...
40. [ʒ]	...	...	...	...
41. [tʃ]	...	...	...	...
42. [dʒ]	...	...	...	...

SENTENCES FOR PHONETIC
INVENTORY

1. Some people reason that seeing is believing. They feel they are frequently deceived.
2. Bill saw a big pickerel swimming in the ripples. He licked his lips in anticipation of a delicious fish dinner.
3. The agent remained away all day. Late at night he made his way to the place where the sailors stayed.
4. Special regulations were necessary to help the selling of eggs. Several Senators expressed pleasure.
5. Sally banged the black sedan into a taxicab. It was badly damaged by the crash.
6. I am unable to understand my Uncle Gus. He mutters and mumbles about nothing.
7. John started across the yard toward the barn. His father remarked calmly that he'd better not wander too far.
8. Is Shaw the author of "Walking on the Lawn"? I thought it was Walter Hall.
9. Don't go home alone in the snow. You'll be cold and soaked and half-frozen.
10. Captain Hook pushed through the bushes to the brook. From where he stood it looked like an ambush.
11. As a rule we go canoeing in the forenoon. The pool is too cool in June.
12. Hugh refused to join the musicians' union. His excuse was viewed with amusement.
13. Fowler wants to plow all the ground around his house. Somehow I doubt if the council will allow it.
14. The tile workers were fighting for higher prices and more time off. They tried to drive back the strike-breakers.
15. The boys toiled noisily in the boiling sun. They enjoyed the work that Roy avoided.
16. First the girls turned on the furnace. Then they worked on burning the dirty curtains.
17. I'll undertake it sooner or later. Perhaps after another summer is over, in September or October.
18. Our barn is covered with brilliant red roses. The broad crimson roof draws admiring crowds from far and near.
19. Lawyer Clark held his little felt hat and his black gloves in his lap. He silently placed the will on the table.
20. Mr. Miller had climbed many mountains, but the chasm before him was the mightiest in his memory.

21. Laden down by their burdens, Dan and Ned ran from the barn into the open. The tornado was not far distant.

22. The monks had no inkling that anything was wrong. Suddenly the strong tones of the gong rang out.

23. Did you ever speculate on the uses of the familiar onion? On the value of a yellow yam?

24. Wait until the weather is warm. Then everyone will want to walk in the woods.

25. "What is that?" he whispered. Somewhere from the left came the whistle of a bobwhite.

26. Hurry back, anyhow, Harry. It will help if you only hear half the rehearsal.

27. Part way up the slope above the pool was a popular camping spot. Many people stopped there for picnic suppers.

28. The British were not bothered about the robbery. They believed they could bribe the Arab to betray his tribe.

29. After waiting for twenty minutes the train left the station. The excited recruits sat and talked all night.

30. The doll's red dress was soiled and muddy, but the ragged child hugged it adoringly.

31. Old Katy had a particular dislike for hawks and crows. She called them "wicked creatures."

32. The big dog began to dig under the log. Gary forgot his hunger and grabbed his gun.

33. "For breakfast," said father, "I find that coffee is the staff of life. Grapefruit is a food for infants."

34. I believe I'll save this heavy veil. The vogue might be revived eventually.

35. We thought that the theory was pathetic, but we had faith that something would lead to the truth.

36. My father finds it hard to breathe in this weather. Even the heather withers.

37. The successful student does not assume that class exercise is sufficient. He also practices by himself outside.

38. My cousin's play, "The Zero Zone," is amusing, but it won't be chosen for a prize because it doesn't deserve it.

39. The fishing ship was in shallows near the shore. In one motion a wave crushed it on the shoal.

40. I make no allusion to sabotage, but an explosion near that garage is unusual.

41. Mitchell was a righteous old bachelor. He watched for a chance to chase the children out of his orchard.

42. All but Judge Johnson pledged allegiance to the legislation. He objected that it was unjust to the soldiers.

Pronunciation

Pronunciation is the act of expressing the sounds and accents of words so that they conform with accepted standards. In addition to aiding understanding, appropriate pronunciation has much to do with the way an audience evaluates and judges a speaker. Adapting and relating to varying standards and groups to which you may belong again points up the utility of bidialectation. In old Milwaukee the word theater was typically pronounced "the-*ay*-ter," a compromised carry-over from the German pronunciation of "das Theater" (tay-*ah*-ter). In Detroit we hear "the-*uh*-ter." Some localities may say "drammer" for drama. The invaluable dictionary is a little awkward on some pronunciations because there are three generally accepted dialects in the United States (eastern, southern, and general American). The most prevalent dialect is general American, and our dictionaries and national mass media are geared to this dialect. That there are others is obvious.

The problem of showing desired or different pronunciation of a word on paper is awkward at best. One way is to agree upon and memorize a common code of symbols based strictly upon sound and free of unphonetic spelling. Thus, the International Phonetic Alphabet was born. It has one symbol for every different sound in the language. The news services use a system of respelling similar to what was used earlier in this section. Dictionaries use diacritical marks and relatively stable words as pronouncing criteria. Accent or stress is indicated as primary (') or secondary (,).

EXAMPLES OF PRONOUNCING SYSTEMS

Word	Diacritical System	International Phonetic System	Respelling System
chaotic	\kā-'ät-ik\	[ke'atɪk]	kay-otic
theatre	\'thē-ət-ər\	['θiətɚ]	the-uh-ter
nativity	\nə-'tiv-ət-ē\	[ne'trvətr]	nay-tiv-ity

A guide to pronunciation and the dictionary diacritical system is carefully explained in the introduction to any good dictionary[11] and is well worth your reading.

The principal sounds of our culture in the alphabet of the International Phonetic Association (IPA) are tabled below; also shown are the written

---

11 See especially *Webster's Seventh New Collegiate Dictionary* (Springfield, Mass.: G. & C. Merriam Company, 1969).

symbols used from our spelling alphabet, key words with the sound in italics, the diacritic symbols, and (for the vowels and diphthongs) the name we give the sound.

Some of the more common pronunciation errors in the English language are improper stress, errors in spelling-phonetics (pronouncing words as they are spelled), sound substitutions, sound additions, sound reversals, and sound subtractions. The system of indicating pronunciation shown on pages 103–104 is used by permission from Webster's Seventh New Collegiate Dictionary, © 1969 by G. & C. Merriam Co., Publishers of the Merriam-Webster Dictionaries.

Phonetic Alphabet

CONSONANTS

Phonetic Symbol	Written Symbol	Word	Diacritic Symbol	Sound Name
[p]	p	*p*ip	p	
[b]	b	*b*e	b	
[m]	m	*m*e	m	
[t]	t	*t*ea	t	
[d]	d	*d*o	d	
[n]	n	*n*o	n	
[k]	k	*k*ill	k	
[g]	g	*g*o	g	
[ŋ]	ng	si*ng*	ŋ	
[θ]	th	*th*ink	th	
[ð]	th	*th*is	*th*	
[f]	f	*f*or	f	
[v]	v	*v*ile	v	
[s]	s	*s*ip	s	
[z]	z	*z*oo	z	
[ʃ]	sh	*sh*oe	sh	
[ʒ]	zh	a*z*ure	zh	
[tʃ]	ch	pic*tu*re	ch	
[dʒ]	j	*j*udge	j	
[r]	r	*r*are	r	
[l]	l	*l*ove	l	
[h]	h	*h*im	h	
[w]	w	*w*it	w	
[hw]	wh	*wh*en	hw	
[j]	y	*y*es	y	

VOWELS

[i]	ee	senior	ē	long e
[ɪ]	i	sit	i	short i
[e]	a	chaotic	ā	half-long a; long a
[eɪ]	a	day	ā	long a
[ɛ]	e	bet	e	short e
[æ]	a	cat	a	short a
[ɑ]	a	father	ä	two-dot a
[ɔ]	o	ought	ȯ	circumflex o
[oʊ]	o	go	ō	long o
[ʊ]	oo	took	u̇	short double o
[u]	u	too	ü	long double o
[ʌ]	u	sun	'ə	short u
[ə]	a	above	ˌə	short u
[ɝ]	ea	heard	'ər	"er" sound
]ɚ[	er	percent	ˌər	"er" sound

DIPHTHONGS

[ju]	u	use	yü	half-long u
[aʊ]	ou	out	au̇	
[aɪ]	i	ice	ī	long i
[ɔɪ]	oi	oil	oi	

IMPROPER STRESS

prag'matist instead of pragmatist
super'fluous instead of su'perfluous
com'parable instead of 'comparable
tele'graphy instead of te'legraphy

ERRORS OF SPELLING-PHONETICS

salmon\'sal-mən\	instead of	\'sam-ən\
rancid\'ran-kid\	instead of	\'ran(t)-səd\
hearth\hürth\	instead of	\'härth\
zoologist\'zü-alə·jəst\	instead of	\zō-'äl-ə-jəst, zə-'wäl-\

SOUND SUBSTITUTIONS

just\jist\	instead of	\'jəst\
tremendous\tri-'men-jəs\	instead of	\tri-'men-dəs\
sieve\sēv\	instead of	\'siv\
ask\äsk\	instead of	\'ask\
catch\kēch\	instead of	\'kach, 'kech\
heinous\'he-nəs\	instead of	\'hā-nəs\

SOUND ADDITIONS

elm\ 'el-əm\	instead of	\ 'elm\
film\ 'fil-əm\	instead of	\ 'film\
umbrella\ əm-bər-'rel-ä\	instead of	\ ,əm-'brel-ə\
wash\ 'wȯrsh\	instead of	\ 'wȯsh\
athlete\ 'ath-ə-lēt\	instead of	\ 'ath-ˌlēt\
indict\ in-'dīkt\	instead of	\ in-'dīt\

SOUND REVERSALS

larynx\ 'lar-ningks\	instead of	\ 'lar-iŋ(k)s\
cavalry\ 'kal-vərē\	instead of	\ 'kav-əl-rē\
perspiration\ 'pres-pi-rā-shən\	instead of	\ ,pər-spə-'rā-shən,
		ˌpər-'sprā\
tragedy (trăd'ĕjĭ) \ 'trad-əjē\	instead of	\ 'traj-əd-ē\

SOUND SUBTRACTIONS

popular (pŏp'lēr)\ 'päp-lər\	instead of	\ 'päp-yə-lər\
eighth\ 'āt\	instead of	\ 'ātth\
geography\ 'jäg-rə-fē\	instead of	\ jē-'äg-rə-fē\
history (his'trĭ) \ 'his-trē\	instead of	\ 'his-t(ə-)rē\
picture\ 'pich-ər\	instead of	\ 'pik-chər\

Summary

Your voice contributes much to your total communication signal; it may be the most important code you emit. Voice and articulation are thought to be defective when they deviate so far from the majority that they call undue attention to themselves.

Some common problems are fast rate, wrong pitch, loudness, and faulty articulation.

The vocal process involves: an *energy* source, or our breathing machinery; a *vibrator,* or our vocal cords; *resonators* such as the cavities in our heads; and finally, *modifiers* such as our lips, teeth, tongue, jaw, and palate. The alteration or modification of the size, shape, and texture of these agents is the primary factor involved in producing speech.

There are certain attributes of voice over which you have considerable control. These are *rate, loudness, pitch,* and *quality.* The rate characteristic is influenced by assimilation, duration, pauses, phrases, and rhythm. Loudness includes considerations of intensity, volume, and vocal variety. Pitch includes considerations of central, habitual, and optimum levels and range. Quality factors considered most critical are nasality, breathiness, and harshness.

Articulation involves the interacting of the speech organs as they help fit or join the various sound units into agreed-upon patterns that we call speech. Your habits and training of such organs as teeth, tongue, lips, palate, and jaw are of great importance to proper articulation. Some of the more common mechanical faults are *lazy lips, locked jaw,* and *mushy mouth.*

Pronunciation is the act of expressing the sounds and accents of words so that they are best adapted to your total communication. There are three general dialects in the United States: eastern, southern, and general American. Our mass media and dictionaries are geared to the general American dialect.

The problem of showing different pronunciations in print is solved in part through pronouncing systems such as the International Phonetic Association alphabet, respelling, and the diacritical mark system; the last is preferred by our dictionaries.

Some of the more common pronunciation errors in the English language are: *improper stress, spelling-phonetics, sound substitutions, sound additions, sound reversals,* and *sound subtractions.*

Preparing and Organizing the Speech 7

Preparing the Speech

In Chapter 4 we discussed the *general* purposes for speaking, namely, to inform, to persuade, and to entertain. In this chapter we are concerned with the *specific* purpose, the specific audience, and methods of locating, organizing, and outlining materials.

The Specific Purpose

The specific purpose is the specified *outcome, objective,* or *response* that your speech is supposed to achieve. A teacher, for example, talks in terms of lesson plans (outlines); the specific purpose is typically called a learning outcome (desired objective or response). A geometry teacher has the general purpose of *informing* (about geometry). His specific purpose or learning outcome for a given class might be to inform the class about the applications of geometry to map and chart reading.

If you are interested in flying, you might start your speech preparation with the general idea (purpose) of informing the class about flying. It is obvious that the general subject of flying is far too big a subject or goal for a short speech. You will want to restrict your subject to what you can reasonably cover in the time available. You might state your specific purpose as follows: to inform the class about the principle of aerodynamics

106

that allows a wing to "lift." Or you might talk about weapon and propeller synchronization in World War I Jennys. The more specifically you can state just exactly what it is you are trying to say or do, the more systematic and intelligent will be your preparation and your communication. In some speeches to persuade, you may not wish to orally state your purpose to the audience; however, in terms of preparation and outlining, you should always start with a clear, precise statement of your specific purpose.

The Audience

Close on the heels of your specific purpose should come a careful consideration of your audience. In fact, if you know your audience, you should really be considering your specific purpose and audience at the same time. Most often, one knows the general type of audience he will meet (for example, businessmen, teachers, housewives). In the case of your classroom speeches, you will have an opportunity to know the specific audience. The introduction speeches give you a marvelous opportunity to gain insights into your specific audience.

Suppose your specific purpose were "to explain the five managerial functions of planning, organizing, controlling, coordinating, and communicating to an audience of management personnel." Your preparation and organization would be different if in checking on your specific management audience you discovered that they were executive vice-presidents rather than first-line foremen. Both groups use these principles, but the application might vary widely. You might revise your specific purpose to include this important specific audience factor so that it became "to explain the five managerial functions of planning, organizing, controlling, coordinating, and communicating to an audience of *executive level* personnel."

Pertinent factors to be considered before you can most efficiently and intelligently collect speech materials are the occasion, the environment, and the general descriptive measures of an audience (size, age, education, and so on).

OCCASION. The speech subject, the language you use, the clothes you wear—all these and many more are often directly related to the purpose of the gathering. The question in part is, "Why have I been chosen to speak?" Are you a second or third choice? Are you being paid? Is this a special meeting called for the express purpose of hearing you? Did the audience pay for this experience? Were they forced to come? Is this perhaps a regular meeting in which they routinely ask interesting people to speak to them? Are you the main bill of fare, or are there other events or speakers on the program? If so, when, in what order, and for how long does each person speak? All these questions are critical to a speaker's preparation for an adaptation to an audience.

A speaker should if possible know the special rules, habits, rituals, and practices he is apt to encounter. For example, organizations such as the Kiwanis, Rotary, Lions, Eagles, and Elks have relatively standard meeting formats. Many of these same organizations have certain "fun" rituals, which, though great sport if you are forewarned, can also be a nightmare if you are caught unaware. A speaker was once fined $1 before saying his first word because he was wearing a red necktie! Know your occasion so well that you can predict these things and actually work them into your preparation.

Part of the occasion is the inevitable speech of introduction. (If you *are* the introducer, read Chapter 13 now). A bad speech of introduction can make life very difficult for the speaker. Seldom does the introducer mean any harm; quite the contrary. His lengthy speech is meant to be complimentary. He may even be so enthused about your subject that he will give part of your speech for you. The chairman or introducer almost always asks the speaker for help, and the novice or reckless speaker almost always says with a blush, "Oh, it doesn't really matter." But it *does* matter, so *do* give him help. He will appreciate it and you will cut down your risks at the same time. On one occasion, a speaker was asked to give a ten-minute critique on a championship debate held before a business audience. His university public relations department had sent a standard release to the chairman of the debate. This release consisted of about four pages of biographical material, including a careful listing of every award and publication with which the speaker had ever been associated. You can guess what happened. The well-intentioned chairman read off every word and took ten embarrassing minutes to do it. This terrifying experience for the critique speaker evoked the somber comment, "Make a careful study of the occasion and then expect the worst!"

ENVIRONMENT. Closely related to the occasion is the general location, that is, the room or the building in which the speech will be made. The same speech delivered in a church, a restaurant, or a fraternity house will be altered communicatively by the location alone. People have different expectations for different types of buildings. Your proximity to the audience is also a factor. If you are on an elevated platform far removed from the first row of the audience, the style of your delivery will be qualitatively different than if you are close to the group. The seating arrangement of the audience makes a difference. Dr. Furbay, for example, experimented with different seating patterns in terms of attitude shift and retention of material and found generally that audiences were more easily persuaded if seated in a scattered rather than compact manner.[1] In terms of comprehension of

---

[1] Albert L. Furbay, "The Influence of Scattered Versus Compact Seating on Audience Response," *Speech Monographs*, XXXII, No. 2 (June, 1965), 144–48.

the largely factual information used in this experiment, both arrangements did equally well. It would appear compactness of itself does not mean greater susceptibility to all types of speeches. It is probably true that logical, factual type persuasion is more effective when listeners are separated, and that physical closeness is most amenable to emotional appeals.

Another environmental factor is the use of a Public Address (P.A.) system. If you do have a P.A. system, it may seriously affect the way in which you use your visual aids. Most microphones will fade if you get more than two feet away from them. It is a good idea to check such things *before* you speak. The noise level of the room is often a problem, as is the lighting and ventilation. Many of these factors can be controlled (or at least better adapted to) if you will consider them early enough.

Effectiveness of visual aids is closely related to all these practical environmental factors. The size of the visual aid is related to the size of the room and the size of the audience. A chart big enough for a group of 25 may be hopelessly lost in a group of 300. A series of slides may be useless if the room will not darken, and a tape recording can be almost lost in a room filled with echoes.

The time for which the speech is scheduled may make a difference. It has happened that A.M. and P.M. have been falsely assumed. The concept of "their" time or "company time" often pertains, and a speaker might regulate not only the content, but the length accordingly. It has been noticed that industrial and business audiences are often more generous when they are listening on company time.

GENERAL DESCRIPTIVE MEASURES. Always evaluate your audience according to the following factors:

1. *Age.* It is obvious that an audience of 10-year-olds will call for considerably different preparation than will a group of 40-year-olds, even if the subject is Little League baseball. Just a few children in an otherwise all-adult audience sometimes presents a problem. Even if you choose (or are advised) to ignore them, you can rest assured that the *audience* will not ignore them and will establish norms of appropriateness and understanding in terms of the youngsters. A risque story is less well received when even a single child is present.

2. *Sex.* An audience of 20 men often differs considerably in outlook from an audience of 20 women. An audience of 10 men and 10 women is still more different than either of the homogeneous audiences. An audience of 19 men and 1 woman may cause a speaker to alter many of his jokes and examples not necessarily *because* of the 1 woman, but because of 19 men's expectations that the speaker will be conscious of the 1 woman. Ignore the women in your audience and the men will be unhappy. As one wag put it, "Treat them all equal and the women will be unhappy."

3. *Education.* A man's education is the sum total of his learning. Do not confuse schooling with education, for schooling is no guarantee of an education. There are many uneducated college graduates! Nevertheless we feel that formal schooling is a faster and more systematic way of learning than some other ways. A person's schooling level may therefore be useful information in planning your speech. Language and vocabulary should be adapted as was suggested earlier. The kind of schooling will also be a factor. That is, an audience with a highly technical education demands a different approach than one with a religious or a liberal arts background. Again, the problem of mixed education levels presents itself. Time invested in this kind of audience analysis is usually well spent.

4. *Occupation.* The procedure of typing a person by his occupation is as dangerous as classifying him according to schooling. Nevertheless, this information is often predictively useful. Income level and the things related to income can often be predicted by knowing the typical occupation of your audience. A group of teachers can be expected to have college degrees, a group of top management executives may have relatively similar opinions about certain pieces of labor legislation, and so on.

5. *Primary Group Memberships.* Most of us belong to so many groups that prediction even for a uniform audience is often shaky at best. For example, an audience at a political convention may be 100 percent Republican or Democrat and yet may be split ever so many ways on other group memberships such as religion, ancestry, and occupation, not to mention key issues. However, the more you can learn about the groups an audience does or does not belong to, the more intelligently you can prepare your speech.

6. *Special Interests.* Whatever our differences on some of our primary group memberships, we often find audiences highly polarized if there is some secondary or special issue that they all have in common. A small community with a winning high school basketball team can unceremoniously ignore a guest speaker if he is not aware of this special interest. Sometimes these special interests are temporary, but a speaker will do well to look for those special interests which the audience *expects* him to know something about.

7. *Audience-Subject Relationship.* This part of your analysis concerns an audience's *knowledge* about your speech topic, its *experience* and *interest* with the subject, and its *attitude* toward your specific purpose. It is often valuable to know the extent of audience uniformity about your subject.

Audiences are sometimes very firm in their beliefs, whatever the level of knowledge or experience. Specific methods of preparing strategy for these occasions are covered at length in Chapter 9. In general, an audience is interested or apathetic toward your speech *subject,* but attitude is a special dimension of interest in your *purpose*. A useful scale for determining the general audience attitude toward your speech purpose is as follows:

		ATTITUDE SCALE		
Hostile	*Opposed*	*Uncertain*	*Cordial*	*Favorable*
−2	−1	0	+1	+2

Your speech preparation and arrangement of material will be heavily dependent upon this kind of analysis.

Locating Materials

Once you have thoroughly considered your specific purpose and have related it to the analysis of audience and occasion, you are ready to start locating and collecting the materials and details that will constitute the speech itself. Obviously this collection of speech details should be closely related to your specific audience as well as to your specific purpose. The question now is, "Where do I find these materials?"

Your own knowledge and experience may give you a head start. Conversations with knowledgeable people can be invaluable. However, any serious interviewing or corresponding should usually be preceded by some modicum of reading and observing. The purpose of starting your more formal research early is to help you better understand what the important questions are. If, for example, you were going to interview an electrical engineering professor on "Information Theory," you would be well advised to browse through one or two of the classic books or articles in the field to get the maximum value out of the interview. The same would be true if you were going to interview a speech professor on such subjects as "Semantics," "Psycholinguistics" or "Congruency." Your probable question right now is, "Where do I find these sources to browse through?"

The simplest answer is your *library card catalogue*. This obvious source represents a vast treasurehouse of information, so take advantage of it. Almost every library has the *Readers' Guide to Periodical Literature*. This source lists magazine articles by author, title, and subject matter. It is typically bound into annual volumes and is located in the reference section of the library. You use it much as you would the library card catalogue. You may also look through the *Cumulative Book Index* and its predecessor, the *United States Catalog;* these sources do for books approximately what the *Readers' Guide* does for magazines. The *Book Index* is arranged according to author, title, and subject. While in the library, see if they have the *New York Times Index*. This is the only complete newspaper index in the United States and can be a real time-saver for you.

A good set of general encyclopedias (such as *Britannica, Americana, New International*) or special ones (such as the *Encyclopedia of the Social Sciences, Catholic Encyclopedia, Jewish Encyclopedia,* and the *Encyclopedia of Religion and Ethics*) are found in many libraries and very often represent the best short statement on a given subject to be found anywhere. These encyclopedias are typically kept current by annual supplements called yearbooks.

When in need of statistics and short statements of factual data, see *The Statesman's Yearbook, The World Almanac and Book of Facts,* and *The Statistical Abstract of the United States.* Smaller general encyclopedias such as the *Columbia* or *Everyman's* will also give compact statements and facts.

To learn more about the authority you may wish to discuss, to interview, or to quote in a speech, consult some of the better known directories and biographical dictionaries such as *Who's Who in America, Who's Who in American Education, Who's Who in Engineering, American Men of Science,* and the *Directory of American Scholars.* For prominent Americans of former years, see *Who Was Who in America, The Dictionary of American Biography, Lippincott's Biographical Dictionary,* and *The National Cyclopedia of American Biography.*

Most professional or trade associations publish journals of their own. Some of these organizations are the *American Bar Association,* the *American Bankers' Association,* the *American Medical Association,* the *Speech Association of America,* the *American Psychological Association,* the *American Federation of Labor,* and so on. Many of the journals emanating from these organizations are indexed by special publications often available in your library (for example, *The Agricultural Index, The Art Index, Index to Legal Periodicals, Index Medicus, Psychological Abstracts,* and many more).

In addition to the *Statistical Abstract of the United States* mentioned earlier, other government publications can be a huge source of speech materials. The *Commerce Yearbook* and the *Monthly Labor Report* provide much invaluable information. The *Congressional Record,* particularly, is a fertile source for speech students. It includes a daily report of the House and Senate debates, it is indexed according to subjects, names of bills, and Congressmen, and an appendix covers related articles and speeches, which occurred outside of Congress.

Other rich sources of materials are the thousands of organizations that issue pamphlets and reports often at no cost. You can write directly to these organizations for information and in some cases receive a speech outline or manuscript in the return mail (for example, *The American League to Abolish Capital Punishment, Inc.* and the *World Peace Foundation,* the *American Institute of Banking,* and the *AFL-CIO*). If you would like to know the address of these or other organizations refer to the *World*

Almanac, which carries the addresses of a large number of them under the heading "Associations and Societies in the United States."

If you do not have enough information from the sources previously indicated, or if you would like to *start out* with a printed bibliography on your subject, it may surprise you to know that there is available in some libraries a bibliography on bibliographies—an index of bibliographies called the *Bibliographic Index*. Check with your librarian for this material.

Note Taking

While you are reading and absorbing all the materials discovered through the devices discussed above, you must consider problems of selecting, sorting, evaluating, and finally recording the material. It will become evident that you need an almost mechanical system of taking notes if you are not to be overwhelmed by the sheer amount of information available to you. The problem of not remembering exactly what you read or where you read it is frustrating indeed, but if this failure of memory is serious enough to prompt a return trip to the library, you have lost preparation time as well.

A very general "yes-no" selection of your potential major sources is usually possible after rapid browsing or scanning. After this preliminary rough sorting, you are ready to record the details that are most apt to support your specific purpose and most likely to coordinate with your audience analysis. One more general consideration is in order before you actually write things down. You may wish to revise, alter, or enrich your specific purpose as a result of your browsing and the subsequent important guidelines that emerge in terms of kinds of materials, issues, causes, or perhaps in your order of presentation. In other words, devise tentative categories or classifications. You can add, delete, or subdivide later as your search becomes more specific. This will also give you a head start on the eventual organizing and outlining of the speech itself.

Now you should start taking systematic notes. The emphasis is on the word *system*. As long as you have done the rough sorting suggested above and are not taking notes purposelessly or haphazardly, you may use any system that is meaningful to you. The most common system for library searches involves the use of 3×5 or 4×6 file cards. You may have noticed debaters actually carrying small metal file cases filled with cards arranged either alphabetically or according to the issues pertinent to their debate subject. You should keep only one subject, source, classification, and note on each card. The big advantage over a notebook is that you can rearrange file cards and thus reclassify or subclassify very easily. This shuffling of cards is very useful when you are actually ready to organize and outline your speech.

The next problem is what to write on the card. If you have a general source, which you "may or may not" wish to use later, a short summary in your own words may be in order. You will then be better able at a later time to decide whether you wish to reread the article. If you find a statement by an authority that you may wish to use, take it down verbatim and put quotation marks around it. Be sure to get the authority's name and qualifications recorded. In testimony or statistics make sure you record the date. It is a well known fact that people change their minds. If you insert explanations or interpretations of your own, put brackets around the words so that at a later date you will not confuse your words with those of your source.

In your English class you may have been schooled in a system of taking notes for a source theme. It should be useful here. Whether you use classifications at the top of the card and a footnote at the bottom will depend in part upon your training and preferences as well as the nature of your specific purpose and subject. Some samples are shown in Figures 33–36.

Organizing the Speech

One can start his thinking about organization in terms of the specific ideas and speech details he has collected or in terms of the general parts into which speeches can conveniently be divided. Let us first look at some useful principles for organizing the raw materials and then analyze ways of dividing or arranging the parts of a speech.

Methods of Organizing Ideas

CHRONOLOGICAL METHOD. In this method, your materials are arranged according to the order in which a number of events took place. In dis-

---

(Subject) *Creativity*   (Classification) *Mental Functions*

1. Absorptive—the ability to observe, and to apply attention.
2. Retentive—the ability to memorize and to recall.
3. Reasoning—the ability to analyze and to judge.
4. Creative—the ability to visualize, to foresee, and to generate ideas.

Source: Alex F. Osborn, *Applied Imagination,* 3rd ed. (New York: Charles Scribner's Sons, 1963), p. 1.

Figure 33

(Subject) *Prehistoric Man*   (Classification)   *Dinosaurs*

". . . you will often see cartoons showing cave men being chased by dinosaurs. But this could never have happened. The physical anthropologists tell us which bones are the bones of the prehistoric men who lived in caves. The paleontologists tell us which bones are the bones of the giant reptiles. The geologists tell us that the human bones come from layers of earth that are 50,000 years old, and the dinosaur bones come from rocks 150,000,000 years old."

Source: Donald Barr, *Primitive Man* (New York: Wonder Books, 1961), p. 10.

Figure 34

cussing "Life on Earth," we would probably take the periods chronologically: (1) Archeozoic, (2) Proterozoic, (3) Paleozoic, (4) Mesozoic, (5) Cenozoic, (6) Present. Most historical subjects lend themselves readily to this method; so do processes of a 1-2-3 order, such as film developing. Remember, however, that these subjects may be handled in different ways. History is often more interesting and meaningful if discussed topically.

TOPICAL METHOD. In this method, the material is ordered according to general topics or classifications of knowledge. To continue the example of history, we might concentrate on the history of religion, war, government, education, or science. The topical importance may or may not violate chronology and is a very useful way to start breaking down very broad topics. One can, for example, look at integration of the races in a myriad of topical ways—educationally, socially, militarily, economically.

SPATIAL METHOD. This method is particularly useful in certain types of

(Subject) *Problem Solving Systems*   (Classification) *General Background*

Chapter 2 (Reasoning) of this book covers four special readings, including some special problems. Included are the following: 1. Reasoning in Humans; 2. An Exper. Sty. of P. S.; 3. The Sol. of Prac. Probs.; 4. Prob. Sol. Proc. of Col. students. [Looks impressive]

Source: T. L. Harris, and W. E. Schwahn, *The Learning Process* (New York: Oxford University Press, 1961), pp. 29–79.

Figure 35

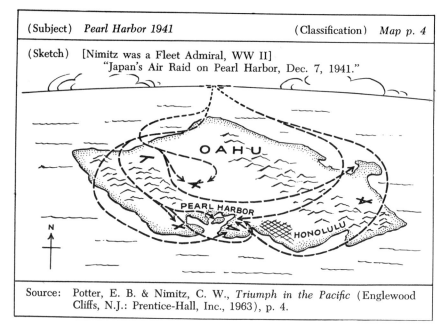

(Subject) *Pearl Harbor 1941*   (Classification)   *Map p. 4*

(Sketch)   [Nimitz was a Fleet Admiral, WW II]
           "Japan's Air Raid on Pearl Harbor, Dec. 7, 1941."

OAHU

PEARL HARBOR

HONOLULU

N

Source: Potter, E. B. & Nimitz, C. W., *Triumph in the Pacific* (Englewood Cliffs, N.J.: Prentice-Hall, Inc., 1963), p. 4.

Figure 36

geographical or physical-order subjects. In a speech about the United Nations, one might first describe each building, then discuss the offices in each building one floor at a time, that is, organize the ideas spatially. It could also be done topically if the audience were familiar with the general political structure of the United Nations. In discussing "Nationalism in Africa," one might use geographical space and simply divide the ideas from north to south and east to west. It is obvious that chronological history might also be a useful method.

LOGICAL METHOD. This method involves generally accepted or obvious cause-and-effect relationships whether they range from the fall of the Japanese empire to the building of a house or a boat. When the order is natural or inherent in the subject or when man generally accepts the association of ideas, it may be convenient to organize our speech materials accordingly. Audience analysis is imperative for this method.

DIFFICULTY METHOD. For some subjects, particularly those of a technical order, it may be advantageous to organize your materials according to an ease index or difficulty order, that is, proceeding from the easiest aspect to the more difficult or complex. In discussing general principles of electricity, we might arrange a series of ideas as follows:

1. The flashlight.
2. Switches.
3. Dry cells.
4. Light bulbs in a series.

5. Light bulbs in parallel.
6. Electromagnets.
7. Current and electrons.

NEED-PLAN METHOD. This method involves the organization of materials according to problems (needs) and solutions (plans). An affirmative debate team concerned with a resolution on government health programs will typically divide its material into these two general categories. The first speaker will concentrate on the various needs in our present situation or in our present programs. The second speaker will discuss the various plans and indicate why one is better than the others. The needs can be subdivided into many useful types such as economic needs, health needs, and social needs.

Methods of Arranging the Parts

Various sets of terms refer to the *parts* of a speech: *Beginning, Middle, End; Introduction, Body, Conclusion;* or in a more classical sense, *Proem, Statement, Argument, Epilogue.* Other *parts* are the speech details and ideas you have already collected and perhaps partially organized into one or more of the general sequences discussed in the last section.

Before an analysis of these parts, let us look at certain rhetorical principles that have a bearing on the ordering and arranging of the parts. They are *Unity, Coherence* and *Emphasis.*

UNITY. In discussing tragic drama, Aristotle said that a play must be so constructed that omission of any part damages the whole, and that each part of the plot must contribute to making inevitable the purpose or end of the play. By analogy, he said, it must have a total unity in the same manner of a living organism. We still use the term *organic unity* to express this concept. With regard to a speech, it means that the material should be unified to the point that it can be summarized in a single statement of purpose. In some speeches, it takes the form of a resolution or proposition, which is forthrightly announced; in other cases, for purposes of strategy, such a proposition might be suppressed; but in all cases, the speaker must understand his purpose if the speech is to have unity. This consciousness of specific purpose helps the speaker evaluate the materials and ideas during preparation. The arrangement of the parts of a speech should be so unified that there is a welding of audience, speaker, and purpose.

COHERENCE. Coherence refers to the specific sequence of the parts of the speech; it therefore involves the various methods of ordering and arranging ideas and speech details already considered. To *cohere* is to be connected by a common principle or relationship. It involves logically consistent subordination of ideas. The actual connecting of the various parts and ideas of a speech is done through words or phrases. Unlike the writer, the speaker cannot go back and recheck to locate a lost thread of meaning. Thus he must be especially careful of his connectives, often repeating and clearly labeling them. Coherence must therefore always involve the audience. A speaker may lose his audience when going from one point to another by assuming that the audience will see the connection, because the relationship or subordination of ideas is logically consistent to him.

To achieve coherence, we must carefully consider the connecting words of transition. Some of the types of links or connectives possible in our language are as follows:

TYPES OF CONNECTIVES[2]

1. *Indicating time:*	previously, formerly, at an earlier period, anterior, contemporary, at the same moment, in the same period, throughout this period, during this time, meanwhile, in the meantime, upon this, then, by that time, already, now, since then, after this, thereafter, in the end, at last, at length, at a later time, henceforth, now that.
2. *Making evident:*	thereof, thereby, thereto, therein, therefrom, in this case, in such a case, at such times, on such occasions, under these circumstances, in all this, in connection with this, together with this, here again.
3. *Returning to purpose:*	to continue, to return, to report, to resume, along with . . . , as I have said, then, now, again, once more, at any rate, at all events.
4. *Making reference:*	in point of, with respect to, as related to, concerning, as for.
5. *Citing:*	for instance, for example, to illustrate, by way of illustration, another case, a case in point is . . . , under this head.
6. *Excepting:*	with this exception, this exception made, except for

---

[2] For a more complete discussion of connectives see Ernest Brennecke, Jr. and Donald L. Clark, *Magazine Article Writing* (New York: The Macmillan Company, 1930), pp. 139–42.

	this, waiving this question, leaving this out of account . . . , excluded, exclusive of . . . , irrespective of . . . , excluding this point.
7. *Summarizing:*	to sum up, to recapitulate, on the whole, briefly, in a word, in brief, in short, we have traced. . . , as we have seen, up to this point, yes, no.
8. *Concluding:*	to conclude, finally, lastly, in conclusion, last of all.
9. *Explaining:*	that is, to explain, in other words, this is as much as to say, that amounts to saying.
10. *Marking a change in tone or in point of view:*	at least, seriously, in all seriousness, jesting aside, to speak frankly, for my part, in another sense, as a matter of fact, in fact, to come to the point, in general, of course, you see, as the matter stands, as things are.
11. *Comparing:*	parallel with . . . , allied to . . . , comparable to . . . , from another point of view, in the same category, in like manner, in the same way, similarly, likewise, as similar view, yet more important, of less importance, next in importance, in contrast with this, conversely.
12. *Emphasizing:*	indeed, moreover, add to this, furthermore, besides, further, even without this, in addition to this, all the more, even more, into the bargain, especially, in particular, how much more, yet again, above all, best of all, most of all.
13. *Judging:*	so, therefore, consequently, accordingly, thus, hence, then, in consequence, as a result, the result is, we conclude, because of this, for this reason, this being true, such being the case, under these circumstances, what follows.
14. *Conceding:*	certainly, indeed, it is true, to be sure, it must be granted, I admit, true, granted, admitting the force of . . . , no doubt, doubtless.
15. *Opposing:*	yet, still, nevertheless, however, on the other hand, at the same time, none the less, only, even so, in spite of this, the fact is . . . , after all.
16. *Refuting:*	otherwise, else, were this not so, on no other supposition, on the contrary, no, never, hardly.

EMPHASIS involves the location, space, form, and order you give your most important ideas. Should you put your most important idea first, last, or in a climactic order? Does the amount of space you give the idea affect emphasis? (Your main point ordinarily is not buried under some sub-sub-point.) Since a number of really important ideas may compete for attention, to which should you give the most emphasis? These questions can be best answered in terms of your subject, your knowledge, your audience, and the occasion. Location, space, form, and order do make a difference and do affect emphasis. The function of emphasis is to use these devices in harmony with the relative importance assigned to each part or idea in your speech.

SYSTEMS OF ARRANGEMENT. Aristotle used the Greek word *taxis,* which denotes division or arrangement, to explain what he thought was the most obvious and logical arrangement of parts or elements of a speech, particularly a persuasive or argumentative speech. He felt that the following elements were most closely related to the thinking habits of man: Proem (Introduction), Statement, Argument, and Epilogue (Conclusion).[3]

For Aristotle the proem and epilogue are primarily used as aids for memory and attention. The main *body* of the speech is the *statement* of purpose and the proofs or *argument.*

In the twentieth century, H. L. Hollingworth[4] indicated the fundamental tasks or steps of a speech as: attention, interest, impression, conviction, and direction. Just as Aristotle suggested that for some occasions a proem or attention step was less necessary, so too does Hollingworth explain the shortening or actual elimination of some of the elements as the audience becomes more selected, organized, concerted, or polarized.

In still more recent times Alan H. Monroe,[5] a speech psychologist, has suggested that the fundamental elements are attention, need, satisfaction, visualization, and action. Like Hollingworth, Monroe feels that the emphasis given each element depends upon the audience disposition and knowledge as well as the nature of the speech. A speech to inform might use only three elements while a speech to persuade might call for all five.

These systems and many more are very useful in that they point up the complicated interaction of subject, audience, speaker, and arrangement. Any system is undoubtedly an understatement or a dangerous generalization in terms of unbelievably complex communication problems.

That other divisions or participations are possible is evident. The *general* purpose of your speech (to persuade, to inform, or to entertain) will dictate how much of a system you will need to include under the general divisions of introduction, body, and conclusion. For example, in Chapter 8 a special system of organizing is recommended, which borrows not only from the systems above, but also from learning theories; it includes attention, overview, information, review. In Chapter 9, several useful systems

---

[3] Lane Cooper, *The Rhetoric of Aristotle* (New York: Appleton-Century-Crofts, 1932), pp. 220–40.

[4] H. L. Hollingworth, *The Psychology of the Audience* (New York: American Book Company, 1935), Ch. III, pp. 19–32.

[5] Alan H. Monroe, *Principles and Types of Speech* (Glenview, Ill.: Scott, Foresman & Company, 1967).

are discussed and illustrated, one of which is attention, need, plan, objections, reinforcement, action. Let us view these five in terms of the more common arrangement of introduction, body, conclusion.

SOME GENERAL SYSTEMS OF ARRANGEMENT

Proem	Attention	Attention	Attention	Attention	Introduction
			Overview		
Statement	Interest	Need		Need	
Argument	Impression	Satisfaction	Information	Plan	Body.
	Conviction	Visualization		Objections	
Epilogue	Direction	Action	Review	Reinforcement Action	Conclusion

More will be said of these specific deviations in related chapters. We will now look at the general requirements of a good introduction, body, and conclusion.

INTRODUCTION. The previous analysis of systems indicates that in all cases the concept of attention is an important aspect of any introduction. We also learned in the discussions of emphasis and arrangement that the amount of attention devices or efforts depends on what attention level the audience has already achieved. In other words, if the audience is on the edge of its seats and in a state of readiness to hear what you have to say, a lengthy introduction designed to arouse attention would be superfluous. More will be said about attention in chapter 9.

Arousing attention is only one requirement of an introduction. Your introduction should also strive to establish or reaffirm good will between you, the group you represent, and the audience. In those rare cases where good will is hard to come by (hostility), then perhaps "establishing a climate for a fair hearing" is a better way of putting it.

In some situations, a function of the introduction is *orientation;* the speaker must sometimes supply certain background explanations or definitions to promote audience comprehension of the main body. A brief historical sketch often helps an audience gain perspective and orientation. Certain terms or language may be either vague or unknown, and *not* to define them is to confuse the audience (for example, cybernetics, carcinoma, data processing, method acting, afram, hippie, communists, juvenile delinquents, and so forth).

The introduction seeks to make your purpose clear; it is often a kind of preview of what is to follow in the main body. This involves a certain amount of repetition, but remember that an *audience,* unlike a *reader,* cannot go back to a previous page. Therefore more repetition is called for.

In sum, the general functions of an introduction are: (1) to secure *attention;* (2) to establish *good will;* (3) to assure a *fair hearing;* (4) to *orient* your audience to the subject; and (5) to make your *purpose* clear.

You can achieve good introductions in many different ways; however, all of them should ideally be related to both the subject and the situation. An unusual story of your troubles in getting to the meeting is acceptable, especially if you can relate it to your subject. This is also true of humor. Although the research is inconclusive on this point, most experts generally agree that if you are going to use jokes they should be in some way related to the subject or situation.

As an illustration of all the functions and requirements of a good introduction, let us quote from the 1961 Inaugural Address of John F. Kennedy.

My fellow citizens:

Attention

We observe today not a victory of party but a celebration of freedom—symbolizing an end as well as a beginning—signifying renewal as well as change. For I have sworn before you and Almighty God the same solemn oath our forebears prescribed nearly a century and three quarters ago.

Orientation and Good Will

The world is very different now. For man holds in his mortal hands the power to abolish all form of human poverty and to abolish all form of human life. And, yet, the same revolutionary beliefs for which our forebears fought are still at issue around the globe—the belief that the rights of man come not from the generosity of the state but from the hand of God.

Fair Hearing

We dare not forget today that we are the heirs of that first revolution. Let the word go forth from this time and place, to friend and foe alike, that the torch has been passed to a new generation of Americans—born in this century, tempered by war, disciplined by a cold and bitter peace, proud of our ancient heritage—and unwilling to witness or permit the slow undoing of those human rights to which this nation has always been committed, and to which we are committed today.

Purpose

Let every nation know, whether it wish us well or ill, that we shall pay any price, bear any burden, meet any hardship, support any friend, or oppose any foe in order to assure the survival and success of liberty.

This much we pledge—and more.

Another powerful example of a good introduction is taken from a 1959 speech by Richard Nixon, then Vice-President of the United States, entitled "The Heart of the American Ideal." The speech was given to a Russian audience attending the opening of the American National Exhibition in Moscow.

Attention 〔 I am honored on behalf of President Eisenhower to open this American exhibition in Moscow.

Good Will 〔 Mrs. Nixon and I were among the many thousands of Americans who were privileged to visit the splendid Soviet exhibition in New York, and we want to take this opportunity to congratulate the people of the U.S.S.R. for the great achievements and progress so magnificently portrayed by your exhibition.

Fair Hearing 〔 We, in turn, hope that many thousands of Soviet citizens will take advantage of this opportunity to learn about life in the United States by visiting our exhibition.
Of course, we both realize that no exhibition can portray a complete picture of all aspects of life in great nations like the U.S.S.R. and the United States.

Orientation (Preview) 〔 Among the questions which some might raise with regard to our exhibition are these: To what extent does this exhibition accurately present life in the United States as it really is? Can only the wealthy people afford the things exhibited here? What about the inequality, the injustice, the other weaknesses which are supposed to be inevitable in a capitalist society?

Purpose 〔 As Mr. Khrushchev often says: "You can't leave a word out of a song." Consequently, in the limited time I have, I would like to try to answer some of those questions so that you may get an accurate picture of what America is really like.

In still more specific terms, an introduction may utilize appreciation, personal reference, quotations, humor, related stories or experiences, and so on. When the purpose is relatively obvious and the speaker and subject well known, a related story, incident, or narrative with built-in attention often serves to reinforce the purpose and give a fresh orientation.

Booker T. Washington's introduction to his address at the Atlanta exposition is a case in point.[6]

Attention 〔 Mr. President and Gentlemen of the Board of Directors and Citizens: One-third of the population of the South is of the Negro race. No enterprise seeking the material, civil, or moral welfare of this section can disregard this element of our population and reach the highest success.

---

[6] A. Craig Baird, *American Public Addresses: 1740–1952* (New York: McGraw-Hill Book Company, 1956), p. 189.

Good Will
> I but convey to you, Mr. President and Directors, the sentiment of the masses of my race when I say that in no way have the value and manhood of the American Negro been more fittingly and generously recognized than by the managers of this magnificent Exposition at every stage of its progress. It is a recognition that will do more to cement the friendship of the two races than any occurrence since the dawn of our freedom.

Fair Hearing
> Not only this, but the opportunity here afforded will awaken among us a new era of industrial progress. Ignorant and inexperienced, it is not strange that in the first years of our new life we began at the top instead of at the bottom; that a seat in Congress or the state legislature was more sought than real estate or industrial skill; that the political convention or stump speaking had more attractions than starting a dairy farm or truck garden.

Orientation
> A ship lost at sea for many days suddenly sighted a friendly vessel. From the mast of the unfortunate vessel was seen a signal, "Water, water; we die of thirst!" The answer from the friendly vessel at once came back, "Cast down your bucket where you are." And a third and fourth signal for water was answered, "Cast down your bucket where you are." The captain of the distressed vessel, at last heading the injunction, cast down his bucket, and it came up full of fresh, sparkling water from the mouth of the Amazon River.

Purpose
> To those of my race who depend on bettering their condition in a foreign land or who underestimate the importance of cultivating friendly relations with the Southern white man, who is their next door neighbor, I would say: "Cast down your bucket where you are"—cast it down in making friends in every manly way of the people of all races by whom we are surrounded.

During World War II, President Roosevelt also used a story in one of his introductions to the many appeals he made for the purchase of war bonds.[7]

> Once upon a time, a few years ago, there was a city in our Middle West which was threatened by a destructive flood in a great river. The waters had risen to the top of the banks. Every man, woman, and child in that city was called upon to fill sandbags in order to defend their homes against the rising waters. For many days and nights destruction and death stared them in the face. As a result of the grim, determined community effort, that city still stands. Those people kept the levees above the peak of the flood. All of them joined together in the desperate job that had to be done

---

[7] *Vital Speeches of the Day*, IX, No. 23 (1943), 703.

—businessmen, workers, farmers, and doctors, and preachers—people of all races.

To me that town is a living symbol of what community cooperation can accomplish.

Body. The major discussion of the speech material takes place here. This is where the bulk of the information or argument is located. All the previous discussions of organization, rhetorical principles, and arrangement come into focus here. The specific arrangements pertinent to the general purposes will be discussed in later chapters on information and persuasion; and the typical forms of the body will subsequently be explained and illustrated under "Mechanics of Outlining."

Conclusion. The words from the arrangement chart on p. 121 are *epilogue, direction, action, review,* and *reinforcement;* we could add *visualization, restatement,* and *summary.* These are devices all calculated to rekindle attention and to assist the memory. You will recall that it was Aristotle who suggested that the major purpose of the conclusion was to help the memory.

The conclusion is generally shorter than either the introduction or the body. It may and generally should include a short summary for clarity and reinforcement. In some cases it will call for explicit directions where certain actions are part of the speaker's purpose. Where your purpose has been inspiration, you may need a more impressive conclusion. Some of the devices suggested in the discussion on introductions (impressive quotation, incident, or experience) are applicable here.

Most important, make it evident when you are finished; carefully consider your exit lines. It is frustrating to an audience and awkward for a speaker who does not know when he is going to finish. This is the dangling or never-ending conclusion caused either by the "ham actor" in all of us or by improper preparation, which leaves you with so many things to tie together that you literally cannot conclude in any unified manner. The lessons are obvious. Prepare your conclusion as carefully as the rest of your speech. It serves as a good check on organic unity. And quit while you are ahead. Do not let an audience so mesmerize you that you ruin a good speech by an overly long or overly dramatic conclusion.

Mechanics of Outlining

Where to Start. You might start by rereading the material just previous to this section! The mechanics can be hollow indeed if they are not enriched with an understanding of: (1) subject, audience, and occasion analysis; (2) methods of locating materials; and (3) methods of organization and arrangement.

The outline is to a speech what a blueprint is to a house. A good, clear outline can help you discover mistakes, weaknesses, and unnecessary information *before* you speak, just as the builder or architect can often save costly mistakes by a hard look at his plans before he starts to build the house.

Begin by reviewing your specific purpose for speaking, which may evolve into a proposition or a thesis. This review serves to narrow and unify the subject matter further, and should result in a precise summary statement of purpose. Your statement of purpose attempts to capture the gist of the entire speech in one sentence, but should not be confused with a title or a general subject area, although they may be closely related.

Start your serious outlining with the body of the speech. The introduction and conclusion, though very important, are nevertheless only enrichers, preparers, or reinforcers of the content-loaded main body. State your main points or ideas in terms of your purpose and locate your supporting material under the appropriate main points. After roughing out the body of your speech, proceed to outline the introduction and conclusion.

Your rough outline should eventually evolve into a complete sentence outline. This will force you to *think* your way through the material and help avoid embarrassing moments on the platform. The sentence outline will also make it easier for your instructor to evaluate and help you with your speech planning. If you intend to use the speech again or if others may have to speak from it, the value of filing a complete sentence outline becomes obvious. After this kind of thorough outlining, you may prefer to redo the outline in a topical or key-word form for actual use on the platform. An outline is an aid to clear, orderly thinking. It is a blueprint of the speech.

TYPES OF OUTLINES. The complete sentence outline suggested above is the most detailed and specific of all the forms. All main and minor points are written out as complete sentences so that their relationship to each other is graphically clear. In all probability, however, your first try at outlining a given speech will be a topical, skeleton form. The phrases or groups of words that carry the essential meanings are typically written as grammatically incomplete sentences. The disadvantage of the topical outline is that your memory may fail you and the topics may suddenly be difficult to visualize as complete sentences or thoughts. Its advantages are fewer notes, more extempore potential, and quick comprehension—*if* you are thoroughly familiar with the concepts involved. A key-word outline is an abbreviated topical outline. In terms of indentation and symbols (see the following section), it looks the same as the complete sentence outline. The key-word outline is usually easier to remember and greatly facilitates extemporaneous resequencing of ideas when the situation calls for such adaptation.

Combinations of these forms are often advisable when you are speaking on a subject with which you are thoroughly familiar. The main points might be complete sentences, the subpoints phrases, and the sub-subpoints key words. Some of these variations are illustrated on pages 128–131.

HEADINGS AND FORMS. We are here concerned with the mechanics of outline symbols and indentations. Logical outlining involves: (1) subdivisions of ideas, and (2) subheadings for amplification or support. If a topic is divided, there should be two or more parts. In other words, if you are going to have a *1*, you should also have a *2;* if you are going to have an *A*, you should also have a *B*. If your *2* or *B* is not important to your speech, the first point should be incorporated into its superior heading: For example,

> A. Wagon trains.
>   1. Role in development of West.

becomes

> A. Wagon trains as factor in development of West.

The numbers and letters used as labels must be consistent. Let your symbols clearly show the relationship of main ideas to each other and the relationship of subpoints to main points. Do not extend any portion of any statement beyond its symbol.

The standard system of symbols and indentations is as follows:

OUTLINE FORM

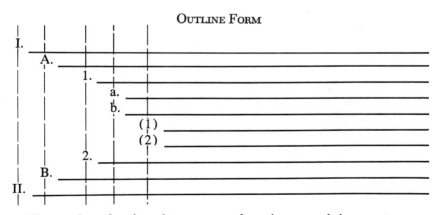

The number of main points you may have in a speech is open to some debate. If you use more than four or five, your listeners will have difficulty relating the points to each other and retention becomes more difficult. Your main points, in order to be true main points and not subdivisions, should be of approximately equal weight or importance. Each main point should be carefully and completely worded and should contribute to the central purpose of the speech. The order or sequencing of your main points should be such that it facilitates retention, logical development, motivation, and understanding.

The format of your outline may vary with your general end and your instructor's preference. You may use *Introduction, Body, Conclusion* or some of the other formats discussed previously. In any case you should probably capitalize, but not number such words as *Introduction, Body,* and *Conclusion,* and perhaps put other words such as *attention, overview, need,* and *reinforcement* in the margins.

Some actual student examples illustrating the use of symbols and indentations follow. The marginal notes in parentheses indicate other systems of arrangement.

OUR FUTURE FIVE WONDERS[8]

General End: To inform.

Specific Purpose: To inform the class of the future five wonders of the world and to explain their functions and how they differ from the old seven wonders.

Introduction

I. Let me briefly remind you of the seven wonders of the Ancient World. (Pictures)
    A. The Great Pyramid of Cheops.
    B. The Hanging Gardens of Babylon.

(Attention)   C. The Tomb of Mausolus.

(Interest)   D. The Temple of Diana at Ephesus.
    E. The Colossus of Rhodes.
    F. Phidias' Statue of Zeus.
    G. The Pharos of Alexandria

II. The future wonders which I will explain are as follows:
    A. Australia's Snowy Mountains Scheme.

(Overview)   B. The United States' Chesapeake Bay Bridge Tunnel.

(Impression)   C. The Netherlands' Delta Plan.
    D. The United States' New York Narrows Bridge.
    E. The Mont Blanc Tunnel Between France and Italy.

Body

I. Each of the future wonders will be of real benefit to man.
    A. The Snowy Mountains Scheme will provide an additional 650 billion gallons of water per year in the Australian desert.
        1. This will be done by forcing the wasted water of the Snowy River through the mountains in long tunnels.

---

[8] From a student speech by Gary Carotta, Wayne State University.

　　　　　　　2. This project will cost $1 billion.
　　　　　　　3. This project will consist of many facilities.
　　　　　　　　　a. 9 major dams.
(Information)　　　 b. 10 power stations.
　　　　　　　　　c. 100 miles of tunnels.
　　　　　　　　　d. 80 miles of aqueducts.
　　　B. The Chesapeake Bay Bridge Tunnel will connect Norfolk, Va. with the Delmarva Peninsula.
　　　　　　　1. Travel time will be 30 minutes.
　　　　　　　2. Longest span over exposed navigable water.
　　　　　　　　　a. Both tunnels and bridges are used (diagram).
　　　　　　　　　b. It is 17.6 miles long.
　　　　　　　　　c. It will cost $140 million.
　　　C. The Netherlands' Delta Plan will prevent ocean storms from overrunning the land (map).
　　　　　　　1. Prevent damage to property and life.
　　　　　　　2. Prevent salting of fertile land as in 1953.
　　　　　　　3. Five massive dams will cut off the sea arms.
　　　　　　　　　a. This is first attempt to hold back this much sea.
　　　　　　　　　b. The cost will be $750 million.
　　　D. The U.S. N.Y. Narrows Bridge will cross the narrows at the entrance to N.Y. harbor.
　　　　　　　1. The world's longest suspension span, 4260 feet.
　　　　　　　2. The world's largest and most expensive bridge.
　　　　　　　　　a. Will have 12 traffic lanes.
(Visualization)　　 b. One granite block weighs 410,000 tons.
　　　　　　　　　c. Can be seen 20 miles at sea.
　　　　　　　　　d. Will cost $325 million.
　　　E. The French-Italian Mont Blanc Tunnel will permit travel *under* the Alps.
　　　　　　　1. The tunnel was a joint venture.
　　　　　　　　　a. French drilling company.
　　　　　　　　　b. Italian drilling company.
　　　　　　　2. The first all-year route from Paris to Rome.
　　　　　　　　　a. Cuts distance by 140 miles.
　　　　　　　　　b. Cuts time from a day of mountain roads to 15 minutes' tunnel time.
　　　　　　　3. A brilliant coordinated engineering feat.

Conclusion

I. These new five wonders have practical and useful purposes for man.
　　A. Snowy Mountains Scheme will make Australia's desert lands places of lush vegetation.

(Review)
(Reinforcement)

B. Chesapeake Bay Bridge Tunnel will enable man to travel more easily from Norfolk to the Delmarva Peninsula.
C. The Netherlands' Delta Plan will secure the land from the damaging storms of the sea.
D. The New York Narrows Bridge will allow traffic to cross the entrance of New York Harbor.
E. The Mont Blanc Tunnel will allow travel through the Alps all year around.

II. These constructions are more wondrous than the ancient ones.
   A. Ancient wonders were noted primarily for art, size, and beauty.
   B. The modern wonders each have all of these plus unchallenged utility.

A shorter topical and key word form of outline is illustrated below:

THE LEFT WING[9]

General End: To inform and entertain.
Specific Purpose: To inform the audience about left-handed people, their problems, theories as to why some people are left-handed, and what is being done to help them.

Introduction

I. Are you one of those people who have been described as temperamental, unstable, unintelligent, pugnacious, or in a word, left-handed?
II. Even if you are not, you should know some facts about this persecuted group.

(Attention)
(Overview)

   A. Their number.
   B. Their difficulties.
   C. Assistance given.
   D. Theories as to why.

Body

I. Who are the Southpaws?
   A. Number.
      1. ¼ North Am. originally left-handed.
      2. Schools report an 8% increase.

(Information)

   B. Some are famous.
      1. Present-day lefties.
      2. Historic lefties.

---

[9] From a student speech by Robert Willard, Wayne State University.

II. Southpaw advantages and disadvantages.
    A. Advantages
        1. Mirror writing.
        2. Sports.
    B. Disadvantages.
        1. Eating.
        2. Musical instruments.
        3. Knitting.
        4. Office machines.
III. Help for left-handers.
    A. The Association for the Protection of Rights of Left-Handers.
        1. Oaths.
        2. Saluting.
        3. Fellowship.
    B. Manufactured goods for lefties.
        1. Golf clubs.

(Visualization)
        2. Musical instruments.
        3. Reversed turnstiles.
    C. Theories concerning Southpaws.
        1. Cerebral dominance.
        2. Inherited.
        3. Present opinion.
           a. Surveys.
           b. Tests.

Conclusion

I. If you are left-handed be comforted in that:
    A. Though your numbers are small you are not inferior.

(Review)
    B. Your disadvantages are being reduced.
    C. The theories make you more interesting.
    D. Society is trying to help.
II. You righties should now have a right attitude about the left wing.

Summary

One of the most important aspects of preparing, organizing, and outlining a speech is to achieve a clear understanding and statement of your *specific purpose,* that is, the outcome, objective, or response, which your speech is supposed to accomplish. Of almost equal importance is a careful consideration of the audience and situational factors (the occasion, the environment, and the various descriptive measures of an audience—size, sex, age, education, occupation, primary group memberships, special interests). The relationships between audience and subject as well as between audience and speaker are other critical factors.

When you have thoroughly considered your specific purpose and have related it to an analysis of audience and occasion, you are ready to start locating and collecting the materials and details that will constitute the speech itself. This chapter provides an extensive list of sources and procedures for making the task much easier than it may first appear. Taking notes from your readings and sources should be done systematically, necessitating only a minimum of rereading and returning to the library. Use of file cards rather than a notebook will also facilitate the eventual organizing and arranging of the various parts of the speech.

The principal ways of organizing ideas for speech purposes are by the chronological, topical, spatial, logical, difficulty, and need-plan methods. The arrangement of the parts of a speech (beginning, middle, end; introduction, body, conclusion; and other variations) is related to your general end as well as your specific purpose. These are all closely interwoven and can usually be coordinated with a simple introduction-body-conclusion system. The rhetorical principles of unity, coherence, and emphasis also have a strong bearing on the arranging of the parts.

The general functions of a good introduction are: (1) to secure attention; (2) to establish good will; (3) to assure a fair hearing; (4) to orient your audience to the subject; and (5) to make your purpose clear.

The conclusion is generally shorter than either the introduction or the body. It may, and generally should, include a short summary for clarity and reinforcement. In some cases it will call for explicit directions where certain actions are part of the speaker's purpose. It is important to make it evident when you are through; carefully consider your exit lines. It is frustrating to an audience and awkward for a speaker who does not know when to finish. Prepare your conclusion as carefully as the rest of your speech; it is a good check on organic unity; remember to "quit when you're ahead." Never ruin a good speech by an overly long or overly dramatic conclusion.

An outline is an aid to clear, orderly thinking. It is a blueprint of the speech. Start your serious outlining with the body of the speech. State your main points or ideas in terms of your purpose and locate your supporting material under the appropriate main points. After roughing out the body of your speech, proceed to outline the introduction and conclusion. Your rough outline should eventually evolve into a complete sentence outline. After completion of a thorough outline, you may then redo it in a topical or key-word form for actual use on the platform.

Your outline numbers and letters used as labels must be consistent. Let your symbols clearly show the relationship of main ideas to each other and the relationship of subpoints to main points. Let each division have at least two headings and do not extend any portion of any statement beyond its symbol. The number of main points in a speech should seldom go beyond four or five. Your main points should be of approximately equal weight or importance. Each main point should be carefully worded and should contribute to the central purpose of the speech. The order or sequencing of your main points should be such that it facilitates retention, logical development, motivation, and understanding.

Presenting
Information   **8**

How We Learn

One of the most frequent reasons for speaking or communicating is an attempt to inform people about something. In a sense you play the role of a teacher; you have the obligation of presenting your material not only in a clear and interesting way, but also in the way which makes it easiest for your audience to learn, remember, and apply the information. To achieve these goals, we need to know something of the way in which man learns.

Known to Unknown

In Chapter 1, we learned that man understands a message primarily as he brings his previous experience and knowledge to bear on the stimulus. It follows that a teacher or speaker must arrange and select his material so that he best utilizes the knowledge and experience the audience already has. In describing or explaining something, the rule might be stated: Go from the known to the unknown. For example, in trying to explain the relationship between wire size and electric current, an electrician compared the rule for selection of size to a garden hose (known) and the excess strain put upon it when one restricted the opening with the nozzle. Having once burst a garden hose by turning the nozzle off, the writer understood his explanation. It was clear, interesting, and easy to apply.

134

On the assumption that everybody knows the size of an English sparrow, a robin, and a crow, birdwatchers typically relate the size of all unknown or unidentified birds to one of these three. This simple relating of known to unknown has made the communicating and sharing of much information far less frustrating for serious birdwatchers.

Serially

People tend to learn more readily when things are arranged sequentially or in some serial order, especially when they are aware of the order. We teach youngsters addition and subtraction before multiplication and division. Though we could start with algebra, it is deemed more efficient to use a sequencing based upon difficulty, part-responses, and cumulative effect. In history courses, we often use a chronological order; at other times, an order or sequence based on social issues might be preferable.

The particular ordering of the parts to be learned is based upon the previous knowledge of the audience, the complexity of the subject, and the specific information or skill the speaker wishes to impart. Typically, the audience is said to be learning (serially) when it is able to connect each portion of the sequence to the one that comes immediately after it.[1] In learning to drive a car, one must learn a great many specifics, but he has not really learned to *drive* until clutching, breaking, steering, and other operations are so connected that the necessity of one arouses automatically the next appropriate action.

Reinforcement

Perhaps in an education or psychology course you have heard the expression $S R X$. In discussing the involved subject of learning, theorists use S to stand for stimulus, R for response, and X for reinforcement. This X may be a reward for responding in the desired way, a punishment, some form of known association, or perhaps some form of repetition. The exact nature and mode of operation of reinforcement is highly complex and is the subject of considerable academic debate. For some theorists SR is explanation enough, as long as there is some form of time-related proximity or what they refer to as temporal contiguity.[2]

For the speech and communication theorist, both temporal contiguity and reinforcement have great practical usefulness. The previous discussion of the advantages of serial learning and relating new information to things

---

[1] J. A. McGeoch and A. L. Irion, *The Psychology of Human Learning,* 2nd ed. (New York: David McKay Co., Inc., 1952), p. 89.

[2] McGeoch and Irion, *The Psychology of Human Learning,* p. 46.

already known is an application of temporal contiguity. The teacher who "feeds back" criticism by a smile, a frown, or a high grade is practicing reinforcement. So is the drill sergeant with a really loud voice. This enhancement of a desired response is an application of reinforcement whether it be by repetition, loud voice, or some other form of emphasis.

A most interesting communication experiment regarding the relative effectiveness of various modes of emphasis was conducted by Dr. Raymond Ehrensberger. A 15 minute speech was delivered to various audiences in what may be described as a relatively neutral mode of emphasis; experimental speeches on the same subject to similar audiences made much use of various kinds of emphasis. All 21 audiences were given tests on the material covered in the speeches to see which kind of treatment affected the greatest retention.

Some of the primary devices of emphasis studied were:

1. Verbal emphasis ("Now get this," and so on, preceding a remark).
2. Three distributed repetitions.
3. Immediate repetition early in the speech.
4. Speaking slowly (half normal rate).
5. Immediate repetitions late in the speech.
6. Pauses.
7. Gestures (hand and index finger only).
8. Four distributed repetitions.
9. Two distributed repetitions.
10. Soft voice (aspirate).
11. Forceful voice (almost bombastic).

An analysis of the retention test results is shown below. The numbers represent the percentage of right answers (of 100 items) that each specific audience scored. When the difference between a specific experimental mode of emphasis and the neutral treatment is greater than might be expected by chance, it is referred to as a significant or very significant difference.

This is strong evidence of the value of emphasis, whether it be done verbally, vocally, gesturally, organizationally, or by some combination of the above. However, some serious warnings are also implied for the speakers. You will note that while three repetitions was a very significant factor in retention, four repetitions fell off considerably and two appeared to cause no effect. Although the results of one limited experiment in no way suggest that three is a magic number, they do imply that too much repetition is as bad as too little. All of us have grown weary of certain TV commercials that continually repeat the product name. By the same token, you have probably learned to appreciate the teacher who repeats and reviews things often enough, making it easier to understand and to recall the

THE RELATIVE EFFECTIVENESS OF A MODE OF EMPHASIS COMPARED TO A
NEUTRAL TREATMENT*

Rank	Device	Experimental Mode % Right Answers	Neutral Mode % Right Answers	Statistical Analysis†
1	"Now get this" (verbal emphasis)	86	53.2	Very significant difference
2	Three Distributed Repetitions	78	51.4	Very significant difference
3	Repeat (Early in Speech)	72	50.7	Very significant difference
4	Slow	76	59.8	Very significant difference
5	Repeat (Late in Speech)	67	50.7	Very significant difference
6	Pause	69	55.4	Very significant difference
7	Gesture	66	53.2	Very significant difference
8	Four Distributed Repetitions	60	51.4	Significant difference
9	Two Distributed Repetitions	58	51.4	No real difference
10	Soft Voice	56	55.4	No real difference
11	Loud Voice	51	59.8	Significant negative difference

* R. Ehrensberger, "An Experimental Study of the Relative Effectiveness of Certain Forms of Emphasis in Public Speaking," *Speech Monographs*, XII, No. 2 (1945), 94–111.

† Very significant difference = 1% level of significance; Significant difference = 5% level; No real difference = below the 5% level; Significant negative difference = 5% level favoring neutral mode.

important items. It is also interesting to note that voice volume made a difference in this experiment. Although this does not mean that we should never use a loud voice, it does demonstrate that a loud voice under certain communication circumstances may actually interfere with retention and recall of information. In sum, take care not to overdo a good thing or to draw superspecific rules from limited experiences. Reinforcement in the form of verbal, vocal, gestural, and organizational emphasis can be a real asset to the speaker presenting information—as long as he is careful to adapt the amount and kind of reinforcement to his particular subject, situation, and audience.

Primary Objectives

One of the primary objectives in presenting information is *clarity;* we utilize what we know about the psychology of learning to facilitate understanding. Perhaps not quite so evident is the fact that an audience's *interest* or motivation to want to learn may seriously affect how much they retain or remember. The third primary principle is *organization*.

Achieving Clarity

The scope of your purpose (the amount of information you wish to cover in a given period of time) is a vital factor in clarity, as are the organization of the material and the choice of language. The use of audio-visual aids represents still another method of enhancing clarity. These special factors will be discussed later; this section is primarily concerned with verbal forms of clarity.

ILLUSTRATION OR EXAMPLE. An education major who was also a practice teacher had as her specific purpose, "To inform the class of the basic principles of overcoming discipline problems in the fourth grade." She could have explained "projections of insecurity and overt cognitive intellectualization assistance from an interacting teacher." The class was fortunate because she elected instead to draw specific examples from her own experience to illustrate and make clear the profound problems of discipline, and this approach was much more interesting. She opened her speech directly with an experience involving George C. and his persistence in putting gum in little girls' hair. She followed this with the story of Rupert B., who, though a gifted child, took a special delight in swearing. Next she explained the psychological reasons for such behavior, the things not to do, and the proper principles of discipline to apply. In a sense, the whole speech was an extended example, which served the purpose of making her point clear. The more detail and the more vivid the incident, the more interesting it generally is. Very often verbal illustration can be quickly and efficiently enhanced through tangible examples like pictures or actual objects (perhaps a recording of Rupert B.'s language).

If your subject is one with which you have had no firsthand experience, you can often draw your examples from people who have. An excellent speech on aerial acrobatics was delivered by a student who had never been in an airplane, but who used examples drawn from the actual experiences of three veteran stunt pilots.

An illustration or example may be hypothetical (that is, a made up or contrived story, which is reasonable and fair to the facts). It usually starts "Suppose you were flying at 10,000 feet . . ." or "put yourself in this predicament. . . ." The hypothetical example does not carry the proof of a real or factual illustration, but it does have the attribute of adaptability to the point being made, since you may tell it as you please. The major problem is an ethical one. Make sure the hypothetical example is never taken for a factual one, and make sure it is plausible and consistent with known facts.

Illustration or example represents a powerful, efficient way of clarifying and supporting a point. In choosing your illustrations, make sure that they are truly related to the point being made and that they are representative. An example out of context or a very real example that is an exception to the general rule only inhibits clarity in the long run. In addition to being reasonable and fair, your illustrations and examples should contain enough specific details and excitement to add to the interest of the subject.

ANALOGY OR COMPARISON. The analogy is often the most useful device a teacher or speaker can use in making a point vivid and clear. It agrees with the learning theory discussed earlier, in that the nature of analogy is to point out similarities between something already known or understood and that which is not (in other words, going from the known to the unknown). If we were trying to give meaning to the size of our vast solar system to people who really had no such concept, the following analogy[3] should be both vivid and useful.

Figure 37. If a Molecule of Water Could Be Magnified as Large as a Pea, a Baseball on the Same Scale Would Be Larger than the Earth.

Abraham Lincoln made good use of analogy and comparison not only for vivid clarification, but also for persuasion. During the Civil War, there were those who loudly criticized his method of conducting the war. At that time, a tightrope walker named Blondin became famous for walking and for riding a two-wheel bicycle on a rope strung across Niagara Falls. In

___

[3] "Scott's Scrapbook," *The Daily Tribune* (King Features Syndicate, Inc.), Oct. 21, 1961, p. 15.

explaining the dangerous position of the nation, Lincoln directed the following at his critics:

> Gentlemen, I want you to suppose a case for a moment. Suppose that all the property you were worth was in gold, and you had put it in the hands of Blondin, the famous rope-walker, to carry across the Niagara Falls on a tightrope. Would you shake the rope while he was passing over it, or keep shouting to him, "Blondin, stoop a little more! Go a little faster!" No, I am sure you would not. You would hold your breath as well as your tongue, and keep your hands off until he was safely over. Now the government is in the same situation. It is carrying an immense weight across a stormy ocean. Untold treasures are in its hands. It is doing the best it can. Don't badger it! Just keep still, and it will get you safely over.[4]

STATISTICS. The use of figures or numbers to help make a point more clear or specific is not as simple as it may seem. Statistics are frequently used to support a point in a persuasive speech, but they are only powerful evidence if they are (1) meaningful to the audience and (2) related to the point under consideration. However, when statistics are overly precise and complicated, we may cloud rather than clarify an issue. Have you ever been given directions like the following by a local resident: "You go down Norfolk street exactly 3.2 miles to Baker street, then 2.4 miles to a Y intersection, turn about 120° on Charlie street for .3 of a mile, then right for 150 yards and you're there." Some specifics are most helpful, but not these! Even if you *were* able to keep them straight, you would probably cause an accident by watching your odometer instead of the road. Of course the other extreme is: "You go up Norfolk quite a little piece and then a couple of miles or so on Baker to a kind of wide angle left turn and then. . . ." A little piece or a "fur" piece can vary by a good many miles.

By themselves, statistics are abstract. Make them more concrete by relating them to known things. To say that South America has serious economic problems because the average family income is $150 per year is reasonably clear, but it is clearer when this figure is compared to the $8400 of the United States or when shown that $150 comes to only 41¢ a day.

We live more and more by predictive statistics. From Univac's vote predictions to insurance rates, from the number of cancers in a carton of cigarettes to the average number of cavities in a given group of children, we are involved in an age of specific, predictive statistics. We have learned to combine statistics with analogies or comparisons to make sense out of the

---

[4] *Town Meeting,* XI (October 11, 1945), 24.

astronomical numbers of outer space. We also explain speed as Mach 1, 2, 3 instead of miles per hour and distance in terms of light years.

The use of statistics can give a speech a sense of specificity and precision if we remember to relate the statistics to known things and to make them meaningful to the audience.

TESTIMONY. Like statistics, testimony has great use in speeches to persuade, but is also valuable for the sake of clarity. In a speech to inform, it may add considerable *interest* to what might otherwise be straight explanation.

In describing the course of events on D-day in Europe, one might more vividly express the story by a series of datelines and statements from a dozen G.I.'s who hit the beaches:

> *0400* Pvt. Johnson, "There were ships and little boats and men all tangled up in one maze of confusion."
>
> *0430* Pvt. Sandrin, "The men coming down the cargo nets to the LCI's (Landing Craft Infantry) seemed to be 20 feet from the deck one minute and a step away the next."
>
> *0500* Pvt. Brown, "The LCI to our left just seemed to evaporate."
>
> *0600* Sgt. Glover, "Where the hell is the air cover?"
>
> *2300* Lt. Rucks, "This has been the longest day of my life."

The explanation of events is often clearer and more impressive through the use of testimony. More will be said of this subject under "Authority" in Chapter 10.

RESTATEMENT is more than simple repetition. It is saying the same thing in a different way. This is particularly useful if the material is complex or the vocabulary specialized. The value of restatement in terms of learning theory, particularly the concept of reinforcement, was made evident earlier in this chapter.

If you were to reread Chapter 1 of this book, you would find the process of communication defined in many different ways, all trying to say the same thing. One descriptive definition was a whole page long, another consisted of a short paragraph, another reduced the definition essentially to encoding and decoding. This is an example of restatement for clarity. If it was not clear one time because of sentence structure or another because of vocabulary, you were given still more choices. If you understood all the definitions at first glance, fine. Assuming that it was not too extended, this repetition should have reinforced the learning. To restate the point of this clarity factor—it involves more than simple repetition, it includes saying the same thing in different ways for reinforcement of learning, and it is particularly useful if the subject is complex or if the vocabularly may be specialized or strange to the audience.

Developing Interest

The second of the two primary principles in presenting a speech to inform, *interest* refers to the motivation of the audience to want to listen or learn. The problem is to hold the attention of your audience while you are practicing all the clarity suggestions just discussed. What are the categories of things that tend to interest all of us? How can they be applied to your subject in such a way as to motivate the audience to pay attention and want to learn? Much of a speaker's *interest* is of course dependent upon his style of delivery and his use of vocal variety; however, we are here concerned primarily with speech content. Some of the more useful qualities of content that stimulate interest are as follows:

SPECIFICITY. When a speaker says, "Let me give you an example of what I mean by dog-tired," you probably pay closer attention than if he were simply to give you some general, academic explanation. Suppose he used the following example:

> The men of hurricane Camille's Red Cross rescue group thought after two days of forced march through wreckage strewn coastal areas that they were dog-tired. Then they saw the remote victims of the storm who seemed to be moving on sheer instinct and determination alone. They staggered through their broken homes with drooping shoulders, so physically drained that it seemed to take every last ounce of strength to put one foot in front of the other.

Specificity, reality, or concreteness are more interesting than vague generalities or the abstract. Instead of saying, "A boy was run over," be specific. Call him by name; indicate his age; identify the car. "Mark Scott, age 6, dashed into the street to greet his mother approaching from the other side and was thrown to the pavement by a 1970 Thunderbird traveling at the 30-mile speed limit."

CONFLICT. The TV westerns always seem to pit "bad guys" against "good guys." This conflict and fighting pay off in viewer interest. Can you imagine a Bonanza story without conflict, uncertainty, or antagonism? Sports contests, even when you know that Otterbein College will surely beat Stanford, still conjure up interest. Disagreement and opposition have elected and destroyed many a politician, but almost always in an interesting way! If in your examples, illustrations, and explanation, you can utilize the factor of conflict without seeming to set up sham or mock battles, your speech should have added interest for the audience.

NOVELTY means essentially that which is different, unusual, contrasting, or strange. Of course if the subject is so unique that a listener cannot relate it to his previous knowledge and experience, interest may actually be lost rather than gained.

Novelty is not limited to uniqueness or oddness, however. Relatively average things become novel if the world about them is in contrast. At one time, a bikini bathing suit would have been an interesting novelty, primarily because of its contrast to other more conservative swim suits. In our time, a girl would probably gain more attention wearing one of the old-fashioned neck-to-ankle suits of the early 1900s or an ultramodern "topless." Of course, as one student put it—"It depends on the girl." New Yorkers find nothing unusual or novel about their tall skyscrapers, but a visitor might himself become a novelty to the natives by his trancelike stares into the low clouds that hide the Empire State Building from view.

The unusual, the contrasting, the unique, the strange, the rare, and the generally different things in life are more interesting than the run-of-the-mill. Let your examples, analogies, and explanations be novel for added audience interest.

CURIOSITY. One of the more marvelous and exasperating aspects of young children is the seemingly endless questions they persistently ask about an infinity of subjects. Grown children (men) are not really much different, except that they may become a little more specialized about the subjects and the questions they ask. Man seems to have a compulsion to find out what lies around the corner or beyond the stars. Each new discovery in space now leads to suspense about what the universe is really like and to the big question, "Is there life out there?"

Unanswered questions, uncertainty, suspense—these are the ingredients that may be effectively utilized by speakers to arouse curiosity and thereby to enhance interest.

IMMEDIACY. By immediacy is meant those matters of the moment or specific occasion that will quickly arouse and arrest attention and interest when related to a speaker's subject. A company training director has the uncanny ability to memorize names of people along with other pertinent facts after just one informal meeting. He once startled a group of 40 executives on the second day of the course by randomly calling off their names throughout a two-hour period: "Mr. William Sandy what do you think of. . . ." Needless to say, interest was high. You never knew when he would call your name, cite your job description, and ask your opinion.

A reference to a previous speaker or some incident that is proximate and known to the audience may have similar effects in garnering interest. In a speech to businessmen in Grand Rapids, Michigan, a speaker noticed several members of his audience staring out the window at the falling snow, probably through apprehension rather than a lack of interest. In any event, he too looked toward the window, paused, and commented, "Misery loves company. We have 18 inches of snow in Detroit and you have 42 inches.

The weather man is predicting clearing skies in the next few hours." The audience seemed more interested after that. Not only had a distraction been acknowledged, but the audience felt more closely identified with the speaker.

Learning about the speech occasion, the audience, the last-minute headlines, and all similar matters of the moment is time well spent in trying to devise methods of making your speech interesting.

HUMOR. If you feel you do not tell a joke well or find it difficult to be a humorous speaker, perhaps you need not be too concerned. The limited speech research on the impact of humor on an audience seems to indicate that at least in *persuasive* speeches it did not make any difference. In a study by P. E. Lull,[5] it was found that audiences listening to humorous and nonhumorous speeches on socialized medicine were equally persuaded by both speeches and in both directions of the attitude scale. D. Kilpela[6] had the same results with a more recent study, using government health insurance as the topic. Both methods were effective, but they do not vary significantly in effectiveness. A study by J. Douglas Gibb[7] comparing humorous and nonhumorous *informative* lectures did show significantly better student *retention* of the humorous lecture. Lull and Kilpela were quick to point out, however, that the type of humor in their studies may not have been of a real professional nature. In other words, a Bob Hope, or a Bill Cosby might indeed have produced significant persuasive results. In any event, funny anecdotes (if told well and in good taste) have probably helped many an otherwise dull speaker, subject, or audience.

If you do decide to try humor in the form of anecdotes for interest, make it as professional as possible. There is no feeling quite so desperate as that which comes upon viewing a poker-faced audience after you have told your best joke. Make sure that the anecdote is related to either the subject or the occasion; make sure you can tell it fluently; make sure you remember the punch line, and make sure it is not seriously offensive to your audience. The best advice of all—try it out on a small group of your friends first. In other words, *practice*.

VITAL FACTORS. If you had the FM radio playing while you were reading this book, and the announcer were suddenly to say, "Alert! Alert! Please turn to your Conelrad frequencies at the civilian defense white triangles on your radio dial," you would undoubtedly stop your reading and turn the dial as instructed. The reason is obvious. Staying alive, pro-

---

5 P. E. Lull, "The Effectiveness of Humor in Persuasive Speeches," *Speech Monographs,* VII (1940), 26–40.

6 Donald Kilpela, "An Experimental Study of the Effects of Humor on Persuasion" (Master's Thesis, Wayne State University, 1961).

7 J. Douglas Gibb, "An Experimental Comparison of the Humorous Lecture and the Nonhumorous Lecture in Informative Speaking" (Unpublished Master's Thesis, University of Utah, 1964).

tecting your loved ones, defending your home—all these are things of vital concern to you, and you are interested because you have to be.

Vital factors, if truly vital, will arrest attention through personal involvement. Those things which affect our self-preservation, our reputation, our property, our sources of livelihood, our freedoms—are truly vital factors. More will be said about the role of each of these factors in Chapter 9, "The Psychology of Persuasion."

Organizing Effectively

The learning theory previously discussed should have provided you with the rationale and background material to organize information effectively. What does it tell us? It tells us of the necessity of early attention and continued motivation; it tells us of the value of serially or sequentially ordered material; it tells us of the need for reinforcement and for preparing states of readiness to learn or listen.

One durable and effective method of organizing informative material, which roughly meets the requirements above, was voiced by the gifted speaker Chauncey Depew, the late state senator from New York: First, tell them what you're going to tell them; second, tell them; and third, tell them you've told them. We shall add the concept of an early-attention step to motivate a desire to listen and shall then revise the language to better suit our purposes as follows: *Attention, Overview, Information, Review.*

The interest factors discussed earlier are all excellent suggestions for gaining attention. Your immediate purpose is to motivate a desire to hear more about the information you have to offer. If the audience is already highly motivated, your attention step becomes proportionately less important.

In a recent student speech "to inform the class about some of the sociological problems facing India," the speaker opened with the following (*attention* and *interest*): "Did you know that half of the world's population is illiterate and that one-third of this half live in India? Did you know that over 300 languages are spoken in India? That 14,000 babies a day are born in India?" He then proceeded to elaborate each of his three points in order. He gave us the detailed *information*. At the close of the speech, he repeated the three facets indicated in the overview, but in addition he briefly summarized some of the salient details from the *information* step. In other words, he *reviewed* the speech, or "told 'em what he told 'em." The amount of summary detail you put into your *review* will depend upon the complexity of the subject, the time allotted, and your purpose. In some speeches, you may prefer a brief synthesis of what you have tried to say; in others, perhaps some conclusions which adequately *review* your speech.

The reinforcement value of this development is obvious. Once more, remember that a listener cannot go back and reread or review. The speaker therefore has the obligation to be sure the learning is communicated. Toward this end, an occasional internal summary, review, or preview in the *information* step may facilitate clarity. A study by Fred Miller clearly shows that, other things being equal, audiences listening to better organized speeches score higher on retention tests than do those hearing poorly organized speeches.[8]

Organization, the third primary principle of presenting information, may thus be systematically enhanced by following the fourfold development based upon learning theory: *Attention, Overview, Information, Review.*

Audio-Visual Aids

Teaching or learning aids are used to help make a subject clear, to motivate interest, and to reinforce the message. On all counts they represent a value to the speaker although not without some hazards and problems. The question of what kind of aid to use in what situation is critical. The role of *demonstration* as an aid is especially important to beginning speakers, because teachers almost always ask for a demonstration speech, in part because it causes you to move and thereby work off excess tension. This section will relate the use of audio-visual aids to audience involvement, and will indicate the special role of demonstration.

The Cone of Experience and Types of Aids

Dr. Edgar Dale, probably this country's foremost expert on using teaching aids, has given us a theoretical model for classifying these aids in terms of audience involvement—namely, telling, showing, and doing.[9] The model roughly grades experience and audience involvement according to the degree of abstractness. Those aids that allow the audience to "do" or experience something are more concrete than those aids that simply "show" something, and "telling" is the most abstract form. Hollingworth[10]

---

[8] Fred Miller, "An Experiment to Determine the Effect Organization Has on the Immediate and Delayed Recall of Information" (Master's Thesis, Miami University, Ohio, 1966); also see, E. C. Thompson, Jr., "An Experimental Investigation of the Relative Effectiveness of Organizational Structure in Oral Communication," *Speech Monographs*, XXVII, (1960), 94.

[9] From *Audio-Visual Methods in Teaching*, Revised Edition, by Edgar Dale. Copyright 1946, 1954 by Holt, Rinehart and Winston, Inc. Reprinted by permission of Holt, Rinehart and Winston, Inc.

[10] H. L. Hollingworth, *The Psychology of the Audience* (New York: American Book Company, 1935), p. 73.

thinks of this ladder of abstraction as being ordered in terms of interestingness—that is, the direct, purposeful experience would be the most interesting. Dale is quick to point out the danger of too arbitrary a hierarchical
order based on either interestingness or learning, since the other aspects of
a speech situation are so variable. Audience response is affected by the
previous experience of the audience, the kind of speech subject and its
amenability to teaching aids, the oral ability of the speaker to visualize
with word pictures, the real purpose of the speaker, and the interest level of
the audience. The specific devices in the cone of experience are as follows:[11]

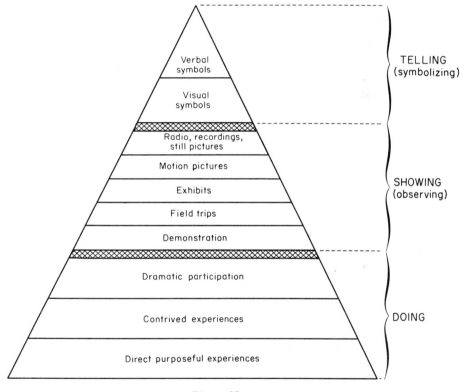

Figure 38

At the top of the cone (the "telling" area) are included the visual
symbols that aid the audience. These are things such as graphs, charts,
cartoons, diagrams, flat pictures, and blackboard sketches.

Some typical forms of graphs that a speaker might use include (1)

---

[11] Dale, *Audio-Visual Methods in Teaching,* p. 39.

pictograms, Figure 39, (2) bar graphs, Figure 40, (3) area diagrams, Figure 41, and (4) line graphs, Figure 42.

Some typical forms of charts include: (1) organization charts, Figure 43, (2) stream or tree charts, Figure 44, and (3) tabular charts, Figure 45.

In the middle of the cone (the "showing" area) are included recordings, motion pictures, exhibits, field trips, and demonstrations. All these items except the last are self-explanatory (more will be said of demonstration in

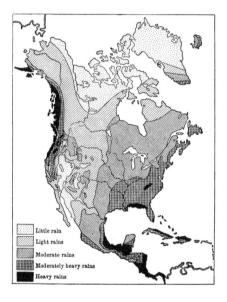

Little rain
Light rains
Moderate rains
Moderately heavy rains
Heavy rains

Figure 39. Pictogram (Pictorial Statistics: Rainfall of North America).[12]

the next section). These are the devices that bring the audience closer to reality than the mere telling, but still not to the real personal involvement found in doing.

The bottom of the cone (the "doing" part) involves contrived experiences and dramatic participations. These would include LINK trainers for pilots, antigravity simulations for astronauts, and other models of mock-ups, as well as the personal involvement caused by semidramatic experiences like role playing or working on case-study problems. Perhaps in grade school you played a Pilgrim landing on Plymouth Rock, an angel at Bethlehem, or Paul Revere. In management training programs today, some

---

[12] From *Essentials of Geography,* by A. P. Brigham and C. T. McFarlane. Copyright 1934, by American Book Company, by permission of Van Nostrand Reinhold Co.

of our top executives are once again role-playing, except that now it is an irate foreman, a shop steward, or an unhappy manager that is portrayed. Why? Because it is thought that this contrived slice of life gets the person more involved in the lesson and more closely approaches the reality of true experience.

The Special Role of Demonstration

The demonstration aspect of teaching aids is especially important in a speech class because this is typically an early type of assigned exercise or informative speech. A demonstration speech reduces anxiety and at the same time enhances the presentation of information. The purpose of a demonstration is to show how a skill, a procedure, a process, or a device is

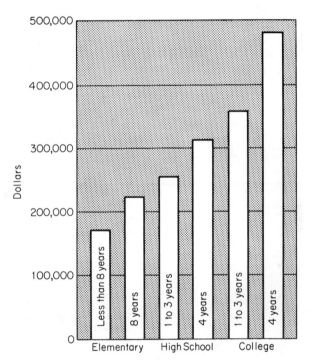

Figure 40. Bar Graph: More Education, More Income[13]; *Lifetime Earnings of Males by Years in School.*

used so that it may aid the audience in learning the skill or acquiring the knowledge. A demonstration combines showing with telling. Many grade school systems now have sessions called "show and tell." These are essen-

---

[13] "More Education, More Income," *200 Million Americans,* U.S. Dept. of Commerce, Bureau of the Census, November, 1967, p. 55.

tially demonstration exercises and are excellent early speech training if conducted by teachers with some basic speech experience.

The value of using demonstration is that the audience can learn by actually seeing. The demonstration helps the speaker remember his material; it appeals to several senses; it reinforces the message; it saves time; finally, it has dramatic appeal and is more concrete than just telling.

The best way to introduce some of the hazards of demonstration is by examples of demonstrations that did not work as planned. Perhaps you remember a certain Betty Furness Westinghouse commercial. While gracefully swishing between refrigerator doors, which were rhythmically opening and closing, she had a door close on part of her lovely, full-skirted dress. Miss Furness finished the commercial without the bottom half of her dress! The point is she finished the speech. We can draw a lesson from this, but first let us recall another. Do you remember when John Cameron Swayze tied a Timex watch to the propeller of an outboard motor, lowered it into a 50-gallon drum full of water, and started the engine? When the motor was withdrawn, the watch was gone. The camera panned down into the drum and there before millions of viewers was a very dead watch badly in need

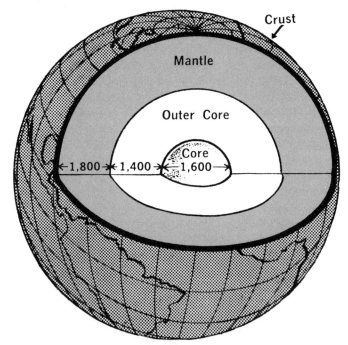

Figure 41. Area Diagram Showing the Four Zones of the Earth's Interior[14]

[14] Special permission granted by *My Weekly Reader*, No. 5, published by American Education Publications/A Xerox Company, Columbus, Ohio.

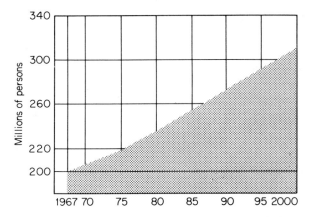

Figure 42.   Line Graph[15]: 100 Million More Americans by the Year 2000.

of reassembly! What would you have done? Incidentally, due to Swayze's handling of this difficult situation, Timex sales actually went up, not down. Sometimes these demonstrations can actually be dangerous. On the old Jack Paar show, a bottle of pills into which Paar had added water and then had shaken to liven the demonstration blew up only moments after it was out of his hand.

Classroom demonstrations are just as much fun and often can be just as hazardous. A student once demonstrated a tear-gas pencil in an over-heated, poorly ventilated classroom with the temperature outside about zero. Talk about audience involvement! Another student, demonstrating the toughness of unbreakable, bulletproof glass, dropped it on the concrete floor. It did not break—it literally exploded. This produced one badly shaken speaker, although a glass company spokesman informed us at a later date that the chances of the angle of impact, the temperature, the force, and other factors being perfectly coordinated (which caused the shattering) were about 1 in 10,000.

The obvious questions are "What can I do to reduce the probability of things going wrong?" and "If something does go wrong in spite of careful planning, what do I do at that moment of truth?"

The answer to the first question is careful planning. Plan exactly *how* you will do it. Make sure you have *all* your equipment and have it in the right sequence. Be sure it *works* in your practice sessions. Emphasize safety precautions. Check for conditions that may vary from the practice session (for example, electric current). Finally, be sure *you* can do it. A flight instructor was teaching cadets the principles of airfoil and how an

---

[15] "100 Million More Americans by the Year 2000," U.S. Dept. of Commerce, Bureau of the Census, November, 1967, p. 8.

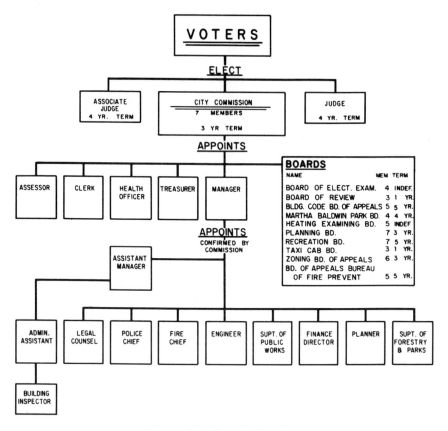

Figure 43. Organization Chart

airplane wing develops lift. To demonstrate, he put a piece of 8½ × 11 paper between his lower lip and his chin. He then blew over it, creating a partial vacuum on the top of the paper, which caused the paper to rise or lift. A new instructor who had observed this demonstration rushed to the next class with no time for practice. Confident that he could do it, he proceeded to blow—with no movement from the paper and with an audience of well disciplined cadets trying not to explode with laughter. There are some moments when defeat is so very evident.

The answer to the second question, "What if it happens anyway?" is again part of planning. More specifically, calculate the magnitude and nature of the risk and then plan emergency alternative procedures for every foul-up you can think of. This is very necessary. You have no time to protect yourself when it does happen, and the shock of the confusion may cause you to react emotionally rather than rationally.

Pilots of high speed aircraft have long talked of calculated risk and alternate procedures. These are preplanned procedures to meet preclassified emergencies. If two engines go out, what do you do? Talk it over? NO, go to alternate plan two on a prearranged signal thereby cutting confusion and perhaps saving your life. There simply isn't time to do it any other way.

The student with the unbreakable glass had a calculated risk of 1 in 10,000. One can hardly blame him for being lax in planning alternate procedures. These are probably better odds than a pedestrian has on the Los Angeles freeway. Nevertheless he could have had two pieces of glass, just as you should always have two bulbs for your slide or movie projector. Extra equipment or spare parts is only part of the answer. The real problem is what you will say. Plan your communication strategy very carefully.

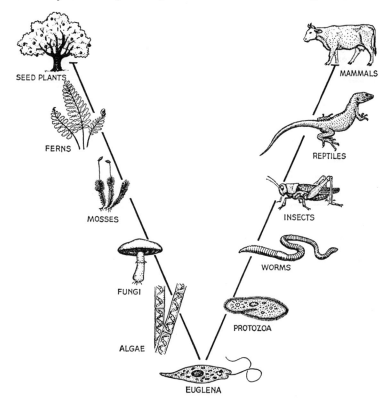

Figure 44. Stream or Tree Chart (Plant Life Is Represented on the Left Side of the "V," Animal Life on the Right)[16]

---

[16] Truman J. Moon, Paul B. Mann, and James H. Otto, *Modern Biology* (New York: Henry Holt and Company, 1947), p. 249. Reproduced by special permission of Holt, Rinehart and Winston, Inc.

Name	Total sample 218	Age 21-40 sample 98	Age 40+ sample 120
Negro	32 %	24 %	36 %
Afro-American	24 %	22 %	26 %
Black	16 %	19 %	13 %
Colored	16 %	19 %	14 %
Other	12 %	16 %	11 %
	100 %	100 %	100 %

Figure 45. Tabular Chart (Negro Identification Preferences, 1968)[17]

When and if the glass should break I will say . . . "the odds on that happening were 1 in 10,000. Let me prove it by beating the next piece of glass with this hammer." If the next piece of glass breaks you may have to resort to an alternate plan involving prayer. You can't win them all!

Some Practical Rules

USING AIDS

1. Never obstruct the vision of your audience; make sure the lectern or stand is out of the way; try not to stand in front of your materials.
2. Use your aids to reinforce, not to distract; introduce them when pertinent, not before (unless for attention).
3. Talk to the audience; "talk" to your visual aid only when you wish the audience to look at it.
4. Make sure you thoroughly understand your own visual aid—precisely how and when you intend to use it; orient your audience to the aid (for example, "This is a top view.").

---

[17] "Negro, Colored or Black?", *Detroit News,* September 8, 1968, p. 1.

PREPARING AIDS

1. Relate your choice of aids to the "cone of experience," a careful audience analysis, your subject, and your specific purpose.
2. Make a visual aid readily visible. Is it big enough? Are the lines heavy and dark enough? (One-eighth to one-half inch thick.)
3. Make each visual aid comprehensible. Do not put too much detail or too many ideas on one aid. Clearly label all the significant parts. Let it be simple enough so that you will be able to easily and quickly orient the audience to the aid.
4. Organize the aid systematically to make it easier for you to recall your speech material.

Summary

Presenting information orally to an audience is similar to the task of a teacher. Teaching is a science as well as an art and involves the serious evaluation and application of learning theory. This same learning theory is therefore useful to any speaker who would attempt to inform. Three critical lessons involve: (1) relating new information to that which an audience already knows; (2) ordering the material in some serial progression that makes it easier for people to follow and relate the significant points; (3) reinforcing or enhancing the message and the response through prudent repetition, verbal emphasis, organization, and voice—connoting importance, reward, punishment and the like. The final lesson from learning theory is that there appears to be a point of diminishing returns with all these devices, this point being related essentially and integrally to the specific and total communication circumstance involved.

The primary principles in informative speaking are clarity, interest, and organization. The factors of clarity are illustration or example, analogy or comparison, statistics, testimony, and restatement. The factors of interest are specificity, conflict, novelty, curiosity, immediacy, humor, and things that are of vital importance to the audience. The method of achieving psychologically sound organization involves: (1) gaining *attention;* (2) preparing the audience through a preview or *overview;* (3) giving the detailed *information;* and (4) *reviewing* the significant points for added reinforcement.

Using teaching aids is a vital part of public speaking, particularly where the goal is clarity. Edgar Dale's cone of experience gives us a good theoretical model for classifying these aids in terms of audience involvement—namely, *telling, showing,* and *doing.* The model helps us make decisions about our selection and use of aids by essentially grading visual aids according to abstractness.

Some typical forms of graphs that a speaker might use are pictograms, bar graphs, area diagrams, or line graphs. Some typical forms of charts include organization charts, stream or tree charts, and tabular charts.

Demonstration is a special form of teaching aid for the speech student. The purpose of a demonstration is to show how a skill, a procedure, a process or a device is used so that it may aid the audience in learning the skill or acquiring the knowledge. A demonstration combines showing with telling. It appeals to several senses, reinforces the message, saves time, is more concrete than just telling, has dramatic appeal, and helps the speaker remember his material and burn off nervous energy.

The practical rules for reducing the hazards of demonstrations all involve planning in advance. (1) Calculate the risks involved. (2) Devise alternate procedures, including what you will say if something goes wrong. (3) Utilize practice runs to make sure you can do it.

The general rules for using all teaching aids are: (1) Make sure your audience can see your aids. (2) Select the proper aids to meet the specific requirements of your subject, purpose, and audience.

Model Informative Outlines

Your instructor may prefer that you follow some prescribed outline form to facilitate his task of appraising them. Two useful types are illustrated below. Both apply the critical principles of attention, overview, information, and review.

INTRODUCTION TO MUSIC[18]

General End: To inform.
Specific Purpose: To state and explain the fundamental concepts of musical theory.

Introduction

I. Play a few bars of music on a violin. (Demonstration)
   A. "I wish I really was good at this."

---

[18] From a student speech by Gary Carotta, Wayne State University.

B. I can't teach you to play an instrument in this short speech, but perhaps I can review musical theory so that you'll feel superior to the three music majors in this class.

II. I should like to cover the following major steps in musical theory:

    A. The kinds of notes.

    B. The musical staff.

    C. Methods of counting the notes.

    D. Relation of these to an instrument.

Body

  I. The kinds of notes.

    A. Neutral notes, A-B-C-D-E-F-G.

    B. Sharp notes, ½ tone up.

    C. Flat notes, ½ tone down.

    (A demonstration and a piano keyboard were introduced here.)

II. Explanation of the musical staff.

    A. The treble clef and melody.

      1. Contains 5 lines, E-G-B-D-F.

      2. Contains 4 spaces, F-A-C-E.

      (A visual aid was shown here.)

    B. The bass clef and rhythm.

      1. Contains 5 lines, G-B-D-F-A.

      2. Contains 4 spaces, A-C-E-G.

      (A visual aid was shown here.)

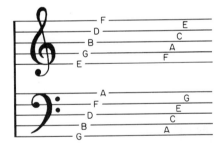

Figure 46

III. Methods of counting the notes.

    A. Whole note gets 4 beats.

    B. Half note gets 2 beats.

    C. Quarter note gets 1 beat.

    D. Eighth note gets ½ beat.

    (A blackboard sketch and demonstration were used here.)

IV. Relation of these points to a musical keyboard.

    (The piano keyboard was displayed here.)

A. The notes (whether neutral, sharp, or flat) correspond with the lines and spaces in the staff.
B. The position of the notes on the staff determines what note or key is to be played on the musical instrument.
C. The type of counting the note receives tells how long the note is played on the instrument.
(A short demonstration here.)

Conclusion

I. I have tried to make clear the following four factors of musical theory:
    A. The kinds of notes.
    B. The musical staff.
    C. Methods of counting the notes.
    D. Relating the theory to an instrument.
II. Now you can start writing your own music or at least sneer at the music majors.

The same material could also be outlined using the four factors of attention, overview, information, and review as major headings instead of introduction, body, and conclusion.

INTRODUCTION TO MUSIC

General End: To inform.
Specific Purpose: To state and explain the fundamental concepts of musical theory.

Attention

I. Play a few bars of music on the violin. (Demonstration)
II. Poke fun at the music majors in the class.

Overview

I. The kinds of notes.
II. The musical staff.
III. Methods of counting the notes.
IV. Relation of these to an instrument.

Information

I. The kinds of notes.
    A. Neutral notes, A-B-C-D-E-F-G.
    B. Sharp notes, ½ tone up.
    C. Flat notes, ½ tone down.
II. Explanation of the musical staff.
    A. The treble clef and melody.
        a. Contains 5 lines, E-G-B-D-F.
        b. Contains 4 spaces, F-A-C-E.

B. The bass clef and rhythm.
   a. Contains 5 lines, G-B-D-F-A.
   b. Contains 4 spaces, A-C-E-G.
III. Methods of counting the notes.
   A. Whole note gets 4 beats.
   B. Half note gets 2 beats.
   C. Quarter note gets 1 beat.
   D. Eighth note gets ½ beat.
IV. Relation of these points to a musical keyboard.
   A. The notes (whether neutral, sharp, or flat) correspond with the lines and spaces in the staff.
   B. The position of the notes on the staff determines what note or key is to be played on the musical instrument.
   C. The type of counting the note receives tells how long the note is played on the instrument.

Review

I. I have tried to make clear the following four factors of musical theory:
   A. The kinds of notes.
   B. The musical staff.
   C. Methods of counting the notes.
   D. Relating the theory to an instrument.
II. Now you can start writing your own music or at least sneer at the music majors.

The
Psychology
of
Persuasion   **9**

The Altering or Creating of
Attitudes

In persuading peo-
ple, we are primarily concerned with alteration of attitudes. "Does oral
argument (speech) affect attitudes?" is a fair question. For centuries we
have answered "yes," based on our subjective observations of speakers and
audiences.

Many teachers, after a particularly exasperating day, may conclude that
nothing happened to the minds of their students. We do have scientific
evidence that some teaching appears to have little effect on student attitudes. As early as 1927, Donald Young found, after measuring class attitudes, that his course in American Race Problems had no effect upon the
racial prejudices of his students at the University of Pennsylvania.[1] If
Young's lectures and assignments be considered oral argument and persuasion, and if he measured the right attitudes at the right time, then we
had better take a closer look at the question of oral persuasion and its
effect upon attitude.

In 1935, F. H. Knower reported specific insights into this question in a
study that has become a classic in speech research. Some of the questions
he asked in designing his study were these:

---

[1] "Some Effects of a Course in American Race Problems on the Race Prejudices of
450 Undergraduates," *Journal of Abnormal and Social Psychology*, XXII (1927),
235–42.

1. Is it possible to produce a significant change in attitude by argumentative stimulation?
2. Is an attitude more markedly changed by an argument which is predominantly factual and logical or one which is predominantly emotional?
3. Does an individual more markedly change his attitude when he hears an argument from a speaker while a member of an audience composed of individuals who hold approximately the same attitude, or while alone in a room with the speaker who presents the argument to him?
4. Is there any difference in the effect of an argument on the change of an attitude in persons of different sex?[2]

This study was carried on in 1931 during the prohibition period in our history. The attitudes experimented with were in regard to this issue. The study was completed before antiprohibition feeling reached its height after the presidential campaign of 1932.

Knower constructed four carefully tested speeches. Two were in favor of maintaining prohibition (dry speeches) and two opposed it (wet speeches). One wet and one dry speech were predominantly factual and logical; the other speech on each side of the issue was an emotional appeal speech. The latter type can be defined as one in which suggestion is employed; stereotypes, sanctions, and taboos are used; vivid illustrations are presented; and appeals to emotional habits are designed to submerge the listener's critical reactions. In the factual appeal, evidence and logical reasoning were brought to the support of contentions and a general attempt was made to arouse rather than stifle critical reactions.

The 607 experimental subjects were first tested to determine their *attitudes before* being exposed to the speeches. They were then divided and grouped into a great many combinations with the four speeches (for example, the wet subjects were divided from the dry subjects). The dry-subject group was split and half given a logical appeal and half a persuasive appeal. The group receiving the persuasive appeal was split and half heard the appeal while members of an audience and half heard the appeal individually. It is to Knower's credit that despite all this subdividing no subject served in the experiment more than once.

Of all the carefully drawn conclusions, the most important in a general sense is that (1) 60 percent of the experimental group made a positive change in attitude, demonstrating that oral argument does affect attitude! Of almost equal importance was his discovery that (2) logical and emotional appeal speeches were equally effective in producing changes in attitude.

---

[2] F. H. Knower, "Experimental Studies of Changes in Attitudes: I. A Study of the Effect of Oral Argument on Changes of Attitude," *The Journal of Social Psychology*, VI (1935), 315–47.

The mean change of attitude occurring in both dry and wet groups as a result of the argumentative appeals presented was statistically significant. The total amount of change occurring in the two groups was almost identical. These data indicate that it is possible to produce a statistically significant change of attitude in a group by presentation of an argumentative appeal.[3]

Other conclusions of interest to us here are as follows: (3) Both logical and emotional approaches were more effective in face-to-face situations than in audience situations. (4) Changes in attitude were more frequent among women than men. (5) Men were more impressed by logical argument than women. (6) Men were more effective with audiences than women. (7) Women were slightly more effective in the face-to-face situations.

In Chapter 1, we discovered that the decoding part of the communication process gives us insight into how people attach meaning to symbols by reaching into their storehouse of knowledge and experience. In Chapter 8, we discussed the learning process to give us the necessary theoretical background for the speech to inform. In this chapter on persuasion, the learning process is also a factor. Learning is usually thought of as involving habitual behavior. Once a habitual form of behavior (including attitudes) is firmly entrenched in a listener, the persuader is hard-pressed to alter it because the listener finds it less necessary to have his sorting and selecting device interpret the message. When he is faced with a specific or attention-getting argument, his hostile attitude and habit patterns may simply cause him to rehearse arguments against your general position and not really perceive your argument. For these reasons, a discussion of attention and a discussion of hostility (of attitude) are now in order. Let us first look to the interesting phenomenon of attention.

The famous psychologist William James said, "What holds attention determines action. . . . The impelling idea is simply the one which possesses the attention. . . . What checks our impulses is the mere thinking of reasons to the contrary. . . ."[4]

Attention may be thought of as a focus of perception leading to a readiness to respond.[5] To think of attention as being literally capable of controlling behavior is a little frightening. This, of course, goes beyond James' meaning, but it does serve to point out the importance of attention in persuasion. If one thinks of hypnosis as a state involving complete,

[3] Knower, "Experimental Studies of Changes in Attitudes," p. 342.

[4] William James, *Psychology: Briefer Course* (New York: Holt, Rinehart & Winston, Inc., 1892), p. 448.

[5] F. L. Ruch, *Psychology and Life,* 3rd Ed. (Chicago: Scott, Foresman & Company, 1948).

undivided attention,[6] it does appear that "that which holds attention determines action. . . ."

In Chapter 8, we found the forms of emphasis useful in terms of transferring information to the audience.[7] The audience was better able to recall and remember things they had been told with emphasis. This is an example of how a speaker can use this attention phenomenon in informative speeches. Although an enhancement of an audience's remembering or interest faculty does not necessarily prove that their attitudes have been changed or even that they are more susceptible to change—*if* attention and interest help determine action and a readiness to respond—then the suggestions for presenting information fit here also.

Our attention, like all perception, is selective. Because of this factor, the persuasive speaker must concentrate on keeping the audience involved in his subject. Other factors are constantly vying for the listener's attention—sounds, sights, people, conflicting ideas, and so on.

Modern research in persuasion also suggests that man alters his attitudes when he feels seriously out of step with himself, as it were. Man seeks a consistency, balance, or consonance among his perceptions and reasonings on a given proposition. Conflicting perceptions, inconsistent appearing facts and confusing logic on a proposition lead to a state of tension, imbalance, or dissonance. This suggests a theory of motivation or persuasion in which man alters his attitudes and behavior to reduce inconsistency, imbalance, and dissonance. These theories are generally referred to as the "balance" or "tension reduction" theories. One of the best known is called cognitive dissonance and was developed by Leon Festinger.[8] According to Festinger, persuasive communications are very effective when they reduce dissonance but ineffective if being influenced would simply increase dissonance. "If a given dissonance exists, and if a person is trying to reduce the dissonance by changing some opinion which he holds, then that person will be very receptive to communications attempting to influence him in that direction."[9] He would likewise tend to be resistant to persuasion attempting to push him in the opposite direction. This does not mean that all behavior is always a consequence of attempts at dissonance reduction, and Festinger is careful to make this clear.

Let us now look to the problem of conflicting, dissonance provoking ideas or antagonistic audience attitudes. Some of the research dealing with

6 Hypnosis is probably more closely allied to normal sleep.

7 R. Ehrensberger, "An Experimental Study of the Relative Effectiveness of Certain Forms of Emphasis in Public Speaking," *Speech Monographs,* XII (1945), 94–111.

8 Leon Festinger, *A Theory of Cognitive Dissonance* (Stanford, California: Stanford University Press, 1957).

9 Leon Festinger, "The Theory of Cognitive Dissonance," in Wilbur Schramm, *The Science of Human Communication* (New York: Basic Books, Inc., 1963), p. 25.

the persuading of relatively antagonistic audiences is fascinating and most instructive for would-be persuasive speakers.

Early in 1945 the Great War had ended in Europe. Perhaps you had forgotten that the war in the Pacific theatre of operations was still raging. This was pre-Hiroshima and Nagasaki. The atom bomb was a carefully held secret. At this moment in history, the United States War Department was deeply concerned about the overoptimism regarding an early end of the war in the Pacific. The general attitude of many of the troops in Europe was, "The war is over—let's go home." The people at home, weary of war, were letting their guard down.

The experiment involved the issue of a long war and overoptimism. The subjects were 625 army personnel. The War Department felt that the weight of evidence indicated at least two more years of war in the Pacific. The specific knowledge sought by the experimenter was: when the weight of evidence supports the main thesis being presented, is it more effective to present only the arguments supporting the point being made, or is it better to introduce also the arguments of those opposed to the point being made?[10]

The persuasion was transmitted with the aid of two radio transcriptions. Both speeches were in the form of a commentator's analysis of the Pacific war. The commentator's conclusion was that the job of finishing the war would be tough and that it would take at least two years after V-E (Victory in Europe) Day.

The first program (A—one side) presented only those arguments indicating the war would be a long one. These very serious issues were distance problems and logistical difficulties, the resources and stockpiles in the Japanese Empire, the size and quality of the main bulk of the Japanese army, which we had not yet met in battle, and the determination of the Japanese people.

The second program (B—both sides) presented all the same difficulties, except that time was also devoted to a brief consideration of arguments for a short war. Some of these arguments were our naval victories and superiority, our previous progress despite a two-front war, our ability to concentrate all our forces on Japan after V-E Day, Japan's shipping losses, Japan's manufacturing inferiority, and the future damage to be expected from our expanding air war.

The experiment was disguised through the orientation program in such a way that the men were not aware of participating in an experimental situation. A preliminary survey of estimates of war duration was used to determine initial opinions. To register a change in attitude a man had to revise

---

10 I & E Division, U.S. War Department, "The Effects of Presenting 'One Side' Versus 'Both Sides' in Changing Opinions on a Controversial Subject"; in Newcomb, Hartley, et al., Readings in Social Psychology (New York: Holt, Rinehart & Winston, Inc., 1947), pp. 566–77.

his estimate of how long the war would continue at least six months or more. An added analysis, which is of interest to students of speech and communication theory, involved the sorting out of scores for the high school graduates and comparing them with men who did not graduate from high school.

The results of this interesting study are shown in Table 1. The researchers' conclusions follow the tables.

The most important finding for our purposes was that the both-sides persuasion was significantly better than one-side persuasion when the audience was opposed to the point of view being presented. Though of less import to the very real issue involved in this study, it is interesting to note that the one-sided arguments were more effective when the audience was already convinced of the point being presented. However, if we knew that

TABLE 1

NET EFFECTIVENESS OF PROGRAM *A* AND *B* FOR MEN WITH
INITIALLY UNFAVORABLE AND MEN WITH INITIALLY FAVORABLE ATTITUDES

Net % Changing to Longer Estimate

1. Initial estimate "unfavorable" (estimated a short war):
   Program *A* (one side only)   36%
   Program *B* (both sides)   48%
2. Initial estimate "favorable" (estimated a long war):
   Program *A*   52%
   Program *B*   23%

NET EFFECTIVENESS OF PROGRAM *A* AND PROGRAM *B*
FOR MEN OF DIFFERENT EDUCATIONAL BACKGROUNDS

1. Among men who did not graduate from high school:
   Program *A*   46%
   Program *B*   31%
2. Among men who graduated from high school:
   Program *A*   35%
   Program *B*   49%

Conclusions

1. Presenting the arguments on both sides of an issue was found to be more effective than giving only the arguments supporting the point being made in the case of individuals who were initially opposed to the point of view being presented.
2. For men who were already convinced of the point of view being presented, however, the inclusion of arguments on both sides was less effective for the group as a whole than presenting only the arguments favoring the general position being advocated.
3. Better educated men were more favorably affected by presentation of both sides; poorly educated men were more affected by the communication that used only supporting arguments.
4. The group for which the presentation giving both sides was least effective was the group of poorly educated men who were already convinced of the point of view being advocated.
5. An important incidental finding was that omission of a relevant argument was more noticeable and detracted more from effectiveness in the presentation using arguments on both sides than in the presentation in which only one side was discussed.

the latter group would be exposed to counterpropaganda at a later date, then what kind of a communication decision should we make?

Fortunately we have another similar study, which throws light specifically on the issue of counterpropaganda. Lumsdaine and Janis[11] compared resistance to counterpropaganda produced by a one-sided versus a two-sided propaganda presentation. This experiment was conducted several months before the President announced to all of us that Russia had produced an atomic explosion. It was a period of self-satisfaction for the United States. We had gloried in World War II; we were well off; we, the only atomic power in the world, were literally sitting on top of the world. The conclusion on the part of the people was that Russia would be unable to produce large numbers of atomic explosions for at least the next five years.

Once again the experimental design involved transcribed radio programs. A one-sided (Program A) and a two-sided speech (Program B) were put together, directed once more at a kind of overoptimism. The main difference between this study and the one previously described is that one week after the speeches, half of the subjects were exposed to counterpropaganda (half who heard Program A and half who heard Program B). A control group heard neither. The subject's opinions were measured again. The net changes in opinion are tabled below.

TABLE 2

COMPARISON OF A ONE-SIDED VERSUS A TWO-SIDED PRESENTATION FOR
GROUPS EXPOSED AND NOT EXPOSED TO SUBSEQUENT COUNTERPROPAGANDA

	Net Change in Opinion
1. Groups not exposed to counterpropaganda	
Program A (one side)	64%
Program B (both sides)	69%
2. Groups exposed to counterpropaganda	
Program A (one side)	98%
Program B (both sides)	39%

In other words, the groups previously persuaded with both-sides argumentation were more resistant to counterpropaganda than those persuaded with one-sided argumentation. Only 2 percent of the later group maintained the desired attitudes when subjected to counterpropaganda, whereas 61 percent of the group previously exposed to both-sides persuasion resisted and maintained the desired opinion. The researchers concluded: "A two-sided presentation is *more* effective in the long run than a one-sided

[11] A. A. Lumsdaine and I. L. Janis, "Resistance to Counterpropaganda Produced by a One-Sided Versus a Two-Sided Propaganda Presentation," in C. Hovland, I. Janis, and H. Kelley, *Communication and Persuasion* (New Haven, Conn.: Yale University Press, 1953), pp. 108–11.

one (a) when, regardless of initial opinion, the audience is *exposed* to subsequent counterpropaganda, or (b) when, regardless of subsequent exposure to counterpropaganda, the audience initially disagrees with the commentator's position."

It is readily apparent that this study supports the War Department study. It shows that we must consider the approach of both-sides persuasion because of the possibility that an audience may be exposed to counterargument.

There are many speech studies, which have in part measured the effects of both-sides persuasion. They often indicate that "other" factors are so important as to make generalizations dangerous. For example, the role of a speaker's prestige or ethos[12] may seriously offset any predicted advantage. There is evidence that in full-blown, emotional, political oratory, a straightforward, argumentative approach may be more effective.[13] The *amount* of opposition to an issue as related to the amount of acceptance may be a serious factor in change of opinion.[14] A study by Jaksa indicates that both-sides persuasion can be very effective in changing or strengthening attitudes for neutral and already favorably disposed people.[15] In no instance in the Jaksa study was the one-sided speech significantly better than one of the three two-sided speeches. However, the one-sided speech was in all cases persuasive. The weight of research evidence appears to favor both-sides (rationalistic) persuasion. However, the specifics and many variables attendant upon each speech and communication situation suggest many problems of application for the speaker. Let us discuss justifications, advantages, and characteristics of both-sides persuasion and suggest applications for your next speech.

Both-sides persuasion has the appeal of objective, rational evaluation. It is a subtle and honest appeal to fair play. An opposed listener is not antagonized by omission of arguments on his side of the issue. Listening should be more favorably oriented because the listener will not be involved in rehearsing counterarguments during your positive (pro side) persuasion. Both-sides persuasion not only helps insulate the audience against counterargument, but also forces the speaker to be more audience-oriented. A

---

[12] Stanley F. Paulson, "The Effects of the Prestige of the Speaker and Acknowledgment of Opposing Arguments on Audience Retention and Shift of Opinion," *Speech Monographs,* XXI (November, 1954), 267–71.

[13] Thomas Ludlum, "Effects of Certain Techniques of Credibility Upon Audience Attitudes," *Speech Monographs,* XXV (November, 1958), 278–84.

[14] I. L. Janis and Rosalind Feierebend, "Effects of Alternative Ways of Ordering Pro and Con Arguments in Persuasive Communications," in C. Hovland, I. Janis, and H. Kelley, *Communication and Persuasion,* p. 115.

[15] James A. Jaksa, "An Experimental Study of One-Sided and Two-Sided Argument, with Emphasis on Three Two-Sided Speeches" (Doctoral Dissertation, Wayne State University, 1962).

speaker is forced to be more sensitive to the audience's attitudes and to the totality of arguments and issues involved in his subject. One student speaker who, after much research on both sides of his speech, reported that he had now convinced himself of the "other" side of the subject. Both-sides persuasion is then: (1) a most effective form of motivation; and (2) a most scientific and rational form of preparation—a new rationalistic persuasion!

Some specific characteristics to be noted in this kind of persuasion are as follows:

1. *Objectivity*—fairness, honesty, bias based on evidence.
2. *Suspended judgment*—avoids superpositive statements, creates doubt, makes frequent use of the hypothesis form.
3. *Nonspecific opponents*—does not identify audience as the opposition, suggests audience is undecided, creates a common ground.
4. *Critical willingness*—arouses audience reevaluation, motivation to reconsider "other" side.
5. *Qualified language*—does not overstate the position and evidence, is careful of overgeneralized statements.
6. *Audience-sensitive*—adapts and adjusts the presentation to the feedback signs, considers alternative actions in advance of the speech.
7. *Ethical*—above all, honest; presents significant opposing arguments in an objective manner; honesty is also pragmatically the best policy.

The Basis of Persuasion

Historical Explanations of Personality

In a very real sense, the sources of persuasion are found in an understanding of human nature and behavior. Since ancient times, man has tried to find simple explanations of what motivates people to do what they do. If one could find universal answers and systems, it was thought that one could theoretically control the behavior of others in ever so many specific ways. To some philosophers the proper study of man is man himself. The assumption is that all men, at least in a general sense, are much alike.

At the physiological level, this presents but few problems, for despite obvious individual differences in height, weight, color, and so forth, the most amazing thing is the striking similarity of all people. We could hardly have a science of medicine were this not true. All doctors use the same anatomy chart, and all search for your appendix in about the same place.

In the nonphysiological aspects of man, the problem is more complicated. Plato argued that to study man one must investigate his environment—for to Plato man was a reflection of his society. In our modern-day thinking, we tend to say that both points of view are necessary to understand man's behavior.

Another explanation of human behavior and personality that stems from the ancients is that these factors are determined by your physiology or some specific psychological classification. One of the earliest typological theories was probably introduced by Hippocrates. The theory was based on what were thought to be the four basic "humors" or fluids of the body. These were yellow bile, black bile, phlegm, and blood. If your yellow bile predominated, you were choleric or hot-tempered; if your black bile predominated, you were melancholic or gloomy and sad; if phlegm predominated, you were phlegmatic or slow and sluggish; if blood were foremost, you were sanguine or cheery and gay.

There have been many other theories for classifying people, including morphological and sociological determinants. Perhaps among psychological types you are most familiar with Jung's *introvert* and *extrovert* classification.[16] Even this useful system evidences the danger of typing people too hastily. Jung himself deplored the either/or system that seems inevitably to follow. He thought rather of all people having introversion-extroversion tendencies, with one or the other tending to predominate on a given continuum. The introvert in a speech class may be a tigerlike extrovert on the football field.

Another theory that is still with us, and like the others has utility with the proper safeguards and qualifications, is the theory of the instinctivist. This is to some extent a perversion of Aristotle's innate human nature theory. If we could locate a long list of urges and drives, which were in no way learned and which were universal in all men, we could select our persuasion systems much more scientifically than it appears we do now. That many people in a given culture react similarly to similar stimulations seems obvious; however, to suggest that learning plays only a minor role or that man has absolutely no choice, which the word *instinct* implies, seems unrealistic and unobjective. As a matter of record so many so-called instincts were "discovered" that a social psychologist in 1924 recorded 6,000 different kinds.[17]

Among behaviorists, J. B. Watson typified the belief that learning and conditioning were satisfactory explanations for complex emotional patterns. However, Watson did argue that there were three innate emotional patterns—fear, love, and rage.[18] In experiments with children, it was discovered that all youngsters expressed *fear* when exposed to loud noises or

---

[16] C. G. Jung, *Psychological Types* (New York: Harcourt, Brace & World, Inc., 1922).

[17] L. L. Bernard, *Instinct: A Study in Social Psychology* (New York: Holt, Rinehart & Winston, Inc., 1924).

[18] J. B. Watson, *Psychology from the Standpoint of a Behaviorist* (Philadelphia: J. B. Lippincott Co., 1924).

sudden loss of support. It was also found that youngsters responded with *love* in the form of gurgling and cooing when stroked gently; and finally, that they expressed *rage* when their movement was seriously restricted. If these are reasonably universal behavior patterns, whether innate or learned, they may represent some basis for theorizing about persuasion.

These classification systems have an obvious utility, if only in terms of more detailed descriptions of the receiver who must decode our communications. Their danger and error to human communication is the tyranny of quick and often permanent labeling of people or groups of people. When extended to ethnic group, national origin, and religion, the problem of overgeneralization is with us, and any practical utility may be completely lost.

Classification of Needs

If man is to continue living, it is obvious that like all other animals he must satisfy certain biological requirements or needs. It is essential for survival that man have oxygen, food, water, rest, and exercise. All men have need of these and all men have roughly the same limitations in terms of pain, temperature, and denial of physiological requirements. Although these needs for self-preservation originate within the body, it is evident that once the body's reserves are in jeopardy the requirements must come from outside the body. The state of imbalance in the body calls upon man to select those things in the outside world that specifically meet the requirement. If he is slow in meeting these internal needs, the demands intensify and the entire body mobilizes for concerted action. Thus, our actions and behavior are triggered by our biological needs, and these needs are associated with goals. The goals, even at the basic level of food and water, offer us choices in the world over which we have some control; however, whether we choose milk or beer or orange juice, we must satisfy our basic need for fluids.

In our culture, we seldom have reason to check on the operation of our biological needs. It is only in great stress situations that a biological imbalance may cause serious conflicts. Nevertheless these biological motivations are constantly with us, affecting our behavior and the intensity with which we search out related goals.

In any attempt to classify needs, one must begin with biological or physiological needs. A system that starts with this kind of survival motivation as a cornerstone is supplied by A. H. Maslow and is particularly useful to the psychology of persuasion.[19] His five general categories of needs, in

---

[19] A. H. Maslow, "A Theory of Human Motivation," *Psychological Review,* L (1943), 370–96.

the order of their importance, are *Physiological, Safety, Love, Esteem,* and *Self-Actualization.*

Maslow takes a position quite opposite to the trait-psychologists and believes that most behavior is multimotivated. One act could engage all the needs. The theory is a general-dynamic one involving the integrated wholeness of the organism that is man.

PHYSIOLOGICAL NEEDS. These are the biological needs referred to previously. They are directly related to survival and self-preservation. Although they are generally rated first in importance, their importance diminishes if they are satisfied or in a state of equilibrium. A starving man may live in a world which to him is dominated by thoughts and visions of food, but for most of us these physiological needs do not completely dominate our behavior. The primary or survival needs may be indicated as follows: (1) oxygen, (2) food, (3) water, (4) rest, (5) exercise, (6) avoidance of bodily damage, and (7) excretion.

SAFETY NEEDS refer to our desire for a sense of security and to our aversion to personal violence, harm, or disease. We most often prefer a safe, predictable environment or world to one plagued with unknown and unpredictable events. It is this protective desire that may prompt us to be concerned with insurance and jobs that offer security first and high wages second. We are here primarily concerned with psychological safety rather than the physiological safety discussed previously.

Like physiological needs, our safety needs are not all-consuming in our lives except in times of emergency or danger. However, many people are seriously concerned with threats to their security and safety. A change in a work routine, even when carefully explained, often causes visible anxiety. A change in environment, such as a college freshman experiences, is often an extreme threat to his safety needs, and he may be quite amenable to persuasion that promises more security in groups, housing, trips home, and friends. The first year of military service represents a similar constellation of events. The desire for psychological safety is a strong need for all of us.

LOVE NEEDS. Some social scientists use the term *belonging* to designate this group of needs. Man must be loved and in turn must express his love. The sharing of life with others is important to man, and he will often react quickly to even the suggestion of a denial of this desire. Man finds satisfaction for this need most generally through his family and close friends, but the category extends beyond this area. We desire the approval and acceptance of our classmates, our fellow workers, and the many groups of people with whom we associate and with whom we tend to identify ourselves. We quite obviously alter our behavior and perhaps even our standards to be accepted, to belong, to be loved by our chosen friends and groups.

The most significant aspect of this set of dynamic needs is the realization that its satisfaction involves both giving and receiving. Man, to be well adjusted, must also give of his love. Our lonely-hearts clubs owe their very existence to this powerful need to give and share love. Unscrupulous persuaders have often taken advantage of this need through fraudulent campaigns to help suffering people.

ESTEEM NEEDS. When our physiological, safety, and love needs are satisfied, then theoretically our esteem needs become most important. These needs go beyond the more passive belongings or love needs into a more active desire for recognition and self-respect. It involves evaluation of self and, according to A. H. Maslow, is of two slightly different types or *sets:*

> . . . the desire for strength, for achievement, for adequacy, for confidence in the face of the world and for independence and freedom . . . secondly, we have what we may call the desire for reputation or prestige (defining it as respect or esteem from other people), recognition, attention, importance, or appreciation.[20]

In our culture this becomes a very important need. We are often accused as a people of being egocentric. A threat to our ego or self-esteem, real or fancied, often prompts swift reaction. Our radio and television commercials appeal to our esteem needs in selling the more expensive, prestige cars or in suggested threats to our station in a group should we be offensive or only "half-safe."

The satisfaction or partial satisfaction of esteem needs leads to self-confidence and a feeling of personal worth. Esteem needs are often fraught with many frustrations and personal conflicts, for man desires not only the recognition and attention of his chosen groups, but also the self-respect and status that his moral, social, and religious standards call for. It is when the former groups call for behavior that is in conflict with the latter that man must often make heroic choices to remain an integrated, whole organism.

Man plays many roles to satisfy some of these different groups, and the problem of explaining the precise extent of his motivation is wrapped up in the complex dynamics of his entire system of needs. For some poorly adjusted people, esteem needs are so great that they will strive for achievement (or what they consider achievement) at the great price of their own self-respect, morals, and ideals. This is not to say that the so-called achievement motive is abnormal. Much has been written about the need for achievement as a motivating force.[21]

SELF-ACTUALIZATION NEEDS. This term, first used by Kurt Goldstein,

---

[20] Maslow, "A Theory of Human Motivation," p. 382.

[21] See D. C. McClelland, *The Achieving Society* (Princeton, N.J.: D. Van Nostrand Co., Inc., 1961); also, S. W. Gellerman, *Motivation and Productivity* (American Management Association, Vail Ballou Press, 1963), ch. 12.

pertains to what might be called *self-fulfillment*—or *self-realization*—the desire by man to reach the acme of his own personal abilities and talents. In Maslow's words, "What a man *can* be, he *must* be." Because this need becomes increasingly important as the previous four needs are satisfied, it becomes apparent that in our culture self-actualization becomes a very important aspect of human behavior and motivation. The large number of retired or established people who return to college or take adult courses in art, writing, or drama to satisfy creative urges is indicative of the role of self-actualization needs. At Wayne State University in Detroit (a large metropolitan institution), the *average* age of the student body is 26 years, and many students have full-time jobs. One part-time student is 87 years old; the oldest full-time student is only 82.

The rank order and practical importance of these dynamic needs are subject to the degree of satisfaction attendant upon each need. Because the degree of satisfaction is constantly changing, even among our physiological needs, the communicator is well advised to know his audience. In Chapter 1 it was pointed out that the receiver decodes in terms of *his* past experiences, emotions, and attitudes. More specifically, he decodes in terms of his interacting dynamic needs. At one time his need for *love* may predominate, coloring the meaning he attaches to a communication; at another time his need for *esteem* may be foremost, and his susceptibility to persuasion is altered accordingly. The description of the degree of satisfaction an average man unconsciously or consciously carries about with him in terms of these five needs is an elusive set of figures, which become really confusing if one presumes that these are constant. Nevertheless, such a description gives us a benchmark from which to start. Maslow suggests the following degrees of satisfaction as being attendant upon the average man:

1. Physiological   85%
2. Safety   70%
3. Love   50%
4. Esteem   40%
5. Self-actualization   10%[22]

Since a satisfied need is not a strong motivator, the smaller figures should indicate the areas most amenable to persuasion.

The prerequisites for self-actualization (and therefore for all the basic need satisfactions) are so important to us that they, in themselves, become strong motivators when they appear to be thwarted or in jeopardy: such things as free speech, intellectual freedom, the right to self-defense, the desire for justice, honesty, and orderliness. We will have more to say about these when we discuss motive appeals.

---

[22] Maslow, "A Theory of Human Motivation," p. 389.

Personality and Needs

Our behavior as adults is oriented primarily in terms of what we have learned (experienced). Man acquires his needs, his goals, and his motives from the world in which he lives as well as from certain biological necessities. What we call *personality* is the totality of a man's knowledge, motives, values, beliefs, and goal-seeking patterns. More academically, personality may be thought of as "the entire sequence of organized governmental processes in the brain from birth to death."[23] The major determinants of personality become of primary importance to the persuader and the leader who must seek out those influences that may in part determine goals and motivations.

Kluckhohn and Murray provide us with a practical and intelligent classification of personality determinants or influences: constitution, group membership, role, and situation.[24] If you remember the dynamic theory of human motivation previously discussed, you can better understand the interdependence and interaction of these influences.

CONSTITUTION. In one sense, the most amazing aspect of man is his constitutional or biological similarity. Yet to overlook individual differences is to overlook an aspect of personality influence and motivation. Constitution refers to the total physiological makeup of an individual. This includes environmental factors of diet, drugs, and climate, as well as the hereditary factors. Geneticists are agreed that traits are not inherited as such, but we do have reason for believing that man varies, at least potentially, in his reaction time, energy level, and rate of learning. Man also varies constitutionally in terms of hearing, sight, and the like. A visual impairment or a severe hearing loss offers implications for personality development, even though there are no set patterns. These constitutional factors determine personality, even though the patterns are not completely predictable. Age, sex, characteristics of appearance, strength, and size influence a man's needs and motivations. The feedback he decodes from his society in terms of these constitutional factors may have a profound effect upon his personality and his needs system.

GROUP MEMBERSHIP. In this personality influence we hearken back to Plato. Man in part will reflect the society in which he lives. His family, his school, and his church are all thought to influence profoundly a man's life and personality. This is not to suggest that we are all carbon copies of those of similar exposure. Even the strong aspect of the culture in which

---

[23] C. Kluckhohn and H. A. Murray, *Personality in Nature, Society, and Culture* (New York: Alfred A. Knopf, Inc., 1956), p. 57.

[24] *Ibid.*, pp. 53–72.

we live determines only what we learn as a member of a group, not what we learn as a specific individual. This in part explains why man alters his behavior and motivations in what seem to be most inconsistent ways.

Our subcultures in America become predictable in a general sense. For example, Texans often have distinctive mannerisms, and the "eyes of Texas" may indeed influence their selection of needs and actions. New Yorkers also exercise strong group influences one upon another; their refusal to show surprise, awe, or even amazement is a constant and delightful mystery to the Middle Westerner. Newcomers to the California climate quickly assume a California personality, and the influence of this subculture is rapidly affecting the personality of our entire nation; summer dress in Michigan has become more casual, and even the East Coast partially appears to have accepted a more leisurely and comfortable West Coast way of living.

Living in a special society requires certain standards or patterns roughly agreed upon by the members of that group. Much random and impulsive individual behavior is sublimated in terms of these group codes. This feeling of unification and purpose and value gives us and the group members a rough pattern of prediction and understanding. The *conceptions* a person has of his total group mold personality more than the group itself.

ROLE in part pertains to a more specific aspect of group membership. Some roles are cast upon us by society because of our age or sex, some we assign to ourselves on the bases of our life goals, and some are really disguises of our private personalities for the purpose of being accepted by certain groups. In its most important sense, a *role* is the part we cast for ourself on the stage of life. We may portray many roles to the world, but each man determines, with the aid of society, what his particular role will be, and his personality is influenced by this decision. The professional person is often stereotyped, and we learn to expect certain roles from professors, lawyers, and doctors. Professors who do not act like professors are often real enigmas to society. The doctor who does not play the role patients expect had better develop an interest in research.

Role is determined by both the way in which man views or evaluates *himself* and the way in which society and its subgroups expect him to behave. Personality tends to develop according to this role. Man is surely motivated by appeals to his specific role in life.

SITUATION. The situational determinants of personality refer to those exceptional, nonpredictable, often accidental events that happen to all men. These are events that can seriously alter our lives and cast us into roles that may profoundly affect our emerging personality—a draft notice, a "Dear John" letter, a scholarship, a riot, an insight or perspective suddenly and never before achieved. A stimulating teacher has probably altered the lives and careers of many unsuspecting students.

The events of everyone's specific situation are not always as potent as those indicated above. Often we perceive only a minor event—a chance remark by a respected person, a brief exposure to danger, a book with a message—but it sets in motion, however slowly or rapidly, actions that make a man different than he was before. To that extent, they mold his personality. These random events do not always initiate personality changes in societally approved directions. An accidental opportunity to steal in a moment of great need and weakness might provide a person with an experience that could furnish a severe guilt complex, a new career, or a renewed faith and courage in his moral stature. In any event, the situational factors in our lives have the potential to seriously affect and help determine personality.

Motive Appeals

The needs system and personality determinants give us a basis for understanding the specific stimulants and conditions that are thought to trigger or set in motion these powerful forces. Though modern social scientists are dubious of the universality of any of these so-called wants, appeals, or propensities, such lists of motive appeals are thought to have utility to advertisers specifically and to persuaders in general. When properly related and evaluated in terms of the dynamic needs, personality factors, and communication processes of a specific listener or audience, they can be most helpful.

One of the older and more durable of these lists in speech education includes self-preservation, property, power, reputation, affections, sentiments, and tastes.[25] With all the dangers of overgeneralization in terms of nonspecific audiences as qualifiers, let us look at the explanation of two of these factors:[26]

> *Affections:* "Affections as an Impelling Motive" means the desire for the welfare of others—kindly concern for the interests of mother, father, wife, son, daughter, sweetheart, friends, any being, human or divine. Also it includes desire for the welfare of our town, country, state, and nation, in so far as this desire is altruistic and not selfish.

> *Sentiments:* "The Impelling Motive of Sentiments" includes the desire to be and to do what is right, fair, honorable, noble, true—desires associated with intellectual and moral culture. It embraces duty, liberty, independence, and also patriotism considered as a moral obligation.

From psychology, William McDougall gives us another durable list, thought to have utility today even though the instinct theory has been

---

[25] A. E. Phillips, *Effective Speaking* (Chicago: The Newton Co., 1931), p. 48.
[26] *Ibid.,* pp. 53–54.

rather thoroughly discredited. McDougall called his list "Native Propensities."

1. To desire food periodically (hunger).
2. To reject certain substances (disgust).
3. To explore new places and things (curiosity).
4. To try to escape from danger (fear).
5. To fight when frustrated (anger).
6. To have sex desire (mating).
7. To care tenderly for the young (mothering).
8. To seek company (gregariousness).
9. To seek to dominate (self-assertiveness).
10. To accept obvious inferiority (submissiveness).
11. To make things (construction).
12. To collect things (acquisitiveness).[27]

More modern lists of appeals are quite similar to those indicated above. Advertising studies supply us with a legion of terms, which, like those of an earlier day, have utility for the persuader who is careful to first relate them to his specific audience. A random collection of these terms follows:

MOTIVE TERMS

Cleanliness	Appetizing	Competition
Sanitary	Activity	Ambition
Hunger	Mating	Curiosity
Pleasure	Comfort	Creating
Rest—sleep	Fighting	Enjoyment
Health	Safety	Devotion
Protection	Conformity	Social Distinction
Group Spirit	Anger	Wealth
Fear	Gregariousness	Adventure
Cooperation	Acquisition	Independence
Conflict	Companionship	Property
Value	Sympathy	Achievement
Mothering	Sex	
Approval	Deity	
Domesticity	Quality	
Power	Reputation	

If we were to attempt to categorize these appeals under the dynamic needs discussed earlier in this chapter, it is obvious that we would have a

[27] William McDougall, *An Introduction to Social Psychology* (London: Methuen & Co., Ltd., 1908).

considerable overlap. This is to be expected, because our needs system is dynamic, and all may be operative at any one time. It is in terms of our dynamic needs that these motive appeals may have utility. The following attempt at sorting is deliberately incomplete and is meant to show examples of possible avenues of relationship.

POSSIBLE AVENUES OF RELATIONSHIP OF
MOTIVE APPEALS TO THE DYNAMIC NEEDS

Physiological	Safety	Love
1. Bodily comfort	1. Fear	1. Loyalty
2. Sex attraction	2. Conformity	2. Family affection
3. Physical enjoyment	3. Companionship	3. Sympathy
4. Hunger	4. Saving	4. Mothering
5. Activity	5. Conflict	5. Respect for Deity
6. Rest and sleep	6. Cleanliness	6. Sentiments

Self-Esteem	Self-Actualization
1. Pride	1. Creativeness
2. Reputation	2. Curiosity
3. Power	3. Constructiveness
4. Achievement	4. Ambition
5. Social distinction	5. Independence
6. Appearance	6. Freedom from restraint

The motive appeals must be filtered, evaluated, and decoded by layers of resistance such as dynamic needs, personality determinants, and finally, the momentary "set" or disposition of the man underneath it all. Human motivation is terribly complex; one should be wary of sure-fire persuasive appeals. See Figure 47.

Organizing Persuasive Material

The apparent similarities between human motivation and thinking patterns and learning patterns offer many suggestions for organizing persuasive material.

Probably the most famous "thought" system is the "reflective" pattern of John Dewey. This same system is used frequently in problem-solving and group-discussion courses, and is further discussed in Chapter 12.

(1) suggestions, in which the mind leaps forward to a possible solution; (2) an intellectualization of the difficulty or perplexity that has been felt into a problem to be solved, question for which the answer must be sought; (3) the use of one suggestion after another as a leading idea, or

hypothesis, to initiate and guide observation and other operations in collection of factual material; (4) the mental elaboration of the idea . . . ; and (5) testing of the hypothesis by overt or imaginative action.[28]

Translating this to the organization of material from the viewpoint of a speaker trying to persuade, you are advised to arrange your material and strategy so that your audience will receive and decode it in the following natural thinking order:

1. Attention and awareness of felt difficulty.
2. A recognition of a problem or need.
3. The sorting of objections and counterplans in search of the best solution.
4. An elaborating and visualizing of the proposed solution.
5. An evaluation of the plan leading to acceptance or rejection of the solution.

Persuaders and speech scholars have made many adaptations similar to the one indicated above. Hollingworth[29] indicated the fundamental tasks of a speaker as attention, interest, impression, conviction, and direction. It has also been stated succinctly and clearly by Alan H. Monroe, who calls his system the motivated sequence.[30] The key words are attention, need, satisfaction, visualization, and action.

Thinking patterns and learning patterns have a great deal in common. For theories on how we learn, we consult the educational psychologist. Many learning theories revolve around stimulus-response bonds (SR) and things which tend to stamp in or reinforce the response (reinforcement). Habit or past experience plays a large part, as does frequency of occurrence of the response either intellectually or physically (SHR) (SOR).[31]

The theory of Miller and Dollard [32] is typical. Their categories in the learning process are drive, stimulus, response, and reward.

Other variations or translations of speech organization might include attention, motivation (for drive), stimulus, reaction, and reinforcement. In very general terms, the SRX bond or stimulus-response-reinforcement theory has usefulness to would-be persuaders. These learning and thinking patterns, together with the new rationalism approach indicated at the beginning of this chapter (both-sides persuasion), offer us a wealth of organizational ideas for our persuasive speeches.

---

[28] John Dewey, *How We Think* (Boston: D. C. Heath & Company, 1933), p. 107.
[29] H. L. Hollingworth, *The Psychology of the Audience* (New York: American Book Company, 1935), Ch. III, pp. 19–32.
[30] *Principles and Types of Speech* (Chicago: Scott, Foresman & Company, 1962).
[31] (SHR)—Stimulus (Habit Strength) Response (C. L. Hull).
     (SOR)—Stimulus Oscillation Response (C. L. Hull).
[32] N. E. Miller and J. Dollard in J. A. McGeoch and A. L. Irion, *The Psychology of Human Learning* (New York: David McKay Co., Inc., 1952), p. 54.

A useful system that takes most of the elements into account is the following: attention, need, plan, objections, reinforcement, and action. If we diagram these in terms of barriers (for example, a lack of attention), we can see the complexity of this process and the dangers of oversimplification or overstructuralization. With man in the center of a maze of thinking, learning, persuasion, communication barriers, the situation theoretically appears as follows:

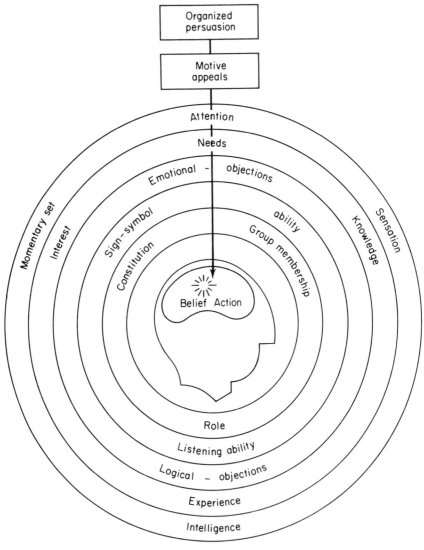

Figure 47.   Persuasion Filters and Barriers

The Gestalt-oriented psychologists remind us that learning is a dynamic interaction of the entire perceptual field rather than simple bonds or associations.[33] Therefore, this is not meant to be a stereotype for organizing persuasive speeches. You are still better advised to use introduction—body—conclusion as a general outline format and to use these other systems of arrangement for further detailing and better understanding. This was explained in Chapter 7. A chart showing some of these persuasion systems in terms of introduction—body—conclusion is useful.

SOME PERSUASION ARRANGEMENT SYSTEMS

	Hollingworth	*Monroe*	*Miller & Dollard*	*Ross*
Introduction	Attention	Attention	Drive	Attention
Body	Interest Impression Conviction	Need Satisfaction Visualization	Stimulus Response	Need Plan Objections
Conclusion	Direction	Action	Reward	Reinforcement Action

Whatever specific organization adaptation you decide upon, the following organizational concepts are at least theoretically involved in all persuasion speeches:

1. Creation of an attention-need and feeling of felt difficulty in order to communicate in the acceptable code.
2. Arousal of interest and problem awareness by relating need to the specific audience through their dynamic needs and motive appeals.
3. Explanation and relation of the solution in terms of the problem, need, previous experience, knowledge, and personality of the audience.
4. Evaluation, when necessary, of all important objections, counterarguments, or alternate solutions.
5. Reinforcement of your message throughout your speech, particularly toward the close, through verbal reminders, reviews, summaries, and visualizations.

Summary

The psychology of persuasion is concerned with the alteration of attitudes. We have reliable evidence that oral speech does affect attitude. The role of attention is vital to persuasion because so many other factors are constantly distracting

[33] J. A. McGeoch and A. L. Irion, *The Psychology of Human Learning,* p. 44.

the listeners. Persuasive communications tend to be effective when they reduce dissonance and inconsistency, and ineffective when they increase dissonance. The use of both-sides persuasion has been shown by experiment to be superior to one-sided persuasion when the audience was opposed to the point of view being presented or when, regardless of initial attitude, the audience was exposed to counterargument. Historic points of view about man's behavior and motivation patterns have utility for us if we are careful to evaluate and qualify them in terms of more scientific modern theories. A useful classification of human dynamic needs is physiological, safety, love, esteem, and self-actualization. Man, the great learner, sees the world and is motivated to a great extent through his personality. The determinants and influences of personality are constitution, group membership, role, and situation. Motive appeals are useful triggers of human needs. They must be evaluated in terms of the layers of resistance indicated as dynamic needs, personality determinants, and the monetary "sets" or dispositions of the listener. Thinking and learning theories offer many suggestions for the arrangement of persuasive speech material. One such theoretical persuasion progression involves attention, need, plan, objections, reinforcement, and action. Human motivation is a highly complex phenomenon involving dynamic interaction of the totality of our previous experiences in the perceptual field. The dangers of oversimplified, overstructuralized, or other sure-fire systems of persuasion are considerable.

Model Persuasive Outline

BUCKLE UP AND STAY ALIVE[34]

General End: To persuade.
Specific Purpose: To persuade the audience to always use the seat belts in their cars.

Introduction

(Attention)

I. A cure for cancer or heart disease! What excitement would be generated if medical authorities made this announcement. Mortality would be reduced to less than one-fifth.

II. For the third leading cause of death, namely auto accidents, there already exists a lifesaving device which relatively few people use.

---

[34] From a student speech by Darlene Uten, Wayne State University.

A. An investigation of the July 4th accidents.
    1. 442 victims, with no belts at all.
    2. Belts would have prevented exactly one-half.

(Physiological and Safety Needs)

B. These statistics are very meaningful to me because last summer I was involved in an accident in which a person without a belt was killed.

Body

I. No medical miracle short of a cure for cancer or heart disease can save so many lives.

(Safety Need)

  A. Auto accidents are the leading cause of death between the ages of 15 to 24.
  B. The risk of death is cut by 80 percent when safety belts are used.

II. Most drivers don't know the facts.
  A. Ejection of occupant is the most frequent factor in serious injury. Investigation of 22 states indicates that you are five times more likely to be killed if ejected.
  B. The typical victim is not a speed demon on a strange road.
    1. National Safety Council found that three out of five fatal crashes occur on roads familiar to the driver.
    2. My accident was on a road I've been traveling all my life.

(Interest)

    3. He is more typically a young homeowner, a wife picking up her husband, or a teen-ager backing out of a driveway.
    4. Fifty percent of all fatalities occur at less than 40 mph.
    5. There is no guarantee against getting struck from behind or side-swiped.
  C. Common misconceptions set straight.
    1. You are not safer if thrown out of your car.
    2. Careful drivers are not immune to accidents.
    3. Local drivers are not immune to accidents.
    4. Driving slowly is no protection.
  D. Some objections set straight.
    1. Don't seat belts often cause injuries?

(Meeting Objections)

      a. Hip bruises—my friend would have traded her fractured skull for a dozen hip bruises.
      b. Submerged in water or on fire:

(Visualization)

        (1) With a seat belt you are more apt to remain conscious.

(2) Seat belts can be released with one hand in two seconds.
2. I don't drive often, far, or fast; why bother?
    a. Three of five fatal crashes are on local and familiar roads, within 25 miles of home.

(Reinforcement)
    b. Fifty percent of all fatalities are under 40 mph.
    c. It takes *two* to tango.

I. Safety belts have been publicized and made mandatory.
    A. All car manufacturers.
    B. United States Health Service.
    C. American Medical Association.
    D. Insurance companies.

II. Always buckle up for safety to save lives and prevent serious accident.
    A. Have everyone buckle up no matter how short the ride.
    B. It takes only six seconds to cut the risk of death by 80 percent.

The
Logical Supports
of
Persuasion **10**

Pathos vs. *Logos*

In the previous chap-
ter, we were concerned with the psychology of persuasion or the psychological supports of persuasion. In this chapter, we shall be primarily concerned with evidence, formal reasoning, and argument—the logical supports
of persuasion. The ancient Greek rhetors used the words *pathos* and *logos*
to make this kind of a distinction, and debates about the nature and advisability of using each approach continue to this day. For our purposes as
communication-conscious individuals, we have need of knowledge about
both *pathos* and *logos;* we cannot exclude either.

Evidence

Aristotle was one
of the first to make the distinction between "extrinsic" and "intrinsic"
proof.[1] *Extrinsic* proof deals with facts in the world about us or statements
based upon such facts—that is, self-evident, observable things. If you were
to go to Baldwin school and count 525 students, it would be a fact that you

---

[1] *Intrinsic* and *extrinsic* are also frequently referred to as *artistic* and *nonartistic*.
See L. Cooper, *The Rhetoric of Aristotle* (New York: Appleton-Century-Crofts,
1932), p. 8.

had observed. It would still be a fact if a document written by the principal said there were 525 students in Baldwin school. *Intrinsic* proof depends upon reasoned effort on our part, that is, the application of rhetoric and logic without which the proof would not emerge.

Essentially, the sources of evidence involve objects or things that are observable and reports about things that *are* observable. The most useful sources of evidence for our purposes are statements by authority, examples, and statistics.

Authority

This evidence or proof is typically in the form of quoted testimony from a person better qualified to give a studied opinion about something than is the speaker. However, the value of an authority depends on how expert the authority is. Perhaps the testimony simply corroborates the observations of the speaker.

The nature of the idea or statement being supported determines in part who the experts are. If you are trying to prove that the man who crashed into your car ran a red light, the expert is the lone man who was standing on the corner and saw the whole thing. With this kind of nonprofessional testimony, you often need more than one witness. If you are trying to prove that you have observed a bird considered extinct, such as the passenger pigeon, you will need the testimony of a qualified ornithologist. He will insist on firsthand observation of a captured bird in this rare case.

Your authority is qualified in two principal ways: (1) his proximity or closeness to a firsthand observation or experience; (2) his training to observe the particular phenomenon in question. He must be an expert *on the topic under discussion.* You would not ask a doctor of medicine to diagnose a problem in an airplane engine.

Other problems of authority involve your audience's knowledge and opinion of the person quoted. The personal interest or bias assigned your expert may be a very real problem. When the audience simply does not know who John Doe is, then you must explain why his testimony is authoritative (for example, John Doe is a Professor of Economics at Cornell University and a member of the U.S. Tax Commission).

Examples

An example is a specific illustration, incident, or instance that supports or brings out a point you are trying to make. A contrived or hypothetical example (as discussed previously) may be a real aid to clarity and is often very persuasive, but it is *not* proof as we are discussing it in this chapter. We are here concerned with real or factual examples.

To prove that man can operate normally in a state of weightlessness, we can cite one example of an astronaut who has successfully done so. However, in some situations *one* factual example, though proving its own case, may be so unique or exceptional that it does not truly support a generalization. If you were arguing that Volkswagens were poorly and carelessly assembled and you supported this statement with only *one* example of a car that was indeed poorly assembled, then your proof becomes suspect. The question in the latter case becomes, "How many specific examples do I need?" This involves the whole question of inductive proof, which will be discussed in the next section.

Statistics

A wag once said, "First come lies, then big lies, then statistics." (Or was it, "Figures don't lie, but liars figure!") Despite the jokes and despite fraudulent uses of statistics, the truth is that we live by statistics. We accept actuarial data on births, deaths, and accidents as facts. However, the very complexity of statistics as a method is what bewilders many people. You do not have to be a statistician to realize that an average (mean) is not always the most representative measure. Let us hypothetically take 11 educators and their yearly incomes as follow:

		Salary		Salary
Educator A	(Administrator)	$22,000	Educator G	$6,000
Educator B	(Administrator)	17,000	Educator H	5,000
Educator C		8,000	Educator I	5,000
Educator D		3,000	Educator J	5,000
Educator E		7,000	Educator K	5,000
Educator F		6,000		

The average (mean) income of these 11 educators is $8545. The problem is obvious. Two educators (administrators) make the figure unrepresentative, particularly if you are talking about "teachers." Counting down half way, we find $6000. This is the median, and is much more meaningful and representative. The average of the teachers less the two administrators is $6111, and the median is again $6000. You could further figure the amount each income deviates from the average and indicate a figure called the *average deviation*. If you were to translate these deviations from the average onto a so-called normal, bell-shaped curve or distribution, you could then determine a figure called a *standard deviation* or *sigma*.

It should now be evident that statistics can very quickly become complicated, capable of many applications, and (if we are not careful) meaningless. The lesson is: (1) select the most appropriate statistics for your point or proposition; (2) make sure they are made understandable to your audience. Statistics (figures) do not lie, but liars *do* have the opportunity to "figure"!

Inductive and Deductive Proof

Induction is that process of reasoning by which we arrive at a conclusion or generalization through observing specific cases or instances. If you were to observe 500,000 spiders, and if each and every one had eight legs, it is a reasonable conclusion that spiders have eight legs. The induction is perfect for the 500,000 cases, since there were no exceptions; to be intolerably scientific, however, it is a prediction when applied to all the spiders in the world, albeit a highly probable one. Assuming one is happy with the generalization "All spiders have eight legs," we can then conclude *deductively* that this eight-legged thing in our garden is a spider. In sum, inductive proof starts with the particular cases and proceeds to a generalization, whereas deductive proof starts with a generally accepted law or principle and applies it to a particular case. Formal deduction involves the use of syllogistic reasoning (see page 189). Requirements for safe inductive reasoning are as follows:

1. The number of specific instances supporting the conclusion must be sufficiently large to offset the probability of coincidence.
2. The class of persons, events, or things about which the induction is made must be reasonably homogeneous.
3. The specific instances cited in support of the conclusion must be fair [representative] examples.
4. Careful investigation must disclose no [unexplained] exception.
5. The conclusion must be reasonable.[2]

Causal Relations

If we were to see a man accidentally shoot a live man and then see the victim fall dead with a bullet in his heart, we could say the *effect* was death and the *cause* the bullet or the man with the gun. Even this simple, observed, cause-to-effect relationship is full of problems. If the shooting were deliberate, would it in any way change the relationship? Let us sup-

---

[2] V. A. Ketcham, *The Theory and Practice of Argumentation and Debate* (New York: The Macmillan Company, 1924), p. 188.

pose you found a dead man (effect of something) with a bullet in his heart. Can we conclude absolutely that the bullet is the cause? This is reasoning from effect to cause, or *a posteriori*. The bullet is certainly a possible cause, even a probable cause, but as any Perry Mason fan knows, the man had been killed by arsenic poisoning and then shot after his death to hide the real cause!

One more—suppose a man dashes into your classroom, shoots a gun at your professor, and dashes out. Your professor falls to the floor and everyone runs out screaming. You observed the cause and concluded that the effect was murder or attempted murder.

Your car battery is weak, you observe that it is 10° below zero, and you come to the conclusion that your car is not going to start. This is Before the Fact, or *a priori* reasoning; the conclusion is based upon circumstances observed before the disputed fact (*cause to effect*).

If when you get up tomorrow morning you say, "It's 10° below zero; my car won't start; I'll be late for school," you are reasoning from *effect to effect*. Both your faltering battery and your tardiness (the thermometer reading too) are the effects of a common cause, low temperature.

In argument from effect to effect, you must first sort out the effect to cause and cause to effect elements and then apply the general requirements for arguments from causal relations. These requirements are as follows:

EFFECT TO CAUSE

1. The alleged cause must be sufficient to produce the effect.
2. No other cause must have intervened between the alleged cause and the effect.
3. The alleged cause must not have been prevented from operating.

CAUSE TO EFFECT

1. The observed cause must be sufficient to produce the alleged effect.
2. When past experience is involved, it must show that the alleged effect has always followed the observed cause.
3. No other force must intervene to prevent the observed cause from operating to produce the alleged effect.
4. The conclusion established should be verified by positive evidence wherever possible.[3]

Syllogistic Reasoning

A brief discussion of the forms and tests of syllogistic argument should help you evaluate your logical supports of persuasion before you present

---

[3] Ketcham, *The Theory and Practice of Argumentation and Debate,* p. 220.

them. Most student audiences, if not all audiences, have a person who argues that you are using only "negative premises," that neither of your premises is a "universal," that you have too many "terms," that you have an "undistributed middle term" and so on. Your listener may not use these terms or even have been exposed to training in formal logic, but this is technically what he is asking. Your answer to him, or better, your logical preparation should be consistent with the discussion of reasoning and argument that follows. Your role as a listener can also be sharpened by a careful reading of the following material.

The syllogism is a formal pattern of logic by which from two known or accepted statements (propositions) we can arrive at a third statement (conclusion) that must follow.

> In a syllogism, we so unite in thought two premises or propositions that we are enabled to draw from them or infer by means of the middle term they contain, a third proposition called the "conclusion."[4]

THE CATEGORICAL SYLLOGISM. When a syllogism involves two statements or premises that are accepted as absolute or universal, that is, needing no qualification, it is called a categorical syllogism. It begins typically with the word "all."

Premise 1: All birds have wings.

Premise 2: All ostriches are birds.

Conclusion: Therefore all ostriches have wings.

You can check your conclusion with simple geometry. Let one circle be "all birds," another be "wings." Because all birds have wings, but not all winged things are birds (insects, airplanes), let the first circle "all birds" be included completely within the circle "wings."

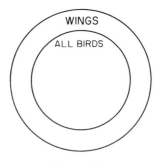

Figure 48

---

4 Lionel Crocker, *Argumentation and Debate* (New York: American Book Company, 1944), p. 114.

The third term, "ostrich," should be conceived as a still smaller circle, for while "all ostriches are birds," all birds (robin, sparrow) are not ostriches.

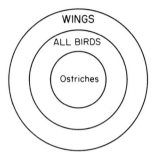

Figure 49

Because the circle "ostriches" is a part of and completely within the circle "wings," it follows that *"all ostriches have wings."* In this example, "wings" is the major term, "birds" the middle term, and "ostriches" the minor term.

The formal science of logic involves eight general rules, which govern every type of categorical syllogism. They are as follows:

1. Only three terms may appear in the syllogism. ("Birds"; "Wings"; "Ostriches."

2. Neither the major nor the minor term may be a universal in the conclusion if it was only a particular term in the premises. ("Ostriches" was universal [all].)

3. The middle term may not occur in the conclusion.

4. The middle term must be used at least once distributively in the premises. ("Birds" is in both premises.)

5. If both premises are affirmative, the conclusion must also be affirmative. (This is our case—affirmative.)

6. Both premises may not be negative; one at least must be affirmative. (Both of ours were affirmative.)

7. If one of the premises is negative, the conclusion must be negative. If one of the premises is a particular proposition, the conclusion must be a particular proposition. (Ours were both positive and both universal.)

8. No conclusion can be drawn from two particular premises; one at least must be a universal proposition. (Both of ours were universal—"all.") [5]

[5] Reprinted with permission of the Bruce Publishing Company from *The Science of Correct Thinking* by C. N. Bittle, O. F. M. Cap. © Copyright 1950 by The Bruce Publishing Company, pp. 187–88.

THE HYPOTHETICAL SYLLOGISM. A hypothetical syllogism has a hypothetical statement as a major premise. There are three types: "if" (conditional); "either-or" (disjunctive); "be and not be" (conjunctive).

The first type may be illustrated as follows:

> If an ostrich has wings, it is a bird;
> An ostrich has wings;
> Therefore, an ostrich is a bird.

> If it is A, then it is B;
> It is A;
> Therefore, it is B.

> If it is A, then it is B;
> It is not B;
> Therefore, it is not A.

The "either-or" or disjunctive type of syllogism appears as follows:

> This organism is either animal or vegetable;
> It is vegetable;
> Therefore, it is not animal.

> It is either A or B;
> It is A;
> Therefore, it is not B.

> It is either A or B;
> It is not A;
> Therefore, it is B.

The "be and not be" or conjunctive type of hypothetical syllogism appears
as follows:

> A man cannot be living and dead at the same time:
> But he is living:
> Therefore, he is not dead.

> He cannot have been in Detroit and Los Angeles at the same time:
> He was in Los Angeles;
> Therefore, he was not in Detroit.

THE ENTHYMEME. The enthymeme is a syllogism that is not presented
in the formal patterns illustrated above. The enthymeme may not have one
or more formally stated premises because: (1) the format would appear
artificial to the audience; (2) it was obvious; or (3) it was deemed more

persuasive to let the audience supply the missing premises. Many times the use of an enthymeme will involve more than one formal syllogism (that is, it is polysyllogistic). For example, take the following syllogisms:

> Actions which cause cancer are evil;
> Smoking is an action which causes cancer;
> Therefore, smoking is evil.

> That which is evil should be made illegal;
> Smoking is evil;
> Therefore, smoking should be made illegal.

The speaker might find it more expedient and more persuasive to use an enthymeme and say, "Any action that causes cancer is evil, and therefore smoking should be made illegal." He might also have used a more formal, abridged polysyllogism called *sorites*.

1. Smoking is an action which causes cancer;
2. Actions that cause cancer are evil;
3. Smoking is evil;
4. That which is evil should be made illegal;
5. Therefore, smoking should be made illegal.

It is useful for the listener to try to put enthymemes into more formal arrangement if he feels the speaker is either in error or in some other way suspect. Some enthymemes fall in place very easily. For example:

> Smoking causes cancer and should be outlawed.

> Any action which causes cancer should be outlawed; ⎫
> Smoking is an action which causes cancer;   ⎬ *not stated*
> Therefore, smoking should be outlawed.   ⎭

The rhetoric experts to this day argue about the exact definition and intended use of enthymemes that Aristotle himself had in mind. For our purpose, we can say that most enthymemes involve unstated premises. These premises may be unstated because of the conventions of our language, because they are considered self-evident, because they would appear artificial, or because the speaker deems it more persuasive to let the audience supply the missing or weakly supported premises. The last statement is of great rhetorical importance, for it suggests the necessity of adapting your logical support or proof to your audience. Particularly when the suppressed premises involve probability rather than universality, a speaker might find it more expedient to use an enthymeme. An enthymeme in the rhetorical sense, then, is effective only when the audience and speaker agree logically, for the audience must supply the predicted and hoped for missing premises.

A searching and definitive article by Professor Bitzer concluded that an enthymeme is an incomplete syllogism, but in a very special sense:

> The enthymene is a syllogism based on probabilities, signs, and examples, whose function is rhetorical persuasion. Its successful construction is accomplished through the joint efforts of speaker and audience, and this is its essential character.[6]

The Toulmin System

This is a system of logic devised by Stephen Toulmin,[7] which gets one from evidence to inference and avoids symbolic relationships seen in the syllogistic models previously discussed. For some, it may be easier to relate to everyday argument, and most importantly, it tries to avoid the "allness" problem often associated with formal syllogisms.

According to this model, we reason from a presumed, or at least stated, piece of evidence or fact (the *Data*) to a statement of an inferential nature (the *Claim*). The two are connected or made reasonable by a more general bridging statement. Toulmin calls these bridges *Warrants*. The last element is the *Qualifier,* which allows for exceptions, qualifications, or reservations. Toulmin symbolizes the relationship between the data and the claim in support of which they are produced by an arrow, and indicates the authority for taking the step from one to the other by writing the warrant below the arrow.

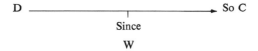

```
D ─────────────────────────────► So C
                 │
               Since
                 W
```

To allow for exceptions, special conditions, or qualifications Toulmin uses the symbol "Q" for such Qualifiers. "R" stands for rebuttal.

```
D ─────────────────────────────► So, Q, C
                 │                     │
               Since                 Unless
                 W                     R
```

    [6] L. F. Bitzer, "Aristotle's Enthymene Revisited," *Quarterly Journal of Speech,* XLV, No. 4 (December, 1959), 408.

    [7] S. Toulmin, *The Uses of Argument* (Cambridge, England: Cambridge University Press, 1958).

For example:

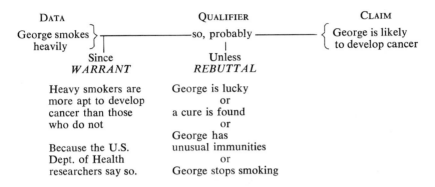

DATA	QUALIFIER	CLAIM

George smokes heavily — so, probably — George is likely to develop cancer

Since

WARRANT

Unless

REBUTTAL

Heavy smokers are more apt to develop cancer than those who do not

Because the U.S. Dept. of Health researchers say so.

George is lucky

or

a cure is found

or

George has unusual immunities

or

George stops smoking

This system stresses the reservations (qualifiers) and should suggest caution to both speakers and listeners in making claims. It also puts a priority on *warrants,* the explicit justification of the reasoning between Data and Claim. It puts new emphasis on the importance of material validity. It should be considered a supplement for syllogistic argument.[8]

Fallacies

Aristotle, in an appendix to his book *Topics,* called the *Sophistic Elenchi,* indicated a classification of fallacies, which is the springboard for all classification systems unto this day. He divided fallacies into two principal types: those in the language of the argument and those in the content or matter of the argument. Fallacies of language were discussed in Chapter 3. The fallacies of matter or (*extra dictionem*) beyond the language—are seven in number. Aristotle himself indicated the problem of his own system, so we may presume to rearrange his list and translate it in terms of the 20th century. For our purposes, we shall examine four basic types of fallacies, together with their respective subtypes. The basic four are *secundum quid* (overgeneralization), *non sequitur* (false cause), *petitio principii* (begging the question), and *ignoratio elenchi* (ignoring or ducking the issue). A *sophism* is a deliberate use of a fallacy for some expected argumentative gain. The intentional use of these devices is called *sophistical reasoning.*

---

8 Jimmie D. Trent, "Toulmin Model of an Argument: An Examination and Extension," *Quarterly Journal of Speech,* LIV, No. 3 (October, 1968), 252.

Secundum Quid

Snap judgments or generalizations based on insufficient evidence or experience belong here. We are not talking about language and the dangers of the word *all,* but rather the concept of *allness* itself. This fallacy results in going from the general case to a specific case, or vice versa. It is similar to the problems of induction and deduction.

It is in the exceptions to generally accepted rules that we often have the most trouble. We would all agree that it is wrong to kill a person. However, a specific application of the rule to a case of killing in self-defense is for most of us an exception. The same could be true of "alcohol is harmful" in many instances.

SAMPLING. A group of star high school football players were being oriented to a certain big ten university campus when they observed 12 of the most devastatingly chic females coming out of a campus building. To a man, the generalization was "Wow! What coeds this place has." The coach did not bother to tell them that these girls were all professional fashion models who had just come from a faculty wives' program. The luck of your sample, as well as its size or representativeness, should cause you to pause before generalizing. A rash of teenage delinquencies may cause some to conclude that all teenagers are juvenile delinquents.

The most insidious part of this fallacy is that it does start with facts. There *were* 12 posh females on a given campus; teenage delinquency *has been* recorded. It is our lack of objective analysis of our sample of experiences or things that gets us into trouble.

EXTRAPOLATION. Stuart Chase refers to this fallacy as the "thin entering wedge."[9] It is also known as the "camel's nose in the tent." It is a form of sampling trouble (as are all overgeneralizations) except that this one is particularly keyed to prediction and probability. The space scientist extrapolates or he does not predict at all. This is also true of the economist and the weatherman. The scientist typically knows the dangers of extrapolation even to the point of couching his predictions in terms of statistical confidence. Chase put it well: "You chart two or three points, draw a curve through them, and then extend it indefinitely!"[10] The scientist draws predictive curves only when he has located enough points to warrant qualified prediction. We are well advised to do the same.

---

[9] *Guides to Straight Thinking* (New York: Harper & Row, Publishers, 1956), p. 6. An excellent book to augment your reading on fallacies.

[10] Chase, *Guides to Straight Thinking,* p. 6.

Non Sequitur

This is the fallacy of assigning a wrong or false cause to a certain happening or effect. It also involves refutation with irrelevant arguments. Superstitions belong here. If you blow on the dice and win, was it the blowing that brought you luck? We still sell rabbits' feet, and most hotels still do not have a 13th floor.

POST HOC ERGO PROPTER HOC. This translates "after this, therefore because of this." The list of superstitions fits here, too, except that in our saner moments we are not really unaware of the fallacy. It is the more subtle type of chronology that hurts us. If a new city government comes into power after a particularly rough winter and is faced with badly damaged roads, it may indeed be easy to hold them responsible as you survey one ruined $30 tire. "We didn't have roads like this until after their election." After this, therefore because of this. The great Roman Empire fell after the introduction of Christianity—care to try that one?

TU QUOQUE. This fallacy translates "thou also" and consists of making a similar, but essentially irrelevant, attack upon one's accuser. A discussion between a Brazilian student and several Americans about Communist infiltration in Latin America became quite heated when suddenly the Brazilian said, "Communists? How about segregation in your country?" The retort was equally brilliant. "How about Nazis in Argentina?" A classic occurred in an army basic-training mess line. The mess corporal put a perfectly good salad right in the middle of a soldier's mashed potatoes. When told what a big ignoramus he was, he retorted in a most effective (if illogical) way, "Yeah, what about those poor guys in Viet Nam?"

CONSEQUENT. This fallacy simply involves the corruption of the inferential process applied to conditional syllogisms. The problem once again is with possible, partial, or even probable truths. If he lies, he will be expelled from school; he was expelled; therefore he lied. (He may have been expelled for poor grades.)

When we use a conditional syllogism and argue from the falsity of the antecedent to the falsity of the consequent or from the truth of the consequent to the truth of the antecedent, we are committing the fallacy of the consequent.

EITHER-OR. Certainly there are things that are either one way or another in this world. You are either living or dead; the lake is frozen or it is not. There is no such thing as a little bit pregnant. However, when a statement or problem with more than two possible solutions is put in a dichotomous either-or context, we have a fallacy. "The fight is either Jane's or Jim's fault." It may be neither's fault, or it may be the fault of both. There are shades of gray in most things. All too often we hear either-or arguments that only slow real solutions: science vs. religion; capitalism vs. socialism; suburbia vs. apartments, and so forth.

LOADED QUESTIONS. The vernacular is probably more clear than *plurium interrogationum* or "many questions." This device usually involves asking two questions as if they were one. It typically puts you in an awkward position no matter how you answer. In a speech, it may take the form of a great many questions, the combination of answers leading to fallacious reasoning. The answers typically sought are yes or no. The classic is, "Have you stopped beating your wife? Yes or no?" If you answer "no," you are a wife-beater. If you answer "yes," you have just admitted you used to beat your wife.

Petitio Principii

This fallacy is commonly called "begging the question," that is, to assume the truth or falsity of a statement without proof. A common form involves using two or more unproved propositions to establish the validity of each other. Other forms involve simple, unwarranted assumption or assertion.

CIRCULUS IN PROBANDO. This form of question begging is called "arguing in a circle." This is the classic example of using two or more unproved propositions to prove each other. Professional boxing should be outlawed for it is inhumane; we know it is inhumane because it is a practice that should be outlawed.

Take the course in Speech and Communication Theory at Northwestern University because it is the best in the country. Why is it the best in the country? Because it is taught at Northwestern University.

DIRECT ASSUMPTION. In this form of *petitio principii,* language may play a large role to help conceal bald assertions. It may be a plethora (excess of language) or just a word or two subtly inserted. In a discussion of big-time college football, an opposition speaker started with the words, "It is my purpose to show that buying professional players is not in the best interest of college football." This statement begged the whole proposition by assuming at the outset that colleges buy professional players. Unless the statement is proven, it remains an assertion.

Ignoratio Elenchi

This is ignoring the issue, or, in the vernacular, ducking the issue. It can be a subtle, insidious, and often a vicious process. It almost always involves using apparently pertinent, but objectively irrelevant arguments to cloud or duck the real issue or argument. There are several types of this fallacy, and each is worthy of a word of warning to the listener and to the naïve or unsophisticated speaker.

AD HOMINEM. When a speaker attacks the personal character of an opponent rather than the issue at hand, he is guilty of *ad hominem*. If intended, the purpose is to change the issue from an argument on the proposition (*ad rem*) to one of personalities. To argue the stage and screen ability of Frank Sinatra by referring to him as "that self-centered, woman-chasing louse" is a good example of *ad hominem*. His alleged stage and screen *ability* have no direct logical connection to his off-stage pursuits. This is not to say that every personal attack is unfair or illogical. If Mr. Sinatra were being evaluated on his public relations abilities, it might be a different matter.

AD POPULUM. This is an appeal to the people in terms of their preju-dices and passions. The symbols of motherhood, the flag, race and sin are typical cases. Vicious and often unsupported attacks have been carried on against liberal-minded Americans in the name of "un-Americanism." "Romanism" was tried again in the presidential campaign of 1960. Hope-fully, baldfaced *ad populum* appeals become less successful as the general population becomes better educated and more sophisticated.

AD VERECUNDIAM involves the appeal to authority and dignity. When the authority is legitimately connected to the subject, as Aristotle is to logic, we have no problem. However, if in our reverence of Aristotle we use him to oppose modern probability theory, we are guilty of *ad verecun-diam*. Joe Namath and Denny McLain are well paid experts in their highly specialized fields. They are probably not authorities on Laser theory or even canned beans or shaving cream. If you are impressed because Dr. Whosis says that alcohol causes cancer, find out if Whosis is an M.D. or an English professor! And check to see if McLain plays the organ.

AD IGNORANTIAM refers to appeals to ignorance—hiding one's weak arguments by overwhelming an audience with impressive materials or oratory in which they are untrained. A 12-cylinder vocabulary can screen many a specious argument. An improper use of statistics (or even a proper one) for people ignorant of the theory or numbers under consideration is a good example of *ad ignorantiam*. This is not to say that vocabulary and statistics are the problem. It is the adaptation to the audience in terms of the speaker's intent.

Summary

In this chapter, we were most concerned with the nature, source, and types of evidence and logical support.

Extrinsic proof deals with facts in the world about us or statements based upon facts, that is, self-evident, observable things. *Intrinsic* proof depends upon reasoned effort on our part, that is, the application of rhetoric and logic without which the proof would not emerge.

The types of most useful evidence discussed were authority, examples, and statistics.

Inductive and deductive proof are differentiated as follows. *Induction* is that process of reasoning by which we arrive at a conclusion or generalization through observing specific cases or instances. *Deduction* starts with a generally accepted law or principle and applies it to a particular case.

Causal reasoning involves cause to effect, effect to cause, and effect to effect. Requirements for legitimate argument from effect to cause and cause to effect are as follows: *Effect to Cause:* (1) alleged cause must be sufficient; (2) no other intervening cause; (3) alleged cause was not interfered with; *Cause to Effect:* (1) observed cause is sufficient to produce alleged effect; (2) alleged effect and observed cause are consistent with past experience; (3) no serious intervening force; (4) verification through positive evidence when possible.

The syllogism is a formal pattern of logic by which from two known or accepted statements we can arrive at a third statement that must follow. When a syllogism involves two statements or premises that are accepted as absolute or universal (needing no qualification), it is called categorical. A hypothetical syllogism has a hypothetical statement as a major premise; three types of hypothetical syllogism are: "if" (conditional), "either-or" (disjunctive), and "be and not be" (conjunctive).

The enthymeme is a syllogism that typically is not presented in a formal pattern; it may have one or more premises unstated. These premises may be unstated because of the conventions of our language, because they are considered self-evident, because they would appear artificial, or most importantly, because the speaker deems it more persuasive to let the audience supply the missing or weakly supported premises. The last statement is of great rhetorical importance, for it suggests the necessity of adapting your logical support or proof to your audience. An enthymeme in the rhetorical sense, then, is effective only when the audience and speaker agree logically, for the audience must supply the predicted and hoped for missing premises.

According to the Toulmin model, we reason from evidence or fact called the *data* to a statement of an inferential nature or *claim*. The two are bridged or related by a *warrant*, which justifies the reasoning between them. The *qualifier* allows for exceptions or reservations. The system attempts to avoid the "allness" problem associated with more formal syllogistic models.

There are four basic types of fallacies: (1) *secundum quid,* or overgeneralization; (2) *non sequitur,* or false cause; (3) *petitio principii,* or begging the question; and (4) *ignoratio elenchi,* or ducking the issue. Specific cases of the last are: *ad hominem,* attacking the personal character of an opponent rather than the issue; *ad populum,* an appeal to popular prejudices and passions; *ad verecundiam,* an unrelated appeal to authority and dignity; *ad ignorantiam,* appeals to or misuse of audience ignorance.

Audience
Participation
Situations **11**

Questions and Interruptions

One of the most elementary mistakes a speaker or panelist can make is to falsely assume that everyone in his audience has heard and understood a question asked of him. To listen to answers without knowing the question is the epitome of frustration for most listeners. In this chapter, you will learn about the situations, principles, and methods of meeting questions and interruptions. The problem of generating and controlling audience participation will also be discussed.

In a sense, every speech situation represents at least potential audience participation. Questions, comments, and objections from the audience may come at any time. You should always calculate the risk of being interrupted or even heckled. Some speakers seem to ask for trouble by pleading with the audience to interrupt for any reason whatsoever. Of course, there are situations when you do wish immediate audience participation, as with some discussion groups or small-group teaching situations. Although one should be democratic and audience-centered, the formal speaker also has an obligation to cover his subject and stay within his allotted time. Unreasonable questions and interruptions have ruined many an otherwise good speech and have shaken many an experienced speaker. The solution to the general problem is in the word *control*. The speaker has to stay in control of the communication situation. He must control the audience participation so as not to do injustice to either the *audience,* the *material* to be covered, or the *time* restrictions placed upon his speech.

202

Most business communication and training programs involve a great deal of audience participation. This is as it should be, for educational psychology teaches us that people learn faster and better when they have a feeling of participation and involvement. In training programs, particularly, the audience is typically invited to interrupt the speaker or teacher. If, however, the speaker chases after every question, relevant or not, he will soon be in serious trouble.

A well-known businessman came to an Institute of Industrial Relations training program as a guest instructor. He was an expert in his field, an above average speaker, and a genuinely nice person. He was given nearly two hours to cover his subject. After a ten-minute break, he was to be followed by another expert whose subject matter demanded that the class be exposed to the previous speaker's material. The situation was similar to an advanced course in algebra making more sense if the teacher in the first course covered *all* the preliminary material and did his job thoroughly. Our man pleaded sincerely for interruptions and *got* them—some good, some bad, some ridiculous, but he tried to react, answer, or comment on each equally. The result was that he was unfair to his audience collectively. The audience's evaluation of him reflected this fact. He finished only one-fourth of his material, and even this part was confused because of the virtual free-for-all participation. Imagine the problem faced by the next speaker!

Another situation in which you may find yourself is the more typical open forum after a speech. The problems indicated previously all apply here, but perhaps to a lesser degree. This is true because you have a much better control of your time and you have probably covered the points you set out to cover. Whatever time is left is controlled by simply cutting off the questions. Life can be miserable, however, when you are given three hours and have only one hour's material. It is just as bad when you have no time for a promised question period.

The third typical audience situation is the symposium forum. Any discussion situation obviously involves participation with the *other* members of the group. However, a symposium forum typically allows one-third of the total time for questions from the general audience. Many convention programs are run this way. The rules and problems once again are similar to the two situations previously discussed, except that often a decision must be made as to which participant should respond. The respondent must now consider both the audience and his fellow panel members. More will be said about discussional speaking in the next chapter.

General Principles

The *first* principle obviously ought to be, "Know your subject and audience." If you know your subject and audience, you are in a position to apply the *second* principle, "Second-guess the situation." Try to guess what areas of your subject are most vulnerable to questions and try to predict what questions this particular audience will ask. *Third,* "Sincerely try to answer or at least react to all questions." Consider and react courteously to even the irrelevant questions and attempt, if necessary, to clarify, delay, or postpone. The *fourth* principle, and one very easy to overlook in your eagerness to meet the question asked, is "Carefully consider the rest of the audience." You not only must try to satisfy the person asking the question, but the total audience as well. You might satisfy the statistician while thoroughly confusing everybody else. *Fifth,* "Do not feel or act as if you have to know everything or win every argument." Finally, *sixth,* "Attempt to encourage good questions and audience participation." It is very easy to discourage questions by even a slightly overbearing attitude (unless you are so overbearing that the audience decides to interrogate you).

People who assume leadership constantly have to be on guard not to intimidate others simply because of their position or rank. The colonel who follows the manual's advice and asks the cadets, "Are there any dumb questions?" is not apt to get many. But he knew that; that was why he said it! When such an attitude is *not* intended, it is even more tragic. A training director for a large corporation sincerely asked the trainees to comment on the meals during their three-week session. He had prefaced his request with some funny stories about the "idiot club," which had registered all kinds of silly complaints during the last session. Most of the complaints *were* silly and even funny. The training director did not mean to intimidate anyone. The trainees did think the anecdotes were funny; nevertheless, not a word was said about the meals. This lack of response, despite numerous private bitter complaints about the food and the preselected menus! The tragic part is that not only did the director fail to get accurate feedback information, but the lack of response was in itself taken as an indication of satisfaction. This is how you can be 100 percent wrong, but worse, this unfortunate lack of communication can be reinforced and may become habitual.

Rules for Answering Questions

Years ago at Purdue University, an audience of about 400 students were listening to a famous philosopher speak. He did a creditable job for a person who came from a school where speech was not in the catalogue. At the close of the speech, the chairman asked for questions from the audience. Most of the raised hands were in the first row, where the philosophy club had gathered. The speaker pointed to a hand in the first row, a mouth opened, and to those near the middle of the audience, the question sounded like this: "I should zzum ug ask hrump zud Hegel?" The speaker moved to the lectern, stroked his chin, and said, "A very good question." He then proceeded to give what I am sure was a very good answer. The problem was that most of the audience did not know the question because they had not *heard* it. The speaker handled three or four more questions in the same manner, the audience becoming frustrated, then restless, and finally in some cases rude as they started to leave.

Repeat the questions is the first rule. This is a good idea even with smaller audiences, for though they are in a position to hear, they may not be listening. Another serious aspect of this all-too-common error is that people will attempt to reconstruct what the question must have been in terms of the answer. You can immediately see the invitation to confused communication that this represents. Counter-questions based on inaccurately reconstructed questions can really raise confusion to a high level.

You may hear a question that is asked in a loud, clear voice, but the wording is awkward or ambiguous. A famous army general was giving a speech at the Ohio State University during the time of the Suez crisis. In the large audience were foreign students from all of the countries involved, including the United Arab Republic, France, England, and Israel. One of these took the general to task in perfectly clear and audible English, except that the question was long, complicated, and included a short preamble and peroration. The general said, "I know what you're getting at," and proceeded to answer for about ten minutes. As the general completed his answer, the foreign student leaped to his feet and proceeded to give another short speech, which said in effect, "But that's not what I asked." The general tried again for five minutes this time, still with no success. After one more unsuccessful attempt, a desperate general finally held up his hand and said, "Let's see if we can agree on what the question is." Sometimes it is necessary not only to repeat but also to *rephrase the questions*. Along with rephrasing, one should always gain the approval of the inquisitor or questioner. Some ways of checking the adequacy of your restatement of the question are to ask the questioner if your phrasing is a fair statement of the question, to look at the person and see if he is shaking his head yes or no, or to pause a moment and see if he objects verbally. You do not always have to rephrase questions; only do so when it is necessary for clarity, and then always seek approval.

Some of the long, complicated questions discussed above deserve careful attention if they are pertinent to the issue and if you are capable of giving some kind of answer or reaction in the time available. When, however, you receive questions which, long or short, are irrelevant, demand a highly technical or complex answer, or would consume all the open-forum time, you have a different kind of problem. Though in principle you do not want to avoid questions, you also owe it to the rest of your audience to stay on the subject and to give more than one person a chance to ask a question. Such a question can ruin an otherwise good speech. Let us therefore formulate our third rule: *Delay or postpone the irrelevant, overly technical, or time-consuming questions.* Postpone these questions until after the official open-forum period or until the end of the period if you have time remaining. In interrupted situations, this rule takes on even more complexity, for a person may ask a question that you had intended to cover later on in the speech. In this situation, you should most often delay the answer until you get to that point (for example, "Could I hold the answer to that for a few minutes? I will cover the issue a little later.") The problem is trying to remember the questions you may have delayed or postponed. One solution is to suggest that he ask the question again, but after you've covered the point at issue.

The loaded-question (see p. 198) is also a danger here. People will sometimes deliberately ask the "Are you still beating your wife?" kind of question, but far more difficult are the unintended, often naïve questions that are loaded. These are difficult to detect because they are often subtle and naïve at the same time and are frequently asked by people who are not troublemakers by reputation. "Why is it that textbook writers have such insatiable egos?" an author was once asked. If you are a writer, try to answer that without condemning yourself.

Rule four: *Label a loaded question.* There are several ways to do this if you are lucky enough to detect one in time. The most effective way is to pause long enough for the audience to label it for you. An audience is often quick to chuckle if they see the speaker faced with a "heads I win, tails you lose" situation. Or the speaker could forthrightly say, "That's a loaded question." A more tactful way might be, "It looks like I'm in trouble no matter how I answer this." Another method of labeling is to ask the questioner to please repeat his question. The audience will listen more closely and may label it for you, or the questioner may "unload" it. After you have successfully labeled or unloaded the question in as courteous a way as possible, you should then attempt to answer. With the proper labels, the audience is not apt to go too far astray in terms of your answers.

The surest way to get in trouble in an open-forum period is to try to bluff your way through a question for which you honestly do not have a good or satisfactory answer. Once an audience senses that you are bluffing, you can expect them to ask more questions specifically on this bluff point. The solution is to know your subject thoroughly—but if you do not have an answer, say so right away and save yourself the ignominy of being trapped later on. No speaker is expected to have all the answers to all the questions in the world. This rule might then be called simply, *"I don't know."*

A graduate student once learned the preceding advice the hard way. It was the occasion of his final oral examination. The committee of examining professors was seated in a circle, ready to fire questions for the next two hours. The very first question was a highly theoretical and complex one, which not even the members of the committee could adequately answer (if indeed it was answerable at all). The candidate, under great emotional pressure, felt that he simply had to answer the first question. He stumbled and fumbled for ten minutes, and a narrow-eyed committee then proceeded to ask ever increasingly specific questions on the same point. After another 20 minutes of torture, the candidate finally blurted out, "I guess I just don't know the answer." The rejoinder from the chairman of the examining committee is worthy of a piece of marble: "We didn't expect you to answer the question, but we expected you to *know when you didn't know*. It is a wise man who knows when and what he doesn't know." The candidate was summarily failed.

However, you cannot escape the hard facts of life by simply saying, "I don't know." In some question-answer situations, you may wish to say, "I don't know, but I have an opinion," or "I don't know, but I can answer in terms of my specialty." The point is that you should answer any question you are capable of answering and yet be honest enough to admit it when you cannot supply an answer.

Generating Participation

In the general principles discussed previously, the last suggestion was to encourage feedback and questions. The dangers of letting an audience run off with your speech were illustrated, as were the dangers of inadvertently intimidating an audience to the point of no participation.

Your general and total speech personality has much to do with the kind of communication climate in which you find yourself. In some cases, audiences just seem to spring into action. In other cases, even for very adept and audience-sensitive speakers, they must be given the proper stimulus for participation. Here are several speaker-originated techniques that might be useful to you.

The Overhead Question

This is a question directly from the speaker or discussion leader to the entire audience. If no questions arise from the audience (or even if they do), you might say, "Let me ask this question to get reaction from an intelligent Middle Western audience." The immediate problem is to make sure you choose a question that will cause a reaction, for if there is silence you may be worse off than before. Sometimes you can react to your own question in such a way as to promote participation. Carefully consider the wording of a few general overhead questions and expected reactions as a method of fostering participation.

The Direct Question

This technique involves choosing a specific member of the audience and directly asking him a question. This is often very effective if the individual listener is known to the rest of the audience or is in some special way qualified to answer. The size of your audience presents a problem insofar as the audience may have difficulty seeing or otherwise determining who has been singled out. Classroom-size audiences or larger groups, if they meet regularly, respond well to this technique. You probably know many good teachers who make excellent use of the direct-question technique. Social and civic groups such as the Lions, Elks, Kiwanis, Knights of Columbus, and Rotary, where the membership knows one another, often make good use of direct questions.

Try not to call on the same person all the time, but do pick those who are most apt to get participation started. Try to tailor the question directly to the individual chosen. The question should be relatively short and clear and should avoid a simple yes or no answer—but if the situation is really desperate, you may have to settle for yes or no.

The Redirected Question

This technique may also be referred to as the reverse or relay method. However, there are some simple differences. In the reverse technique, you simply redirect the question to the person who asked it. "That's a very good question—how would you answer it?" In the relay method, you redirect it to some other person. "A good question; let's see how Mr. Wright would answer it." You might, of course, overhead the question to the whole audience.

There are some guideposts that are useful. As a general rule, do not redirect a question unless you yourself know some partial answer to it, except a simple question of fact upon which you can freely admit ignorance. The story of the beginning teacher who redirected a tough question (to which she did not have the answer) to each individual of the class, only to find that it came right back to embarrass her, is not entirely contrived. A second suggestion is to not redirect so freely that you lose control of the situation.

Priming the Pump

This is the overriding technique of building questions into the speech. When preparing your speech, consider the problems of meeting questions and interruptions during the presentation, not just during an open-forum period. In the main, your questions or implied questions should seek to develop your point, to stimulate thinking, or generally to obtain interest and attention.

Summary

One of the most elementary mistakes a speaker can make is to assume that everyone has heard and understood a question asked of him. To listen to answers without knowing the question is the epitome of frustration. Every speech represents potential audience participation, typically in the form of questions, comments, or objections. You should calculate this as part of the risk. Unreasonable questions and interruptions have ruined some speeches. The speaker has to control the audience participation so as not to do injustice to the audience, the material to be covered, or the time restrictions. The typical audience-participation situations involve open forums, symposium forums, instructing situations, and group discussion before an audience.

Some general principles explained were: (1) know your subject and audience; (2) second-guess the situation; (3) do not begrudgingly grant opposing arguments; (4) answer the question; (5) consider the total audience; (6) generally encourage questions.

Specific rules for answering questions are as follows: (1) repeat the questions; (2) when necessary, rephrase the questions; (3) delay or postpone irrelevant or overly complicated questions; (4) label loaded questions; (5) don't bluff, say "I don't know."

To help generate participation, you may use the *overhead technique*—a question from the speaker directed to the total audience. You may use the *direct question* by directly questioning a specific member of the audience. You may also use the *redirect* technique, which involves reversing or relaying the question. In the reverse technique, you redirect the question to the person who asked it; in the relay, you redirect it to some other person. You are also counseled to *prime the pump;* build questions into the formal part of your speech.

In the participation part of your speech, try not to call on the same person all the time; try to tailor the questions directly to the audience or individuals chosen; keep your overhead or direct questions short, clear and, free of yes-or-no answers. In the main, your questions or implied questions should develop your point, stimulate thinking, and generally obtain attention and interest.

Discussion:
Cooperative
Communication **12**

The Nature of Discussion

This chapter is primarily concerned with systematic, cooperative decision-making in small group discussions. The term discussion is derived from the Latin *discussus,* to strike asunder; that is, to pull it apart, to separate and subordinate the elements and ideas that make up a question or topic. Discussion is not to be confused with debate. Debate is two-sided, discussion many-sided. Debate is competitive, discussion is cooperative. If decision is impossible through discussion, it may very well lead to debate. Debate may then lead to resolution. If not, one might very possibly return to discussion. Premature or unnecessary debate has hung up many group discussions. The nature of a discussion-debate continuum is illustrated by Gulley:[1]

Problem	Definition	Analysis	Suggested Alternatives	Weighing of Alternatives	(Decision Impossible)	Advocacy on Alternatives	(Possible Return to Discussion)	(Possible Vote)	Decision
		DISCUSSION				DEBATE			

---

[1] Halbert Gulley, *Discussion, Conference, and Group Process,* 2nd. ed. (New York: Holt, Rinehart and Winston, Inc., 1968), p. 139.

In terms of the communication theory discussed in Chapter 1, the unique aspect of discussion is that a participant is both sender-receiver and encoder-decoder at the same time—a truly dynamic, interactive, interpersonal communication situation. Feedback and perception take on even greater significance.

Discussion Defined

The experts are in basic agreement about what we mean by group discussion.

Discussion is the process whereby two or more people exchange information or ideas in a face-to-face situation.[2]
. . . they (discussion groups) consist of a number of persons who perceive each other as participants in a common activity, who interact dynamically with one another, and who communicate their responses chiefly through words.[3]
. . . discussion occurs when a group of persons asssemble in a face-to-face situation and through oral interaction exchange information or attempt to reach a decision on shared problems.[4]
. . . an orderly process of cooperative deliberation designed to exchange, evaluate, and/or integrate knowledge and opinion on a given subject or to work toward solution of a common problem.[5]
. . . a number of persons who communicate with one another over a span of time, and who are few enough so that each person is able to communicate with all others, not at secondhand, through other people, but face-to-face.[6]

Hedde and Brigance put it well years ago when they said:

Discussion, then, is a means of thinking together through purposeful conversation.[7]

Assuming then that we have a real, interacting, face-to-face group—that is, persons with some common goal, not just a loose collection of indi-

---

[2] R. Victor Harnack and Thorrel B. Fest, *Group Discussion Theory and Technique* (New York: Appleton-Century-Crofts, 1964), p. 21.

[3] Dean C. Barnlund and Franklyn S. Haiman, *The Dynamics of Discussion* (Boston: Houghton Mifflin Company, 1960), p. 20.

[4] Gulley, *Discussion, Conference and Group Process,* 2nd. ed., p. 5.

[5] Horace Rahskopf, *Basic Speech Improvement* (New York: Harper & Row, Publishers, 1965), p. 348.

[6] G. C. Homans, *The Human Group* (New York: Harcourt, Brace & World, 1950), p. 1.

[7] Wilhelmina G. Hedde and William N. Brigance, *American Speech* (Philadelphia: J. B. Lippincott Co., 1942), p. 40.

viduals, we might synthesize the above by saying that at its best *group discussion is systematic, cooperative, reflective thinking and communication.*

Contemporary Forms of Discussion

The word *form* refers to the type or format of discussion. In its most general sense, group discussion refers to a cooperative thinking endeavor typically among 20 people or less. The basic forms are *dialogue, panel* and *symposium.* Three techniques which may be used in combination with any of the forms include *buzz group, role playing* and *brainstorming.* A *forum* is simply that part of a discussion in which the audience may speak. It could be and often is applied to any of the discussion forms.[8]

A *dialogue* is a two-person discussion which may involve simple conversation, an interview or counseling. If a dialogue is held before an audience and the audience is invited to participate, it becomes a dialogue-forum.

The *panel* discussion is typically composed of 3 to 7 people pursuing a common goal in an informal climate which facilitates spontaneous interaction. An audience may or may not be present. It typically calls for a procedural leader and some agenda.

A *symposium* is a small group (typically 3 to 5) with special knowledge about differing aspects of a broad topic who make individual, uninterrupted speeches before an audience. A procedural leader controls speaker order and time limitation. A forum usually follows except where an audience is not physically present (radio-TV). Frequently the symposium speakers then relate to one another more informally in a panel discussion.

Discussion forms may be used for information sharing, problem solving or decision making, as well as for instructional purposes.

Examples of information sharing groups might include *staff meetings, study groups,* and *workshops.* Overlap is evident and probably unavoidable. A workshop, for example, may be thought of as a study group which has been consolidated into a couple of days or even a few concentrated hours.

Examples of problem solving groups include *committees, conferences,* and governing *boards* or *councils.* These are discussion groups which either have the power of decision or at least the power to strongly recommend action based on their collective problem solving. They are typically closed group discussions.

[8] See especially *Michigan Speech Association Curriculum Guide 3, Discussion and Argumentation-Debate in the Secondary School,* Kenneth G. Hance, ed., (Skokie, Illinois: National Textbook Corporation), 1968.

A *case conference* is simply a discussion about a real or contrived critical incident which hopefully leads to a learning outcome for the participants. It may or may not be conducted with an audience present. It can be evaluated in terms of participant interaction, leadership, agenda setting, and the solution itself.

In large groups where wider forum participation may be desired, the audience may be divided into subgroups of 4 to 6 people to allow more intimate, informal discussion. This technique is known as *buzz*, "Phillips 66" or "Discussion 66." It refers typically to subgroups of 6, which discuss a carefully worded question.[9] The results of these individual buzz sessions are reported to the larger group by a spokesman. The anonymity of the people in the subgroups seems to be an important factor. A person is more apt to speak up in a group of 6 than 600.

If in a group, typically a case conference, roles or dramatic parts are assigned and acted out extemporaneously, it becomes the technique of *role playing* or what Hirschfeld has described as *extemporaction* ". . . a technique that adds experiential kinesthetic and emotional factors to the intellectual learning process."[10] In the Hirschfeld technique, considerably more instructor planning and participation are involved. As a technique, role playing is often a good prelude to the other forms of discussion.

A unique technique that some speech communication instructors use to show the effect of eliminating premature and discussion-inhibiting comments of an arbitrary or critical nature is *brainstorming*. In this technique, an arbitrary, psychological climate complete with penalties is prescribed, which in effect prohibits immediate criticism of ideas. This typically permits more creative ideas to come to light in a short period of time than in the more traditional climate.[11] This technique can also be combined with other forms and used for varied purposes other than instruction. It can be particularly useful when a great many ideas are wanted from a group in a short period of time. It is a good technique for screening attitudes and opinions. For example: "What should this class use as a topic for a project discussion?" This question under brainstorming rules regularly produces 60 or 70 topics in 10 minutes. No evaluative discussion of the topics is allowed until later. Buzz groups are a good follow-up to screen the list more systematically.

---

[9] J. Donald Phillips, "Report on Discussion," *Adult Education Journal,* Vol. VII (October, 1948), pp. 181–82.

[10] From material supplied by Adeline Hirschfeld, director of P.A.C.E. project, "Creative and Sociodramatic Supplementary Educational and Cultural Enrichment Service," Title III, E.S.E.A., Oakland University, Rochester, Michigan, 1967.

[11] Alex F. Osborn, *Applied Imagination: Principles and Procedures of Creative Thinking* (New York: Charles Scribner's Sons, 1953).

Agendas

If group discussion is *systematic, cooperative, reflective thinking and communication,* then we had better explore reflective thinking in detail and see what kind of system or scheme it suggests for orderly agendas or discussion outlines. That orderliness pays off in terms of consensus or agreement is shown in a study of 72 conferences by Collins and Guetzkow. They report "Those meetings in which discussion is orderly in its treatment of topics, and without backward references to previously discussed issues, tended to end in more consensus. . . . When participants discussed but one issue at a time, instead of simultaneously dabbing in two or three, it was more possible for the group to reach consensus."[12]

Reflective Thinking Process

Reflective thinking according to John Dewey is defined as, "active, persistent and careful consideration of any belief or supposed form of knowledge in the light of the grounds that support it, and further conclusions to which it tends," as opposed to nondeliberate, everyday thinking. Dewey thought of reflective thinking as scientific habit, which consisted of acquiring the attitude of *suspended judgment,* and a mastery of the various methods of searching for materials. Maintaining an intelligent state of doubt and systematic inquiry are the essentials of reflective thinking.

Dewey's point of view about general education is also pertinent to group discussion both in terms of agendas and the way you conduct yourself. He thought of the aim of education as the establishment of a kind of *self-discipline* in students. This self-discipline was thought of in terms of *systematic observation, thorough examining,* and most importantly for us, in terms of agendas, *methodical arrangement of thought.* There are five steps in the Dewey system, which are interpreted below.[13]

1. The occurrence or awareness of a *felt difficulty.* You know something is wrong, unexpected, unidentified. You experience a state of disequilibrium.

---

[12] Barry E. Collins and Harold Guetzkow, *A Social Psychology of Group Processes for Decision-Making* (New York: John Wiley & Sons, 1964), p. 111.

[13] John Dewey, *How We Think* (Boston: D. C. Heath & Company, 1910), pp. 68–78.

2. The *definition* of the felt difficulty to see what kind or nature of problem you have, and how serious it is. Look carefully, don't misdefine. Suspend assiduously your judgment regarding solutions.

3. The formulation of alternate suggestions, explanations and, hypotheses as *possible solutions.* Inference and analysis takes place here. (Review Chapters 1 & 10).

4. The rational elaboration of the possible solutions gathering facts, evidence, inference. Further analysis of the consequences of alternative solutions.

5. Further testing, rejecting, or corroborating of the solution chosen in Step 4—by observation, measurement, hypothetical case or model building, or actual experiment if applicable. You now have a reasoned solution in your thoughts.

Agenda Systems

It is obvious that the reflective thinking system just discussed, while addressed to an individual, would make just as much sense for a group of individuals solving a problem or making decisions. More recent research tends to support the Dewey stages or phases. Bales and Strodtbeck divided problem-solving discussions into three periods in terms of the number of interactions. They found that in the first period or phase the communications pertained primarily to *orientation, information, repetition,* and *confirmation.* In the second phase, the interactions involved primarily *analysis, evaluation,* and *communications* seeking or giving *opinions* and *feelings.* In phase three, they found that acts of *control* predominated; that is, communications involving possible directions and ways of action.[14]

The researchers also indicate that as a group approaches the third phase they experience increasing strains on their solidarity and social-emotional relationships. Both positive and negative reactions tend to increase. Tension reduction is apparent as differences are resolved and agreement reached.

The danger of oversimplifying so complicated a process is made clear by the research of Scheidel and Crowell who suggest that the reflective-thinking steps as an agenda system is not a simple linear progression after all, but rather a circular or spiraling course.[15] After studying idea development in ten discussions, they indicate that members spend one-fourth of their comments confirming statements, and another fourth clarifying and

---

[14] Robert F. Bales and Fred L. Strodtbeck, *Phases in Group Problem-Solving,* in Darwin Cortwright and Alvin Zander, *Group Dynamics: Research and Theory* (New York: Harper & Row, Publishers, 1960), pp. 624–38.

[15] Thomas M. Scheidel and Laura Crowell, "Idea Development in Small Discussion Groups," *Quarterly Journal of Speech,* 50 (1964), pp. 140–45.

substantiating. The latter is the outward movement of this spiral model. Its progress towards decision is the onward movement.

The better agenda systems found in the literature are those derived from the findings of research coupled with creative insight. Some excellent examples follow.

Two Phase Agenda

I. The Analysis Phase
    A. Definitions: What does the question mean?
    B. Limitations, if any: What part of the problem do we intend to concentrate on if we cannot discuss the whole problem now?
    C. What are the important facts about this problem?
        1. What is its history?
        2. What are its causes?
        3. What has happened; is happening?
        4. What has happened elsewhere that illuminates the problem under discussion?
II. The Solution Phase
    A. What are the advantages and disadvantages of each alternative course of action?
    B. By what or whose standards must any decision be evaluated?
    C. What decision should we reach?[16]

Six Step Agenda

  I. Ventilation (general establishment of rapport)
 II. Clarification (phrasing the question)
III. Fact-Finding
IV. Discovery (finding hypotheses or solutions)
 V. Evaluation (of proposed solution)
VI. Decision Making (verbal formulation of conclusion)[17]

Six Step Agenda

Problem	1. Problem Formulation
Description	2. Problem Analysis
Phase	3. Problem Reformation (if necessary)
Problem	4. Solution Proposal
Solution	5. Solution Testing
Phase	6. Action Testing[18]

---

[16] Gulley, *Discussion, Conference, and Group Process*, pp. 215–16.

[17] Barnlund and Haiman, *The Dynamics of Discussion*, pp. 86–97. (Parenthesis are this author's.)

[18] Harnack and Fest, *Group Discussion Theory and Technique*, pp. 64–68.

Ross Four Step Agenda

I. *Definition and limitation*—a concise, but qualified statement of the felt difficulty, problem, or goal
II. *Analysis*—The determination of the type or nature of the problem, and its causes.
    a. Puzzles—questions of fact
    b. Probabilities—reasonable predictions—chance
    c. Values—beliefs, attitudes
III. *Establish Criteria*—A group consensus on the standards to be used in judging solutions.
    a. Minimum and/or maximum limits
    b. A rating of hierarchical importance
IV. *Solutions*
    a. Evaluation in terms of the criteria
    b. Decision and suggested implementation or action

A visual aid or chart depicting the agenda may prove helpful to participants.[19]

Agenda System Elaborations

Using the Ross four step system as a point of reference, but with the understanding that what is said here will apply, for the most part to all the possible agenda systems shown, let us look to some of the finer points.

1. THE DEFINITION STEP. In most problem-solving discussions, the suggestion to take stock of the felt difficulty, to ventilate about it, is pertinent. It helps take emotional heat, if any, off the topic; it gives a quick audit of feelings. (For example, there may be more than one felt difficulty in the group.) It helps the group formulate the problem and determine goals.

The first major content aspect is *definition* of the problem, and where pertinent, *limitation* of the problem in terms of agenda. (For example, are we talking about unemployment in Chicago, in Illinois, in the U.S.?) If a group has several different definitions of a problem, and worse yet, isn't aware of the differences, confusion and irritation can be predicted. Discussion time is well spent on the definition aspect. Agree on the problem and/or goal *before* you move on.

In some cases a thorough discussion of the problem may make the solution obvious or known from previous identical situations (for example,

---

[19] John K. Brilhart, "An Experimental Comparison of Three Techniques for Communicating a Problem-Solving Pattern to Members of a Discussion Group," *Speech Monographs,* XXXIII, No. 2 (June, 1966), 176.

POSSIBLE AGENDA SYSTEMS

Dewey	Gulley	Barnlund-Haimen	Harnack-Fest	Ross
1. Felt Difficulty	Definition (ANALYSIS)	Ventilation	Problem Formulation (DESCRIPTION)	Definition & Limitation — Felt difficulty, Problem, Goal
2. Definition	Limitation	Clarification	Problem Analysis	
	Important Facts	Fact Finding	Problem Reformation	Analysis—Nature of Problem — Puzzle, Probability, Value
3. Possible Solutions	Alternate Courses of Action (SOLUTION)	Discovery	Solution Proposal (SOLUTION)	Establish Criteria — Limits, Hierarchical importance
4. Rational Elaboration	Standards	Evaluation	Solution Testing	
5. Further Testing	Decision	Decision	Action Testing	Solutions — Evaluation against criteria, Decision

219

medical diagnosis). Most often, however, a group is now ready to *analyze* systematically its agreed upon problem. Agenda suggestions range from fact-finding and problem restatement to a systematic determination of the essential *nature* of the problem. *Nature* is typically divided into problems of *Fact, Policy, Value,* or in the Ross system, *Puzzle, Probability, Value.* In the former division *Fact* appears obvious. Can it be empirically verified to the satisfaction of group members? One cantankerous professor claims he never has heard a good definition of a fact. For the most part, facts are actions, events, or conditions, which have been properly observed, described, classified, and reported. A question of *Policy* is somewhat easier to explain as being concerned with the feasibility, or desirability of a future course of action. Of course facts will probably be a part of this kind of deliberation also. Questions of *Value* are primarily concerned with judgments about attitudes, beliefs, feelings, very often those things most difficult to quantify. More will be said about value later.

2. THE ANALYSIS STEP. a. *Puzzles.* In the division under nature of the problem, the *Puzzle* dimension refers to questions of *Fact* previously discussed, but more than that, it is easier to apply, if less comprehensive. As an illustration, consider a common jigsaw puzzle. No one would argue that they cannot be difficult or frustrating (or amenable to group effort). Yet there is definitely a solution—there is really only one best solution—and best yet, the solution is recognizable when you achieve it. It *is* the *canals* of Venice! An early detection and agreement on a problem as puzzle can save much time and aggravation. If someone viewed our jigsaw puzzle as a question of value, perhaps a threat to his intelligence, then we have a compounded problem. In any event, it will probably slow the solution (getting the puzzle together).

Some puzzles are complicated. Thus, we use computers to solve engineering problems, and adding machines and cash registers in supermarkets. But they are still puzzles and one is well advised not to get his emotions, his morals, his complete value system involved too quickly.

b. *Probability.* The *probability* dimension refers to common sense reduced to calculation. The suggestion here is that certain problems are of the nature of a probability calculation. They are then theoretically amenable to probability theory or the laws of chance. While the very nature of the word probability indicates that such a problem may never be known with certainty, the mathematical chance or probability itself may often be treated as an operational fact. A gambler can predict his odds with relative certainty. He knows that he has a 50 percent chance of getting a head in flipping a coin. However, even in simple games, determining probability figures can quickly become complicated. If your point is 5 in a dice game (two dice), you have only 4 possible combinations: 1–4; 4–1; 3–2; 2–3. Since theoretical probabilities are multiplied (two 6-sided dice give 6×6 or

36 possible combinations) the odds are 4/36 or 1/9. The 6 combinations yielding the number 7 have a probability of 6/36 or 1/6. The number of rolls is of course a significant variable. The larger the number of rolls, in general, the greater the likelihood of the theoretical probability occurring. All probability and prediction problems are not so theoretically absolute. An insurance company never knows exactly how many accidents, deaths, fires, and so on, will occur among its policy holders, but can make quite accurate predictions on the basis of past experiences. This science of probability prediction is called statistics. From statistics we not only learn to ask "what caused the difference," but also how to test whether a change or difference is merely a random variation or indicates some known or unknown factor at work. There are significance tests that make it possible to express the difference on variations mathematically. This expression or number may be interpreted as an indicator of the "level of confidence" we may justifiably have in the data, or our chances of being wrong. Every discussant need not be a statistician, but he should be aware of the nature of probability type problems and also the role that theory can play in making decisions about problems involving large masses of data.

c. *Values.* The *value* dimension concerns desirability rather than probability or inevitability.

Ethical value structures held by group members are commonly considered as deriving from their past experiences. It is in this light that questions of *ethical* value must, in part, be evaluated.

A person's general value system is determined by his past experiences; his understanding and acceptance of the concept of law as natural, universal, and/or pragmatical; and his personal idea of the various continua from good to bad, pleasure to pain, noble to ignoble, loyal to disloyal, as well as a multitude of minor preferences that often defy any search for principle (for example, food, color, architecture, and so on). With knowledge of the categories indicated above, it is often possible to make fairly reliable, nonnumerical predictions and analyses regarding questions of value.

To the extent that preferences and attitudes may be referred to as values, the problem is slightly less ambiguous. It is possible to determine attitudes (a form of preference) in a quantified way about many things, from the size of next year's cars to the latest high fashion innovations. Differences in attitudes toward a given subject can, in fact, be measured fairly accurately through the use of standard statistical techniques described previously.

Knowledge of preferences (of others) pertinent to the group decision in which you are involved affords you predictive insight of a relatively uncomplicated nature. Some value theorists speak of a "rational-preference-ranking,"[20] which is a way of selecting the preferred or most valued alternative. Comparative preferences on like or similar things have been found to be measurable and meaningful. However, the measurement of comparative and/or cumulative preferences for dissimilar things is less amenable to reliable measurement. An "other things being equal" preference for the color red and another similar preference for Cadillacs does not necessarily add up to a preference for red Cadillacs. The further question of whether a person likes the color red better than he likes Cadillacs, and to what extent, points up a quantification problem that has been a long-time bone of contention among social science philosophers.

While the *value* dimension of analysis is the part most resistant to numerical quantification and measurement, this does not mean we should not try to quantify, to objectify, and to search for systematic analysis. It does mean that we must know our own intelligently derived values and how they may be applied to the group analysis of a specific problem. It also means that we must make every effort to ascertain differences in preferences and values among the people in our group and also those who may be affected by this group's decision. This kind of analysis should lead to better and more prudent group decisions regarding questions of *value*.

3. THE CRITERIA STEP. Whether one thinks of this step as really a continuation of analysis or the beginning of the solution phase is of no great import. It is, however, an important enough agenda item to warrant your close attention. *A criterion is a standard or yardstick by which we may measure or evaluate something.* In the case of group discussion, it refers to an *agreed upon* standard. If a group has reasonably clear and agreed upon criteria in mind, the evaluation or testing of suggested solutions is a lot easier or at least more systematic. If a group were discussing the problem of a club house for their organization, they would want to clearly establish such criteria as *cost, size, location, new or old,* and so on. The concept of *limits* can help a group at this point. If we are talking about cost in terms of $100,000, what do we really mean? Is that the top *limit* or the bottom? If the group really meant $75,000 to $110,000, it should so state it, at least to itself. The same could be said for size and location. Criteria can also be negative. The group could, for example, name locations that it would not consider under any conditions.

The concept of *weighting* your criteria in terms of importance should also be considered. If size is the single most important criterion, then get group agreement, that is, the old club house is crowded and unless the next place is x-amount larger, however beautiful a bargain, it won't solve the problem. If location is next most important (that is, close to where the members live), and then cost, parking, architecture, and so on, you have

---

[20] Donald Davidson, J. C. C. McKinsey, and Patrick Suppes, "Outlines of a Formal Theory of Value," *Philosophy of Science,* XXII (1955), p. 140.

the beginnings of a sub-agenda for evaluating solutions. Your list of criteria then should appear in some kind of rank or weighted order in terms of importance. *Weighting* may be profitably considered by a group if some of the criteria are close together in importance. Assuming a 100 point weighting scale, and the decision that both size and location are very, very important, the group might assign size 90 points, location 80 points, cost 50 points, architecture 20 points, and so on, along with specific upper and lower limits for each. Such a scale gives the group considerably more insight into the distance between its ranked criteria. It further gives you a more logical, systematic approach to the solution step.

4. THE SOLUTION STEP. To continue the illustration of the clubhouse under the criteria step, the group may now consider solutions that individuals may offer. If David W. offers pictures and real estate data on a building he's found, but a matching against the criterion of size indicates it does not meet the lower criterion (and no plan for enlargement is provided by the contributor), then the group is quickly and systematically ready to go on to the next possible solution. It is possible that a group may come up with several solutions that meet the major criteria and the discussion may now focus on the less heavily weighted criteria. This is good trouble and the group is aware of it. Without criteria to go by, the group might engage in lengthy argument about lesser aspects of a problem, and irony of ironies, spend little time on the major aspects none of which may have met the most elementary of unstated criteria.

You may wish to evaluate and discuss your alternative solutions further in terms of the puzzle, probability, value, analysis suggested. You may wish some additional firsthand observation or action testing, but the group is ready for *decision*.

5. AGENDA AND PROCESS. The problem-solving, normal thinking, or decision process being recommended as a basis for agenda building should not be construed as a totally linear function in which each step is equally long and/or independent. Groups often find it necessary to overlap or back up as new insight or information comes to light. A spiral model was discussed previously, which indicates that while a group is moving toward a solution, it is following a circular course in which members spend one-fourth of their comments confirming statements already made and another fourth clarifying and substantiating.

It is then the nature of process as explained in Chapter 1 not to suddenly freeze or hold still, but rather to be a moving, dynamic phenomenon. Stated agendas have a way of becoming much more static and should be worked out carefully with full consideration of the nature of process.

The same qualifications should be applied to your consideration of the nature of problems as puzzle, probability, and value. No problem is typically 100 percent puzzle; most problems have all three dimensions present. The suggestion is that for most cases after a group has determined the nature of a problem, it is well advised to take up the less controversial, puzzle dimension first and the value dimension last. There are exceptions, and this in no way suggests that values are less important than puzzles or probabilities. A person's communication behavior in a group is often qualitatively as well as quantitatively different when he feels his value system is in constant jeopardy.

Discussion Leadership

In general, *leadership* should be thought of as any significant action by any discussant that has influence on group achievement.[21] We may have an assigned or appointed group *leader* whose duties or behavior may range from a modest regulation of participation to near domination and control. It is possible then to be in a *leaderless* group (no appointed leader) and still have considerable *leadership,* should it emerge from the group. By the same token, one could be in a group with a poor assigned *leader,* and, none emerging, have really no *leadership.* The distinction, therefore, between *leader* and *leadership* and *leaderless* and *leadershipless* is a critical one. All group members have a stake and often a role in *leadership.* Thus, what follows applies to all group discussants whether they happen to be assigned group leader, chairman, moderator, or whatever.

Sources of Leadership

Leadership *may* accrue to a person in a group because he was appointed the moderator. It *may* accrue to a person if only on given issues because he happens to be the best informed. It *may* befall a person by reason of his role or status in the group. (For example, he happens to be the boss, a full professor, and so on.) It may also befall a person, particularly in leaderless groups, who happens to perform vital group functions and procedures exceptionally well. He knows about agendas, reflective thinking, democratic leadership, the communication process, and human relations.

Functions of Leadership

Leadership, whatever its source (and all group members have responsibility here) should in general help a group move towards its goal or

---

[21] See especially, Dean C. Barnlund and Franklyn S. Haiman, *The Dynamics of Discussion,* Chap. 13; and Halbert Gulley, *Discussion, Conference and Group Process,* 2nd ed., Chap. 10.

purpose, or help it locate its goals. Leadership should also promote a healthy, democratic communication climate within the group. The major functions of leadership then are related to *goal achievement* (content) and *interpersonal relations* (communication climate).

Aspects of leadership related to *goal achievement* or content include such things as contributing and evaluating ideas, locating issues and consensus, synthesizing and cross-relating the ideas of others, and generally seeking specific content contributions.

Aspects of leadership related to *interpersonal relations* include such things as controlling emotions, setting communication and psychological climate, resolving conflict, regulating the over and under talkative, and generally promoting those actions concerned with the social dimension.

Leadership, particularly where assigned or designated, must also attend to the more specific *procedural* functions such as starting the meeting, agenda making and/or following, clarifying, summarizing, and ending the meeting. Procedural functions may also include advanced planning and the physical arrangements. The procedural leader must review the purposes of the meeting. He should consider the members individually and decide the degree of formality necessary and the specific way he wishes to open or start the discussion. He should consider group goals in terms of the time available. The agenda should be agreed upon by the members unless already prescribed.

The procedural leader is also responsible for participation, that is, preserving order, seeing that only one person speaks at a time, and fairly distributing the right to speak. He may find it necessary to clarify what has been said on occasion, as well as remind the group of the agreed upon agenda.

Styles of Leadership

Style refers in part to method and in part to philosophy. Some styles of leadership are variously described as laissez-faire, non directive, permissive, democratic, supervisory, authoritarian, and autocratic. The above are ordered on a kind of control continuum from "none" to "much."

STYLES OF LEADERSHIP

Laissez-faire	Non-directive	Permissive	Democratic	Supervisory	Authoritarian	Autocratic
1	2	3	4	5	6	7
No Control			Optimum Control			Much Control

As with most things, virtue is near the middle. Everything said so far about discussion advises that a *democratic* style is superior to a highly autocratic or near "abdication of responsibility" style. This is not to say, however, that in some group situations where *goal achievement* becomes unusually pressing, leadership should not go up the scale when it will help. Most union-management discussions are cooperative negotiations. On the other hand, to achieve sincerely healthy *interpersonal relations,* particularly where emotions are strained or unusual personalities are in conflict, it may be advisable to go down the scale.

An interesting study by Simons indicates that the more participative patterns or styles of deliberation, even with relatively large groups (15–20), were more productive in problem-solving discussion than the more formal patterns.[22]

Communication Climate

CLIMATE. A healthy group communication climate might be described as a *cohesive* environment in which the discussants through *interaction* achieve a mental state of relative psychological safety and freedom. According to Shepherd,[23] *cohesion* refers to the forces which bind members of a group, the degree of closeness and warmth they feel for each other, pride as members, a willingness to be frank and honest in their expression of ideas and feelings, and their ability to meet emergencies and crises which may confront them as a group.

Interaction refers to the type and degree of communication behavior directed toward another person or persons when their reaction or reciprocal behavior is taken into account. It pertains directly to one's interpersonal responsibilities in group discussion.

For Carl Rogers,[24] psychological safety involves being accepted as an individual of some worth, operating in a climate where one is not persistently evaluated as a person, and being able to understand (and be understood) empathically, that is from the other person's point of view. Psychological freedom involves group facilitation of a person's symbolic expression, an openness to communicate percepts, concepts, and meanings.

---

22 Herbert W. Simons, "Representative Versus Participative Patterns of Deliberation in Large Groups," *Quarterly Journal of Speech,* LII, No. 2, (April, 1966), 164–71.

23 Clovis R. Shepherd, *Small Groups, Some Sociological Perspectives* (San Francisco: Chandler Publishing Company, 1964) p. 26.

24 See Carl R. Rogers, *On Becoming a Person* (Boston: Houghton Mifflin Company, 1961) pp. 356–59.

This healthy communication climate should also include facilitating situations and facilitating people. It should be a climate where a person's status is not unreasonably threatened, where he feels accepted as a person, where he has the freedom to be wrong, and the freedom to participate based on involvement. This is not a bad communication climate for all matters of learning and personal growth and development.

Congruence is a term by which Rogers meant a matching of experience, awareness and communication.[25] Rogers' general law of interpersonal relationships is useful to us. While it describes a two person relationship, the wisdom is equally pertinent to small groups. For Rogers, it is the perception of the receiver of communication that is most crucial.

> The greater of the congruence of experience, awareness, and communication on the part of one individual, the more [his] ensuing relationship will involve: a tendency toward reciprocal communication with a quality of increasing congruence; a tendency toward more mutually accurate understanding of communications; improved psychological adjustment and functioning in both parties; mutual satisfaction in the relationship.

> Conversely the greater communicated incongruence of experience and awareness, the more ensuing relationship will involve: further communication with the same quality; disintegration of accurate understanding, less adequate psychological adjustment and functioning in both parties; and mutual dissatisfaction in the relationship.[26]

Participant Responsibilities

In addition to the general climate setting responsibilities for which all participants are accountable, certain, more specific participant responsibilities may be described.

Sattler and Miller[27] suggest desirable role descriptions for participants who would help promote the group and its goals:

Encourager	Standard Setter
Harmonizer	Group-Observer
Compromiser	Follower
Gate Keeper (opens channels of communication)	

They also suggest roles that have a negative effect:

---

25 Carl R. Rogers, *On Becoming a Person*, p. 339.
26 Carl R. Rogers, *On Becoming a Person*, pp. 344–45.
27 William M. Sattler and N. Edd Miller, *Discussion and Conference* (Englewood Cliffs, N.J.: Prentice-Hall, Inc., 1968) pp. 330–46.

Aggressor (deflates status of others)   Playboy
Blocker (opposes beyond reason)   Dominator
Recognition-Seeker   Help Seeker
Self-Confessor   Special Interest Pleader

Participants as well as leaders have an interpersonal responsibility whenever these situations arise:

One or two members dominate
Some members will not talk
Some apparently lack interest
Discussion drifts to irrelevant matters
Conflict occurs between members
Discussion "techniques" backfire

Sattler and Miller conclude that the good participant should in general: "(1) use tact, (2) be enthusiastic, (3) exhibit a sense of humor, (4) be cooperative, (5) minimize differences that exist between him and others, (6) be friendly, (7) identify with the group's goals, (8) consider the rewards of group membership, (9) interact, and (10) work to make the group successful."[28]

In this context Shepherd concludes, ". . . the definition of a successful group is a group with high cohesion and high productivity, in which objectives, role differentiation, values and norms, and membership criteria are clear and agreed upon, and in which communication is open and full."[29]

Observing and Evaluating Discussion

One of the most popular observational schemes for small group research was developed by Bales. The system involves a classification of communicative acts where act is defined as verbal and nonverbal behavior. It is called "Interaction Process Analysis." Bales divides an observer's duties into three areas, first the positive social emotional acts, then the "task" acts, and thirdly, the negative social-emotional acts. A modified outline of the system follows:

---

[28] William M. Sattler and N. Edd Miller, *Discussion and Conference*, p. 312.
[29] Clovis R. Shepherd, *Small Groups*, p. 124.

INTERACTION PROCESS ANALYSIS, CATEGORIES OF COMMUNICATIVE ACTS[30]

Major Categories		Subcategories	Illustrative Statements or Behavior
Social Emotional Area	A. Positive Reactions	1. Shows solidarity	Jokes, gives help, rewards others, is friendly
		2. Shows tension release	Laughs, shows satisfaction, is relieved
		3. Shows agreement	Passively accepts, understands, concurs, complies
Task Area	B. Attempted Answers	4. Gives suggestion	Directs, suggests, implies autonomy for others
		5. Gives opinion	Evaluates, analyzes, expresses feeling or wish
		6. Gives information	Orients, repeats, clarifies, confirms
	C. Questions	7. Asks for information	Requests orientation, repetition, confirmation
		8. Asks for opinion	Requests evaluation, analysis, expression of feeling
		9. Asks for suggestion	Requests direction, possible ways of action
Social Emotional Area	D. Negative Reactions	10. Shows disagreement	Passively rejects, resorts to formality, withholds help
		11. Shows tension	Asks for help, withdraws, daydreams
		12. Shows antagonism	Deflates other's status, defends or asserts self, hostile

Key: a. Problems of Communication
  b. Problems of Evaluation
  c. Problems of Control
  d. Problems of Decision
  e. Problems of Tension Reduction
  f. Problems of Reintegration

[30] Based on Robert F. Bales, *Interaction Process Analysis* (Cambridge, Mass.: Addison-Wesley Press, 1950), p. 9; A. Paul Hare, *Handbook of Small Group Research* (New York: The Free Press of Glencoe, 1962), p. 66; and Clovis R. Shepherd, *Small Groups, Some Sociological Perspectives* (San Francisco: Chandler Publishing Co., 1964), p. 30.

A tabulating of acts by observers in various research studies (typically college students) indicates an average group profile of 25 percent positive reactions (A), 56 percent attempted answers (B), 7 percent questions (C), and 12 percent negative reactions (D). As Shepherd stated, "The portrait is of a group in which most of the discussion involves expressing *opinions* and *information* and conveying *agreement,* with occasional expressions of disagreement and tension release (such as joking) and occasional requests for *information* and *opinion.*"[31] A relatively simple and self-explanatory general discussion rating form for observing participants follows:

DISCUSSION EVALUATION FORM—WSU

1-2-3	4-5-6	7-8-9
Weak	Average	Strong

Criteria for Evaluating Discussion Participation Include the Following:

A. Information about the problem. (Breadth, accuracy, and use of information.)
B. Analysis of the problem. (Sensing problem's importance; finding the issues; avoiding irrelevant matters.)
C. Ability to think cooperatively. (Open-mindedness; alertness; willingness to abandon weak arguments; ability to synthesize the contributions of others.)
D. Skill in speaking. (Adapting voice, action, and language to the occasion; ability to state ideas clearly and briefly.)
E. Good manners. (Listening attentively; quoting others accurately; giving others a chance to speak; general courtesy.)
F. General overall effectiveness.

	1	2	3	4	5	6	7	8	9	10	11
Project											
Class Hour											
Date											
A. Information											
B. Analysis											
C. Cooperative Thinking											
D. Speaking Skill											
E. Good Manners											
F. Overall Effect											
Total Scores											
Rank Order of Participants											

General Comments on the Group as a Whole (Use back of sheet as needed):

[31] Clovis R. Shepherd, *Small Groups, Some Sociological Perspectives,* p. 32.

Observing and evaluating discussion can also be approached in terms of diagraming the participation. These chartings are referred to as sociograms and may provide graphic insights into group behavior. One can simply tabulate the number and length of contributions, or also tabulate the contributions according to categories or types (for example, Bales). One can also draw circles on a piece of paper representing the discussants and then with lines and arrows diagram the flow and amount, and so on, of interpersonal communication. One can often find graphic evidence to show to the overtalkative.

Summary

The unique aspect of discussion is that a participant is both sender-receiver and encoder-decoder at the same time. It is a dynamic, interactive, interpersonal communication situation. If decision is impossible through discussion, it may very well lead to debate. Debate is competitive and two-sided, discussion cooperative and many-sided. Assuming a real group, persons with a common goal, not just a loose collection of individuals, we can define group discussion as *systematic, cooperative, reflective thinking and communication.*

Group discussion involves a cooperative thinking endeavor among 20 people or less. The basic forms are *dialogue, panel* and *symposium.* Three techniques which may be used in combination with any of the forms include *buzz group, role playing,* and *brainstorming.* A *forum* is simply that part of a discussion in which the audience may speak.

Discussion forms may be used for information-sharing, problem-solving and instruction. Information-sharing groups include staff meetings, study groups and workshops. Problem-solving groups include committees, conferences, and boards or councils. Instructional formats include case conferences, role playing, and to some extent, all of the forms and techniques.

Maintaining an intelligent state of doubt, and systematic inquiry are the essentials of reflective thinking. There are five steps in the Dewey system: (1) felt difficulty, (2) definition, (3) possible solutions, (4) rational elaboration, and (5) further testing or corroborating. One four-step adaptation involves: (1) *Definition,* (2) *Analysis* as puzzle, probability, and value, (3) establishing *Criteria,* and (4) the *Solution* step. Discussion is a moving dynamic phenomenon, which may be more circular than linear in function as a group moves. Modern research suggests three phases in problem-solving discussions. Phase one involves orientation, information, repetition, and confirmation. Phase two involves analysis, evaluation, and expressions, seeking or giving opinions and feelings. Phase three involves controlling possible directions and ways of action. Five agenda systems thought to creatively reflect and synthesize the literature are shown.

Leadership should be thought of as any significant action by any discussant that has significant influence on group achievement. It is possible to have no appointed leader and still have leadership; the reverse is also true. The distinction between *leader* and *leadership,* and *leaderless* and *leadershipless* is a critical one. All group members have a stake and often a role in leadership.

Leadership *may* accrue to a person through designation, through his information, because of his status, or through his ability in performing vital group functions. The major functions of leadership are related to *goal achievement* and *interpersonal relations.* Leadership, particularly where designated, must also attend to the *procedural* functions.

Procedural functions may include planning, physical arrangement, purposes, degree of formality, goal setting, and considerations of agenda. The procedural leader is also responsible for general participation control and preserving order. Styles of leadership may be described as autocratic, authoritarian, supervisory, democratic, permissive, nondirective, and laissez-faire. The democratic style is recommended.

A healthy group communication climate is described as a cohesive environment in which discussants achieve a mental state of psychological safety and freedom. Interaction involves reciprocal communication between members and pertains to interpersonal responsibilities. Congruence means a matching of experience, awareness, and communication. Rogers' law of interpersonal relationships suggests that with congruence comes: more mutually accurate understanding, improved psychological adjustment and functioning, and a more satisfying relationship. Other specific participant responsibilities are described.

Interaction Process Analysis is an observational system that classifies verbal and nonverbal behavior as communicative acts. An observer's duties are divided into three major areas: positive social-emotional acts, task acts, and negative social-emotional acts. Twelve subcategories for analysis are shown.

A successful group discussion is an interacting, reflective thinking group of people with goals, essential systematic leadership, high cohesion, high productivity, and cooperative interpersonal communication.

Special
Occasion
Speaking 13

"Scope of This Chapter"

All communication occasions are in a sense special, yet many occasions call for surprisingly similar speeches in form and style, if not in content. Speeches of introduction, for example, occur often enough, involve routinely the same principles, and are so frequently unsuccessful that a further and more specific application of the speech and communication theory previously discussed is useful. In addition to speeches of introduction, the following special occasions will be discussed: speeches of presentation; tribute and commemorative speeches; after dinner speeches; and adaptation of speech material to radio and television.

Speeches of Introduction

"I just now met our speaker who is a friend of our chairman and a speaker on human relations. He teaches speech and should be a good example for all of you to follow. It gives me great pleasure to introduce Mr. W. R. D. Forsythe."

How would you like to speak to a strange audience after that introduction? Attention was called to the speaker's oratory instead of his subject. It sounded as if the speaker were foisted upon the group by a buddy in the

233

organization. It was evident that the introducer in this case did not know anything about the speaker and was not particularly interested in "human relations." The only good point about the introduction was its briefness!

Even more devastating as a speech of introduction is a 20 minute nightmare of poor jokes, trite language, and overly dramatic praise of the speaker's virtues. This is especially cruel when the speaker only intends to speak for 30 minutes. What makes the situation really impossible is that the introducer is typically a well-intentioned, sincere, and genuinely nice person, who is simply socially inept at introducing people.

This last fact makes it most difficult for a speaker to recover his poise, because ordinarily he cannot lash back as he is wont to do. However, on one occasion a speaker evened the score. A young instructor was introducing a distinguished Professor to a group of university personnel who knew the professor. He proceeded to give a speech that involved an explanation of every accomplishment and every entry on the professor's bibliography. It was embarrassing to everyone and almost began to sound like satire because of the sheer volume of detail. His final remark was, "Professor, have I overlooked anything?" A plainly irritated distinguished professor rose to his feet, glowered at the introducer, and said, "I caught a big fish once!"

What then are some principles and rules that you can apply to avoid making life intolerable for the speaker?

Remember that the major purpose of a speech of introduction is to create a rapport between the speaker and the audience, which in turn creates a desire for people to want to hear his subject. You want the audience to like him, to respect him, and to be predisposed to listen attentively. Toward this end:

1. *Make sure that you know something about the speaker and his subject.* Consult with him before the meeting if you can; see if there are some things he prefers said or not said.

2. *Be brief but adequate.* Make sure that enough is said about the speaker and his subject to achieve a rapport, but remember that your job is to focus attention on the speaker and his subject. Do not overplay *your role,* for you are not the main speaker.

The length of the speech of introduction is also related to how well the speaker is known to the audience. You might introduce Richard Nixon simply and adequately with, "Ladies and Gentlemen: the President of the United States." Seldom should a speech of introduction run more than three or four minutes.

3. *Stress the importance and appropriateness of the speaker's subject.* However, take care not to give his speech for him. Do not explain the speaker's qualifications to the point of neglecting to create curiosity and attention for his subject.

4. *Speak with sincerity and enthusiasm.* If you are not familiar with the

speaker or his subject or are simply not interested, get someone else to make the introduction. Do not become artificial in your enthusiasm; do not overpraise; do not stress his "oratorical" skill; do not use trite language. In general, speak about accomplishments rather than virtues.

5. *Pay attention to the speaker.* After you have finished your speech of introduction, making sure that his name and subject were announced clearly and correctly, be a model listener. This suggests that the audience also be good listeners. A gabby or hyperactive introducer can ruin the speaker's attention and rapport.

An excellent model is a speech by Professor Glenn R. Capp introducing Dr. A. Q. Sartain to the Baylor University chapter of the American Association of University Professors.

"If a man be endowed with a generous mind, this is the best kind of nobility." This statement by Plato characterizes our speaker for tonight. During the more than twenty years that I have known Dr. Sartain, I have become increasingly impressed not only with his generous and penetrating mind, but with his kindly spirit.

A risk that one runs in introducing a cherished friend is that he may deal in extravagant statements. I find myself in somewhat of a paradoxical situation this evening because a simple factual recital of the training, accomplishment, and contributions of Dr. Sartain appears to be overstatement. I am tempted to dwell at length on such matters as these:

(1) His writings, which include co-authorship of a recent textbook, *Human Behavior in Industry*, his forthcoming textbook to be published by Prentice-Hall, and numerous articles in professional journals.

(2) His important positions, which he has held at Southern Methodist University, where he was first the Director of Forensics, later Professor of Psychology, and now is chairman of the Department of Personnel Administration. He also has more than a passing interest in Baylor University, having taught recently as visiting professor in our summer session.

(3) His membership in important organizations. For example, he served recently as president of the Southern Methodist University chapter of the American Association of University Professors. He is president of the Southwestern Psychological Association, a fellow of the American Psychological Association, and a member of the Association for the Advancement of Science.

Rather than dwelling on these matters, may I say simply that I congratulate you for securing Dr. Sartain for this occasion. I have been impressed with the excellence of his forensic teams, but even more with him as a man—his pleasant disposition, his sense of fair play, his high ethical standards, and his ability as a scholar. I present to you my friend and the friend of all teachers—Dr. A. Q. Sartain.[1]

---

[1] Glenn R. Capp, *How to Communicate Orally*, 2nd ed. (Englewood Cliffs, N.J.: Prentice-Hall, Inc., 1966), p. 351.

Speeches of Presentation

"Thanks for holding down the other end of the log," was engraved on a simple brass plaque and signed by four outstanding graduate students. This award was presented by simply placing it on the center of a professor's desk before he retired from a major university. With this close little group a speech, a banquet, even a personal confrontation was unnecessary. The recipient was honored and felt that his efforts were appreciated and recognized. Most often, however, a speech is called for, and it should seek as its major purpose to show honor, appreciation, and recognition.

The same sense of good will and appreciation can be transmitted under considerably different circumstances. A five minute formal speech was read from a manuscript before a banquet audience of 300 people. It concluded: "For these and his many other achievements, it was unanimously agreed by the Executive Faculty of the Marquette University School of Speech that Dr. James W. Cleary was richly deserving of our Distinguished Alumni Award in the field of Speech Education." The point is that presentations vary widely. The size of the group involved, the nature of the award, and the occasion are all critical factors in how much is said and how formally it is said.

Two general principles for most speeches of presentation are as follows:

1. *The speech should sincerely communicate honor, appreciation, and recognition.* It should not stray from the facts or it becomes insincere. Do not overpraise, overstate, or overemotionalize. Honestly review the recipient's accomplishments and virtues.

2. *Adapt your speech to the occasion and the award.* For annual and routine service awards, only a short, forthright word of congratulations may be necessary, even on a formal occasion. When many similar awards are given, as with forensic contest winners, one short speech can often serve to show honor and recognition for the entire group, each of whom might then individually step forward to receive his medal. This is not to say that the speech should be any less sincere. Make sure the speaker selected to present such awards is thoroughly familiar with the kind of effort and achievement involved.

On some occasions the speaker may also have to consider the donor of the gift. A university giving an honorary degree or a distinguished alumni award deserves some recognition and reflected glory. This is also true of business and industrial concerns who honor long-time employees.

In situations where the award may have a history, a special set of criteria, or where it is otherwise unusual, a short description of these facts may be in order.

As a sample of a speech of presentation, let us turn to the presentation of a Volume of Tributes to Dr. J. W. Crabtree, Secretary Emeritus and founder of the National Education Association, by W. E. Givens.[2]

Dr. Crabtree's record speaks more eloquently than any speaker could. He came to Washington in 1917 and started the office of the National Education Association in one room of his house, with one secretary. On January 1, 1935, when he became Secretary Emeritus, he left a modern, seven-story building on the "Street of the Presidents" six squares from the White House in our nation's capital, and he left there a loyal office force of one hundred and forty-five people, all of whom love and respect him.

He started in 1922 the life membership movement that put up that great building, and that has grown from that time until tonight our great national Association has some 5400 life members scattered throughout this great nation.

Miss Hale read you a few of the letters that he has received. It is my pleasure on behalf of his friends throughout the nation to present to him from you a beautiful volume of some seven hundred letters from his friends, bound in a beautiful binding presented by the publishers of our *Journal* as a compliment to Mr. Crabtree. It is a great pleasure to present this volume to Mr. Crabtree tonight and to assure you all that it is a great honor to be the successor of such a man.

Tribute and Commemorative Speeches

This form of special occasion speaking includes such subclassifications as eulogies, anniversary addresses, dedicatory speeches, and some nominating speeches. The *eulogy* is typically a speech of tribute upon the death of a person or shortly thereafter. It may also apply to the anniversary of the birth or great moments in the life of a historical figure such as Lincoln or Washington. *Anniversary* speeches celebrate and commemorate an event, a man, or an institution. Dedicatory speeches are typically tributes; buildings, monuments, ships, libraries, and other things are generally dedicated in the honor of some outstanding personality, institution, or group of men. In some nominating

---

[2] W. Hayes Yeager, *Effective Speaking for Every Occasion* (Englewood Cliffs, N.J.: Prentice-Hall, Inc., 1940), p. 159.

speeches, it is the practice to pay tribute to the nominee as a way of proving his qualifications for office. Since most organizations now use nominating committees, nominations are made with less oral flourish.

All commemorative speeches involve tributes to men, their ideals, and their achievements. The purpose is to gain or increase respect, emulation, and appreciation of the men involved and their impact upon society or its institutions.

Organizationally, you can proceed chronologically according to the history of the man or institution being commemorated, or, when time is short and the chronology generally well known, you can proceed topically and concentrate on selective aspects of personality, achievement, or societal impact.

Three general rules for most tributes and commemorative speeches are as follows:

1. Develop a sensitive understanding about the subject. To deliver a funeral oration about a stranger would be awkward and embarrassing, if not sacrilegious. Make sure you have *more* than just the immediate facts about the man, the occasion, the memorial, or building being dedicated or otherwise commemorated. Try to capture the personality of the subject in both the large and small incidents of his life that typify his virtues or outlook on life. Know his outstanding achievements well, but do not lose sight of those characteristics of personality that typify the man.

2. Be objective and fair to the facts. Perhaps we should not "speak ill of the dead," but neither should we be totally dishonest. To eulogize a lazy, intemperate, hardheaded, old lady as "this kind, generous model of moral simplicity" is apt to cause outright laughter and do a disservice to whatever virtues and respect to which the woman was entitled. No person is perfect in every way. Washington was not a model tactician at Valley Forge; young Lincoln was defeated so many times at the polls that his political future was in real jeopardy. You will want to magnify and concentrate on the person's virtues and achievements, but let him be human.

3. Utilize a style of language and delivery in keeping with the occasion. The nature of commemorative occasions is often demanding of a slightly more elevated style than that generally prescribed in this book. The expectations audiences have of a speaker in a church or cemetery are somehow special. In paying tribute to the tragically lost astronauts, one can hardly escape the connotative effect of voice and measured cadence that helps express the grief, the reverence, the solemnity of the occasion. There are many happy anniversaries, dedications, and tributes, which will call for different adaptations of style. Probably part of every commemorative speech demands some element of elevated style. The model that follows helps illustrate this point. It was delivered from the floor of the United

States Senate by Senator Dirksen. A formal resolution was read and Senator Dirksen was then recognized.[3]

MR. DIRKSEN: Mr. President, the memory of John Fitzgerald Kennedy lingers in this forum of the people. Here we knew his vigorous tread, his flashing smile, his ready wit, his keen mind, his zest for adventure. Here with quiet grief we mourn his departure. Here we shall remember him best as a colleague whose star of public service is indelibly inscribed on the roll of the U.S. Senate.

And here the eternal question confronts and confounds us. Why must it be? Why must the life of an amiable, friendly, aggressive young man, moved only by high motives, lighted on his way by high hopes, guided by broad plans, impelled by understanding and vision, be brought to an untimely end with his labors unfinished? And why, in a free land, untouched by the heel of dictatorship and oppression, where the humblest citizen may freely utter his grievances, must that life be cut short by an evil instrument, moved by malice, frustration, and hate? This is the incredible thing which leaves us bewildered and perplexed.

One moment there is the ecstasy of living when one can hear the treble cries of scampering children over the White House lawn, the pleasure of receiving a Thanksgiving turkey which I presented to him but three days before the evil deed, the pleasure of conversation over many things, including his hopes for the future, the exciting fact of sunshine and green grass in late November, the endless stream of citizens coming to the President's House, the strident voice of the city rising from the hum of traffic, the animation of saluting crowds, and then the sudden strangling death rattle of dissolution. Who shall say, save that there is a Divinity which shapes our ends and marks our days?

As the tumult and grief subside, as the Nation resumes and moves forward, and his own generation measures his works and achievements, what shall we say who knew him well—we in this forum, where he spent eight years of his life—we who knew him best not as Mr. President but simply as Jack?

We saw him come to this body at age 35. We saw him grow. We saw him rise. We saw him elevated to become the Chief Magistrate of this Nation. And we saw him as the leader of both branches of the Republic assembled to deliberate over common problems.

In this moment when death has triumphed, when hearts are chastened, when the spirit reels in sheer bewilderment, what do we say now that the Book of Life has been closed?

Let me say what we have always said when he was alive, gay, happy, friendly, ambitious, and ready to listen.

He had vision that went beyond our own. His determination to effectuate a test-ban treaty is a living example.

He was his own profile in courage. His unrelenting devotion to equality and civil rights attests that fact.

He was devoted to our system of constitutional government. His attitude toward the separation of church and state looms like a shining example.

---

[3] *Congressional Record*, pp. 21, 596–97.

He had the great virtue of spiritual grace. If at any moment he may have seemed frustrated over a proposition, it was so transitory. If he showed any sign of petulance, it was so fleeting. There were no souring acids in the spirit of John Kennedy.

If at any moment he may have seemed overeager, it was but the reflection of a zealous crusader and missioner who knew where he was going.

If at any moment, he seemed to depart from the covenant which he and his party made with the people, it was only because he believed that accelerated events and circumstances did not always heed the clock and the calendar.

If his course sometimes seemed at variance with his own party leaders or with the opposition, it was only because a deep conviction dictated his course.

On the tables of memory, we who knew him well as a friend and colleague can well inscribe this sentiment:

"Senator John Fitzgerald Kennedy, who became the 35th President of the United States—young, vigorous, aggressive, and scholarly—one who estimated the need of his country and the world and sought to fulfill that need—one who was wedded to peace and vigorously sought this greatest of all goals of mankind—one who sensed how catastrophic nuclear conflict could be and sought a realistic course to avert it—one who sensed the danger that lurked in a continuing inequality in our land and sought a rational and durable solution—one to whom the phrase 'the national interest' was more than a string of words—one who could disagree without vindictiveness—one who believed that the expansion of the enjoyment of living by all people was an achievable goal—one who believed that each generation must contribute its best to the fulfillment of the American dream."

The *te deums* which will be sung this day may be wafted away by the evening breeze which caresses the last resting place of those who served the Republic, but here in this Chamber where he served and prepared for higher responsibility, the memory of John Fitzgerald Kennedy will long linger to nourish the faith of all who serve that same great land.

Perhaps the most eloquent commemorative speech of all time was Lincoln's Gettysburg Address. The speech is shown in the actual hand of Lincoln. This is his first draft and therefore slightly different than other versions you may have studied[4] (see pages 242 and 243).

---

[4] The first page was written in ink in Washington shortly before November 18. It is believed that there was once a second page in ink which was lost. Lincoln completed the draft in pencil in Gettysburg on the evening or morning of November 19. The words, "here to the unfinished work which they have thus far, so nobly carried on," are omitted or lost. He delivered the speech from this draft, but did not follow the text verbatim. See *Long Remembered,* The Gettysburg Address in Facsimile (Washington, D.C., The Library of Congress, 1963), with notes and comments by David C. Mearns and Lloyd A. Dunlap. Library of Congress Catalog Card No.: 63–65145. (Facsimile #3).

After-Dinner Speeches

After dinner speeches are not always "after-dinner" speeches. In our day a banquet may be the setting for a very serious and profound speech to persuade or inform. All the lessons previously discussed obviously apply to these speeches as they would to any other. There is, however, a tradition of after-dinner speaking (with the hyphen), which is rather special in our society. This is the good-humored, light-hearted, genial situation with the major purpose being a sociable dinner and relaxed enjoyment. This is the type of speech situation with which we are here concerned. The audience has been made content with good food and is tolerant and benevolent. They are not in a mood for contentiousness, moral reevaluation, or complex, logical stratagems. These speeches are typically brief, light, and generally humorous. They are not easy speeches to deliver; for some they appear to be well-nigh impossible. You need not be a professional jokester; indeed, unless you tell a good, related joke especially well, you are better advised to seek your humor in another vein. Some general principles to help you are as follows:

1. Select suitable topics. "Great Snafus of the Civil War" was a delightful after-dinner speech at a history buffs' banquet recently. The group was of course interested in the profound aspects of the war, but not at this particular moment. Look on the lighter side of issues for your subjects. If you are going to talk about teachers, concentrate on their eccentricities, and so on.

2. Be good humored. The diners are full of food and full of good will. Enhance the fellowship. Avoid bitter argument and contentiousness.

3. Adapt to the audience. A joke or a story is often funny to one group and not to another. More importantly, it may be offensive. Make sure you know the audience, the occasion, and the program format. Capitalize on this information; tie your good humor appropriately and directly to your specific audience. A canned speech for all occasions is seldom successful.

4. Be clear and brief. Avoid complex organization; stick with one or two obvious main points. Do not use elaborate forms of support. Use primarily examples and humorous illustrations, and above all, be brief. Attention spans are often short after a long day and a pleasant dinner. Plan several cutoff points in your speech to extricate yourself should the total program take more time than expected or should the audience seem unusually restless or quiet (asleep).

A good example is a very funny speech by Dorothy Dix (Mrs. E. M. Gilmer, the original advice-to-the-lovelorn columnist), to elementary school principals after a National Education Association banquet.

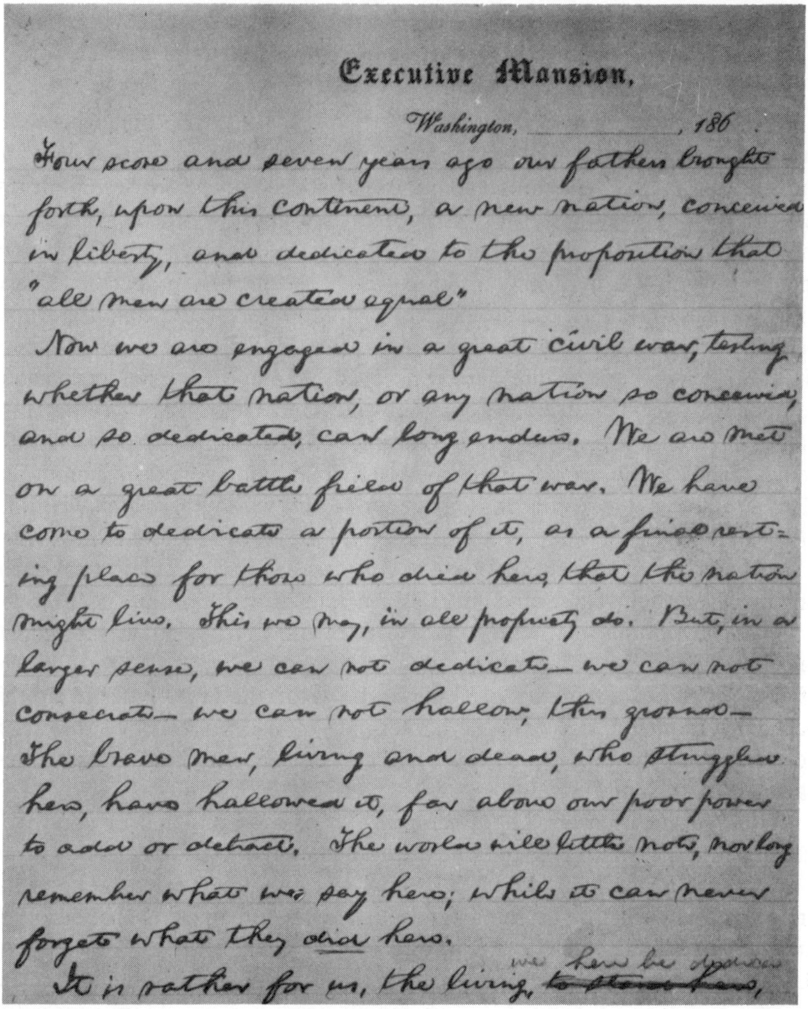

Executive Mansion,

Washington, , 186 .

Four score and seven years ago our fathers brought forth, upon this continent, a new nation, conceived in liberty, and dedicated to the proposition that "all men are created equal"

Now we are engaged in a great civil war, testing whether that nation, or any nation so conceived, and so dedicated, can long endure. We are met on a great battle field of that war. We have come to dedicate a portion of it, as a final resting place for those who died here, that the nation might live. This we may, in all propriety do. But, in a larger sense, we can not dedicate—we can not consecrate—we can not hallow, this ground—The brave men, living and dead, who struggled here, have hallowed it, far above our poor power to add or detract. The world will little note, nor long remember what we say here; while it can never forget what they did here.

It is rather for us, the living, ~~to stand here,~~ we here be dedicated

Figure 50

EXPERIENCES OF A WOMAN COLUMNIST[5]

Not very long ago I received a letter telling me about all the harm I was doing. It read: "Dear Miss Dix: I wonder if you know how much harm you are doing in the world. I was in love with a man who did not notice me at all, and I wrote you to ask you how I could attract him, and you told me how to do it, and I did, and married him, and now I wish I had not!"

---

[5] *Proceedings,* National Education Association, 1937.

ted to the great task remaining before us—
that, from these honored dead we take increased devotion to that cause for which
they here, gave the last full measure of devotion— that we here highly resolve these
dead shall not have died in vain; that
the nation, shall have a new birth of freedom, and that government of the people by
the people for. the people, shall not per-
ish from the earth.

I am very happy to be able to add my own word to the welcome you have
been given in New Orleans. As you know, New Orleans is a convention city,
but we rarely have so large a convention as you have brought us today. I suppose
the principals of the elementary schools also know that the parents of today
have passed the buck, so to speak, and they expect the teacher not only to teach
their children learning, but morals and manners as well. The babies have been

thrown squarely in your laps, so what happens to the country in the future depends on how you bring these youngsters up.

When I was asked to report at this auspicious assembly, I was proud and pleased, but when I was told I was to talk about myself, my various undertakings seemed to have run out on me.

Our favorite indoor sport in talking about ourselves is in talking about our work. In my occupation of writing a love column, there are many things that are really very funny. I do not know why, because love is a most serious thing in the world—it makes the world go round, and is the cause for most of the trouble made and murders committed. I do not know where my work begins or finishes, of course, but I do my bit toward keeping things going.

I have been writing this column for a long time. When I started, things were not what they are today, and nothing amazes me so much as the different questions people ask me. Forty years ago people asked me whether it was proper to help a boy friend with his overcoat when he called; now it is, "Do you think there is any harm to go over and spend a week-end with him?" I have no end to the number of letters where girls have asked me how to keep their husbands. There is hardly any question in the world that comes up between mothers and fathers, and between them and their children, and between husbands and wives, and sweethearts, that in one way or another does not fall into my collection. One person wrote me that she was thirty-five years old, with a peaches-and-cream complexion, and that she was going to be married to a man of forty; that there was nothing in the way now, except that she had false teeth. "Now," said she, "what must I do about it? Should I tell him before I marry him that I have false teeth and disillusion him, or wait until after we are married and run the risk that he might throw them in my face? Shall I break the engagement on some trifling excuse and carry my secret to the grave with me? It is a question. What do you think of it?" I thought long and seriously, and then wrote to her: "Marry your man and keep your mouth shut."

A man not long ago asked me the same question; he also had false teeth. And I told him: "Go on, child, she would not know the difference if she saw you."

You might think, judging by my gray hair, that I was past the marrying age, yet no debutante gets half the proposals that I do, but they always say, "I will not interfere with your career." I spent last summer on a ranch in Colorado, and while there I received a letter from a man who said he had long thought that I would make the kind of wife he wanted. He heard that I was on this ranch, and proceeded to tell me that he was a middle-aged man, owned a huge ranch, and lived ninety miles from a railroad, and then: "I have to come down into your neighborhood anyway, to look over a bunch of beef cattle, so I thought I could come and see how we would like each other." I wrote him that I thought he was better at driving cattle than love on a ranch!

My chores are many, ranging from naming babies to finding ways and means for all sorts of people from all walks of life; but the questions I receive are so unique that I have copied a few from some of the letters I have received:

"My husband tells me to go to hell. Have I a right to take the children?"

"We have been married two weeks, and have not quarreled yet, but are working up to it."

"Shall I tell the boys I stutter?"

"I use Life Buoy soap and still no boy friends."

"I took your advice, Miss Dix, about being a perfect lady, and now I stay at home every night alone."

"I am fifty years old, madly in love with a woman who already has a husband. What is the quickest and most humane way of getting away with same?"

"As soon as I come into the house he yells at me 'you dog' and 'go to hell,' and sometimes he also uses profane language."

"There is nothing you cannot do; thank you in advance for a home, and a husband, and a playmate."

"I have a nice home, a car, a fur coat, jewels—everything a girl marries for."

"I have been a decent girl as far as I can remember."

"My husband beats me until I am black and blue, but my mother advises me to pay no attention and act indifferent."

"Of course we have spats, as all married couples do, and I got one arm broken, but we never have any disagreements of a serious nature."

"There was a great void in my life, so I fell madly in love with a dentist."

"I am married to a bookworm—what is good for worms?"

"A woman depreciates faster than her automobile, and that is going some."

"In high school I was an honor student, with very few friends, and none of them boys."

"Please do not put this in the paper because my girl reads your pieces—she has no sense at all."

"Miss Dix, is my boy friend just a good Catholic, or is he trying to get rid of me; he said he has given me up for Lent?"

"He has bought a license for his dog, and his car—oh, my, why don't he buy a marriage license?"

"My husband and I quarrel like cats and dogs. My birthday is on May 12, and his is on September 15. Are we congenial?"

"My child's father is married, but I am not. What is my relationship to my child's father?"

Some of them are very nice and tell me that I have helped or taught them something. One of the greatest compliments I have ever had in a letter was: "Miss Dix, I usually take my boy friend to dinner, but now I want advice from someone who is really practical, and I am coming to you."

Adapting Material to Radio and Television

93.4 percent of our households have TV today. Seventy million Americans heard and saw the first Kennedy-Nixon debate in 1960. In 1863 only 20,000 Americans heard

Lincoln at Gettysburg. Although it is the point of view of this book that the same basic, oral speech and communication processes and skills apply in principle whatever the media or situation, some pragmatical differences are obvious when dealing with the mass media. Never before has a speaker had access to such a potentially vast audience. Never before could a speaker be more easily ignored.

Despite the practical problems to be discussed shortly, the radio and TV media have marvelous advantages. In addition to potentially giant audiences, the speaker is typically free of audience interruptions such as questions, heckling, and rebuttals, as well as the usual distractions of movement, falling chairs, side conversations, and the like. Through the marvel of closeup TV camera work, you can show small objects and visual aids, which would be impossible to present in regular speech situations. Emphasis and mood can be varied with dramatic effect as the various cameras take closeup shots followed by more distant ones. The viewing screen can be divided so that you can simultaneously and selectively compare or emphasize various objects or concepts pertinent to your message. Audio or video taping for future use gives you the very real advantage of seeing how you appear to the audience, and you also have an opportunity to make changes. The mass media can have an intimacy that is often overlooked— the kind of person-to-person communication that is so very difficult with really large audiences in typical platform speech situations. We are only now learning how to make use of the many instructional and educational advantages of the radio-TV media.

It is not the purpose of this section to explain the engineering, production, and academic intricacies of radio and television performance. We shall instead explain some of the essential differences between platform speaking and the use of microphones and cameras and shall suggest methods of adapting your communication to these differences.

Probably the most difficult problem for a good platform speaker to cope with in radio or television is the lack of feedback from the audience; except for occasional studio audiences, his listeners are unseen and unheard. The truly sensitive platform speaker is constantly checking his audience for signs of fatigue, misunderstanding, confusion, or approval and he paces his rate, volume, and vocabulary accordingly. A radio studio can be a lonely place. A television studio has a few more technicians and a monitor, which allows you to see yourself, but still no important listener feedback.

The next important difference for a good platform speaker is the great number of mechanical and technical distractions and limitations. This is much more of a problem on television than on radio, because cameras as well as lights and microphones call for more cues, more technicians, and more prearranged signals.

If you are the courageous type who uses a great deal of movement on the platform, you will quickly find yourself in trouble with the producer, the director, and just about everyone else working the show; your movement will cause you to be off camera, off mike, or both. The microphones of today are marvelous and are more adaptable to movement than a few years ago, but the camera is still a nemesis for the amateur. Typically, two or more cameras are operating, and you talk to the camera that has its little red tally light on. The TV cameras move quickly and silently, and a momentary glance at your notes or time cues is long enough for the evil eye to appear suddenly right in front of you, so close that you can see yourself reflected in the lens, that is, if the flood lights have not blinded you. The mechanical headaches are indicated here to make sure you take advantage of a preshow rehearsal, which will acquaint you with some of these problems and help prevent you from being caught flatfooted and open-mouthed when you are actually on the air.

If this is not enough to chill the bones of a speaker, there is still one more critical operating difference. Despite the large and diverse audiences available, they are not assembled in large halls in the manner of a great audience listening to a famed orator. They are individually seated, sometimes within a few feet of your face. They are subject to numerous distractions, and are free from the inhibitions of a large hall. A few moments of boredom may cause a change of channels.

In addition, sensitive microphones may make "normal" projection, force, and volume adjustments a liability, not to mention oral style. A teacher once had a radio announcer in class who had difficulty adjusting to a regular classroom audience. He spoke in a beautiful, intimate voice as if he were on mike; consequently many in the room could not hear him. He explained that if he projected and used the platform manner suggested while on microphone, he would soon be out of a job. And he was right. What, then, are some guide lines for adapting your speeches and general communications to the special characteristics of the radio-television media?

1. Consider the advantages of microphone and camera. Utilize the variety of camera shots available for presentation of visual aids, for emphasis, for mood. Let the producer and director help you enhance your presentation. Use the monitor to see how you appear to others.

2. Prepare yourself for a lack of audience feedback. Determine your most likely audience in advance and adapt to them. Try your speech on live audiences of one or two people so that you have a basis for imagining realistic feedback during air time.

3. Accept the differences and limitations of microphone and camera. Limit your movements and bodily action to the range of the equipment. Visualize a small conversational audience rather than a vast multitude assembled in one location. Limit your use of voice and style accordingly. Check your dress and your grooming, particularly for television close-ups.

4. Learn to expect and live with mechanical distractions. Observe a show. Rehearse on the set and learn the cues. Watch the producer, director, or engineer for cues. If you are not sure who's who, ask. In the case of television, follow the camera with the red tally light on. Look right into the camera. Check the monitor occasionally for feedback on yourself. Are you inanimate, listing, grinning? Wear cool clothes; the lights are hot.

5. Prepare your speech material carefully. Time is a major concern. Time your material until it is exactly the right length. Write time cues for yourself in the margins of your script. Prepare time fillers in advance; have omission options for timesavers. Keep your organization simple so that time adjustments and adaptations can be exercised without completely baffling the audience. Remember that despite all the headaches and crises discussed in this section, it is what you have to say, the message, that really counts. In the final analysis, it is that way in all communication situations. Don't let the media become the message!

Summary

All communication is in a sense special, yet many occasions call for surprisingly similar speeches in form and style. Special occasion speaking involves primarily introductions, presentations, tributes and commemorations, after-dinner speeches, and adaptations to radio and television.

The major purpose of a speech of introduction is to create a rapport between the speaker, audience, and subject that produces a desire for people to want to hear his subject. Toward this end: (1) make sure that you know something about the speaker and his subject; (2) be brief, but adequate; (3) stress the importance and appropriateness of the speaker's subject; (4) speak with sincerity and enthusiasm; (5) pay attention to the speaker after he starts to speak.

The two general principles for most speeches of presentation are: (1) the speech should sincerely communicate honor, appreciation, and recognition; (2) the speech should be specifically adapted to the occasion and to the award.

Tribute and commemorative speeches include such subclassifications as eulogies, anniversary addresses, dedicatory speeches, and some nominating speeches. The purpose of all commemorative speeches is to gain or increase respect, emulation, and appreciation of the people involved and their impact upon society or its institutions. The key topical aspects are personality, achievement, and societal impact. Three general rules are: (1) develop a sensitive understanding about the subject; (2) be objective and fair to the facts; (3) utilize a style of language and delivery in keeping with the occasion.

After-dinner speaking refers to the good-humored, lighthearted, genial situation, with the major purpose being a sociable dinner and relaxed enjoyment. These speeches are typically brief, light, and generally humorous. Some principles to follow are: (1) select suitable topics; (2) be genuinely good-humored; (3) adapt to the specific audience; (4) be clear and brief.

Some guide lines for adapting your speeches and general communications to the special characteristics of the radio and television media are as follows: (1) Consider the advantages of microphone and camera; (2) prepare yourself for a lack of audience feedback; (3) accept the differences and limitations of microphone and camera; (4) learn to expect and live with technical distractions; (5) prepare and carefully time your speech material to facilitate adaptation to the media involved. Remember, the message is still the most important part of any speech.

Index

253

F

Facial expression, 25, 80
Fairbanks, G., 91, 94, 97
Fallacies, 195
    ad hominem, 199
    ignoratio elenchi, 198
    (ignoring the issue)
    non sequitur, 197
    (false cause)
    petitio principii, 198
    (begging the question)
    secundum quid, 196
    (overgeneralization)
Feedback, 16
Feierebend, R., 167
Feleky, A., 26, 77
Fest, T. B., 212, 217
Festinger, L., 163
Fonda, Jane, 36
Freeman, J. T., 45
Fright (*see* Speech fright)
Furbay, A. L., 108

G

Garrett, H. E., 26
Generalization, 61 (*see also* Language)
Gerbner, G., 5, 10
Gestures, 25, 81
    descriptive, 82
    reinforcing, 81
Gettysburg address, 242
Gibb, J. D., 20, 144
Goetzinger, C. S., 2
Goyer, R. S., 5, 12, 28
Grades, 3
Gray, C. E., 40
Guetzkow, H., 215
Gulley, H., 211, 212, 217, 224

H

Haiman, F. S., 212, 217, 224
Hance, K. G., 213
Harnack, R. V., 212, 217
Hayakawa, S. I., 60
Heckling, 202
Hedde, W. G., 212
Hellman, H. E., v
Henrikson, E., 37
Hepler, H. W., 8, 9
Hinds, G. L., 29

Hippocrates, 169
Hirschfeld, A., 214
Holliday, Judy, 36
Hollingworth, H. L., 146, 120, 179
Homans, G. C., 212
Hostile audiences, 163
Hovland, C., 164, 166, 167
Hull, C. L., 179
Humor, 144
Hurst, C., 3
Hypothesis theory, 19

I

Ignoratio elenchi, 198
Illustration, 138, 186
Immediacy, 143
Impromptu speaking, 71
Inductive reasoning, 188
Inference, 56
Informative speaking:
    analogy, 139
    audio-visual aids, 146
    clarity, 138
    illustration, 138, 186
    interest, 141
    known to unknown, 134
    learning theories, 134
    model outlines, 156
    objectives, 137
    organization, 145
    reinforcement, 135
    restatement, 141
    serial order, 135
    statistics, 140
    testimony, 140
Interaction, 226
Interaction process analysis, 229
Interest factors, 141
    conflict, 142
    curiosity, 142
    humor, 144
    immediacy, 143
    novelty, 142
    specificity, 142
    vital, 145
Interpersonal relations, 225
Interrupted speeches, 202
    answering questions, 204
    direct questions, 208
    generating participation, 207
    loaded questions, 198, 206
    overhead questions, 207